13TH GEN

Also by Neil Howe and Bill Strauss

Generations

Also by Neil Howe

On Borrowed Time (with Peter Peterson)

Also by Bill Strauss

Fools on the Hill (with Elaina Newport)
Chance and Circumstance (with Lawrence Baskir)
Reconciliation After Vietnam (with Lawrence Baskir)

13TH GEN

ABORT, RETRY, IGNORE, FAIL?

by Neil Howe & Bill Strauss

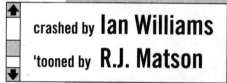

crashed by **Ian Williams**

'tooned by **R.J. Matson**

Vintage Books

A Division of Random House, Inc.

New York

A Vintage Original, April 1993
First Edition

Library of Congress Cataloging-in-Publication Data
Strauss, William.
13th gen : abort, retry, ignore, fail? / William Strauss & Neil Howe ;
crashed by Ian Williams ; 'tooned by R. J. Matson.
p. cm.
ISBN 0-679-74365-0
1. United States—Civilization—1945
2. United States—Social conditions—1960–1980.
3. United States—Social conditions—1980–
I. Howe, Neil II. Title. III. Title: Thirteenth gen.
E169.12.S845 1993
973.92—dc20 92-56350
CIP

Text design and composition: Jennifer Dossin

Manufactured in the United States of America
10 9 8 7 6 5 4

To our children:
Giorgia, Rebecca, Eric, Victoria, and Melanie.

ACKNOWLEDGMENTS

We would like to thank our Vintage editor, Edward Kastenmeier, for believing in this book and in the need for his generation to find its identity. Ditto to our agent, Rafe Sagalyn, for his labors on behalf of this and other projects; to Susan Mitchell for the jacket design; and to Marty Asher, Katy Barrett, George Donahue, Cathryn S. Aison, Jennifer Dossin, Dan Halberstein, Duncan McCarthy, Doug Lea, Brian Ash, Ernest Wilson, Richard Jackson, and so many others whose efforts and ideas have meant so much.

We are grateful to the countless "13ers" with whom we've spoken in recent years, plus the hundreds of writers and artists whose comments adorn the margins.

CONTENTS

session 3: start 10:31:50 pm 11/30/92 (logtime: 2:38:41).
file: c:\13th-gen\part3.doc

>PART THREE: THE 13ING OF AMERICA

PART 1

ABORT, RETRY, IGNORE, FAIL?

>1. We Don't Even Have a Name

Imagine coming to a beach at the end of a long summer of wild go-ings-on. The beach crowd is exhausted, the sand shopworn, hot, and full of debris—no place for walking barefoot. You step on a bottle, and some cop yells at you for littering. The sun is directly overhead and leaves no patch of shade that hasn't already been taken. You feel the glare beating down on a barren landscape devoid of secrets or in-nocence. You look around at the disapproving faces and can't help but sense, somehow, that the entire universe is gearing up to punish you.

This is how today's young people feel, as members of $#+áqs7?taé9

Not ready error reading drive B
Abort, Retry, Ignore, Fail? a
Abort, Retry, Ignore, Fail? a
Abort, Retry, Ignore, Fail? a
Abort, Retry, Ignore, Fail? f

C:> ph-bill

ATDT 1(703)555-0991... Phone number being dialed... Connection made...

<TRAN> bill this is neil are you there? i'm having trouble printing the 13th generation text. can't even "abort" it. sure we need hard copy?

<RECV> no. here's more bad news. our agent says he can't get anyone interested in this book idea. seems publishers all think 1) today's teens and twenties have an attention span no longer than a soundbite, 2) they wouldn't be caught dead near a bookstore, 3) they don't want to read about themselves, and 4) nobody else cares what they are anyway. those publishers must think every 13er is a totally stupid, MTV-wasted eraserhead.

<TRAN> well that's that. so much for fat advances and oprah phil arsenio. guess it's time to trash it.

<RECV> hold off. can't we send our 13th gen file out over USA-TALK, that computer bulletin board you use? what's to lose?

<TRAN> ok let's do it. god knows who's up and watching at this hour.

<RECV> hope it doesn't make anybody too mad. 13ers'll probably hate our yuppie guts for it.

<TRAN> i'm serene. what about our factoids and rj's cartoons?

<RECV> i'll feed them in as you upload the text.

<TRAN> here goes. stay online while i switch to DOS and dial out. set to be a boomer and spout truth?

<RECV> i'm already pouring my classic cola. go ahead.

C: > usa-talk

ATDT 1(202)555-3850... Phone number being dialed... Connection made...

*** Welcome to USA-TALK On-Line Bulletin Board.
*** Your handle is: 2boomers
*** Log on at 10:05:46 pm, 11/28/92.
*** Messages to/from other current USA-TALK users will appear in upper-right cb box. At any time press alt-e to enter cb box.
*** SELECT: (D)ownload, (U)pload, (M)enu, (Q)uit? u
*** Upload channel currently open. Specify file at prompt:

>C:\13th-gen\part-1.doc

*** USA-TALK uploading 13TH-GEN\PART-1.DOC by 2BOOMERS at 10:06:08 pm: stand by...

PART 1
ABORT, RETRY, IGNORE, FAIL?

>1. We Don't Even Have a Name

Imagine arriving at a beach at the end of a long summer of wild go-ings-on. The beach crowd is exhausted, the sand shopworn, hot, and full of debris—no place for walking barefoot. You step on a bottle, and some cop yells at you for littering. The sun is directly overhead and leaves no patch of shade that hasn't already been taken. You feel the glare beating down on a barren landscape devoid of secrets or in-nocence. You look around at the disapproving faces and can't help but sense that, somehow, the entire universe is gearing up to punish you.

This is how today's young people feel as members of what 30-year-old writer Nancy Smith calls "the generation after. Born af-ter 1960, after you, after it all happened." After Boomers. And be-fore the Babies-on-Board of the 1980s, those cuddly tykes deemed too cute and fragile to be left *Home Alone.* Who does that leave stuck in the middle? Eighty million young men and women, ranging in age from 11 to 31. They make up the biggest generation in American his-tory (yes, bigger than the Boom); the most diverse generation—eth-nically, culturally, economically, and in family structure; the only generation born since the Civil War to come of age unlikely to match their parents' economic fortunes; and the only one born this centu-ry to grow up personifying (to others) not the advance, but the de-cline of their society's greatness.

As they shield their eyes with Ray-Ban Wayfarer sunglasses, and their ears with their Model TCD-D3 Sony Walkmen ($229.99 sug-gested retail), today's teens and twenties tone-setters look shocking on the outside, unknowable on the inside. To older eyes, they pre-sent a splintered image of brassy sights and smooth manner. Fami-lies aside, what the older crowd knows of them comes mostly from a

It's like, we don't even have a name. Yours—"Baby Boomers"—is so big we fall in its shadow.

Nancy Smith,
"25 and Pending," in the
Washington Post

The future's so bright, I gotta wear shades

Timbuk 3,
"The Future's So Bright"
(song)

We're street smart, David Letterman clever, whizzes at Nintendo. We can name more beers than Presidents. Pop culture is, to us, more attractive than education.
I don't think we can do this dance much longer . . . .

Daniel Smith-Rowsey,
"The Terrible Twenties,"
in *Newsweek*

mix of film cuts, celebrity blurbs, sports reports, and crime files.

Over-30 moviegoers see them as hard-to-like kids, kids who deserve not a break but a kick, a pink slip, maybe even jail time. They are *The Breakfast Club*'s "brat pack," enduring pointless punishments at the hands of befuddled adults. Hard Harry trying to *Pump Up the Volume* for his "why bother generation." Bill and Ted having adventures that could only seem "excellent" to somebody as terminally stupid as them. Tom Cruise proving he's a *Top Gun* only by breaking a few rules. A *Heathers* wilderness of teen suicides. Death-dosed *Boyz n the Hood*. Rob Lowe's *Bad Influence*. An evil teenage *Hand That Rocks the Cradle* for a baby far more precious than she ever was. Here and there, screenwriters lighten up a little— for example, when Ferris Bueller combs for pleasure in a world gone mad, or when *Edward Scissorhands* becomes an artist with the aid of his deformity, or when Wayne emerges from his parents' basement to find a "Way" in a "No Way" world. But, mostly, the impression is of kids growing up too hard to be cute.

The shortened scripts of TV sitcoms and the quick bites of ads and music videos leave an even brassier image of affluent wise guys and sassy girls more comfortable shopping than working or studying. Ads target them as beasts of pleasure and pain who have trouble understanding words longer than one syllable, sentences longer than three words. Pop music on their ever-declining number of Top 40 stations—the heavy metal, alternative rock, New Wave, rap—strikes many an older ear as a rock 'n' roll endgame of harsh sounds, goin'-nowhere melodies, and poetry that ranges from the clumsy to the foul or racist. There's other stuff—a capella "voicestras," acoustic revival— but not many aging classic rockers ever hear much of it.

TAME
TWENTY NOTHINGS
AMERICA'S WASTED YOUTHS

News clips document a young-adult wasteland of academic non-performance, disease-ridden sex, date-rape trials, wilding, and hate crimes. Today's youngish sports figures often look to elders like American Gladiators, athletically proficient but uncerebral, uncivic, lacking nuance. To older eyes, the Neon Deions differ from the Namaths and Aarons partly in their size, speed, and muscularity, but also in their in-your-face slam dunks, end-zone boogies, and weak team loyalties. Those who, like Mary Lou Retton, do succeed in capturing our hearts invariably set off to "rettonize" themselves and capture our product endorsements. Team logos, once sources of local pride, now mark territory for inner-city gangs. But the Ickey Shuffle, Shark jacket, and Air Jordan high-top aren't the only sporting icons new to this generation: There's also one-armed Jim Abbott pitching in the major leagues, America's world-champion women soccer players, and second-generation black student-athletes like Duke's basketball star Grant Hill (the son of Yale and Dallas Cowboy football star Calvin Hill).

Yes, this is a generation with a PR problem. Its collective reputation comes from young celebrities and criminals, from the biggest stories of success and failure. Yet most in their teens and twenties are quick to insist that *People* cover stories and police blotters tell little about them personally, about their circles of friends, about their lives in school or on the job, about what it means to come of age in 1990s America. And, they insist, their generation will remain a mystery until elders take the trouble to block out the iconography and look more discerningly at the young men and women in daily American life.

In polyglot American cities—New York and Los Angeles especially—we see them as the reckless bicycle messengers (who, like *Bicycle Days* author John Schwartz, like to "live a little faster"), the rollerblading commuters, the pizza and package-delivery drivers, the young Koreans helping their fathers at grocery stores, the local-access cable TV producers, the deal making wannabees whom trader-turned-writer Michael Lewis says "age like dogs" before making their fortunes—or going broke trying. Other times, we notice them as the directionless college "slackers," the non-voters, the wandering nomads of the temp world, the store clerks whose every declaration sounds like it ends with a question mark, the women in tennis shoes lunching at the gym, the computer jockeys loading games onto their office PCs when the boss isn't looking.

***crasher
>well what have we here? this looks interesting.

Ain't no wrong now,
ain't no right
Only pleasure and pain

Jane's Addiction,
"Ain't No Right" (song)

The signs are that this will be a more ambitious, pragmatic, skeptical, selfish, goal-oriented, materialistic generation. They will have narrower goals . . . . Baby Busters probably will not want to teach the world to sing. They probably will not want it all, but are more likely to want what they have earned.

Matthew Greenwald,
president of survey
research firm

We are clueless yet wizened, too unopinionated to voice concern, purposefully enigmatic and indecisive.

Bret Easton Ellis,
"The Twentysomethings:
Adrift in a Pop Landscape,"
in the *New York Times*

In the inner city, they're the unmarried teen mothers and the unconcerned teen fathers. They're the lethal gangsters, the Crips and Bloods—and the innocent hiphoppers who have no illusions about why older white guys cross the street to avoid them. Across the landscape of urban youth, we see more millionaires and more hopelessly poor, more immigrants and more nativist skinheads, more social fractures and cultural fissures than today's 40-, 60-, or 80-year-olds could possibly remember from their own younger days.

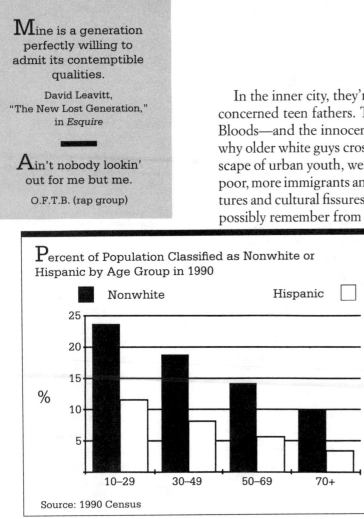

Percent of Population Classified as Nonwhite or Hispanic by Age Group in 1990

Nonwhite ■   Hispanic □

Source: 1990 Census

In 'burb and town life, they are kids at the mall. Kids buying family groceries for busy moms and dads. Kids doing the wave at the ballpark. Kids of divorce. (Omigosh, it's Saturday, and I'm supposed to be with Dad, and I have, like, *so* much homework this weekend.) Kids battling back against drugs and alcohol. Kids in mutual-protection circles of friends, girding against an adolescent world far more dangerous than anything their parents knew. Kids struggling to unlink sex from date-rape, disease, and death.

In school, the diversity of student bodies has never been greater—not just in ethnicity, but also in attitude, performance, and rewards. Asian-Americans (and immigrant children generally) are achieving at a tremendous clip, and black and Hispanic aptitude test scores are rising, while Anglo aptitude test scores remain below levels seen one, even two generations ago. On campus, women outperform men and soar into graduate programs, while collegians of both sexes struggle with a faculty-fueled debate over how to undo their various alleged insensitivities. Their handbills are more likely to promote products than ideologies, their protests more against the immediate scourges of their world—hikes in tuition, cuts in library hours, the hiring of teaching assistants who can't speak English—than against injustice in the world beyond. Most of them support global causes but don't have the money or time to contribute. Besides, they figure, what difference could they possibly make?

As college alumni, these are the grads with the big loans who were supposed to graduate into jobs and move out of the house, but didn't. They had more bucks in their pockets (and more employers in tow) before college than after. Whatever their schooling, these young adults seem to get poorer the longer they've been away from home—unlike their parents at that age, who seemed to get richer. In the work

force, they lower their sights and take jobs as yardworkers, Walmart shelf-stockers, Blockbuster checkers, health care trainees, and as the miscellaneous scavengers and nomads in the low-wage/low-benefit service economy. In unions and corporations, they face career ladders where the bottom rungs have been cut off.

Overseas, the dressed-down kids of '70s-era Amsterdam have been replaced by dressed-up kids of '90s-era Prague: get-it-done types, exporters of U.S. culture, entrepreneurial globalites who know how to make bucks out of social chaos, experts at exploring the brawling world frontiers of capitalism. If they're on the skids at home, what they're good at doing is in demand elsewhere—whether as conquering warriors of Panama and Kuwait, as McDonald's-Moscow managers in Adam Smith ties, or as multilingual aides to the Tokyo and London financiers busy gobbling up American assets.

With each passing year, these young men and women are gradually but surely making their mark on the national character. In them lies much of the doubt, distress, and endangered dream of late twentieth-century America. In them also lies a reason for hope. As a group, they aren't what older people wish they were, but rather what they themselves know they need to be: street-smart survivalists clued into the game of life the way it really gets played, searching for simple things that work in a cumbersome society that offers little to them.

When they look into the future, they see a much bleaker vision than any of today's older generations ever saw in their own youth. Even the hard-pressed youths of the Great Depression saw a path (albeit difficult) to a bright future, under the guidance of wise and determined older adults. But today's teens and twenties aren't singing about any "over the rainbow" reward and see precious little wisdom and determination up the age ladder. They have trouble identifying any path that does not lead to decline for them and their nation. In-

They are resigned to the fact that their tickets are punched but their train is rusted to the rails. They don't expect much, which is why they work so hard to take care of what they've got. They aren't leaving anytime soon. If we threw them out, where would they go?

Henry Allen,
"The Young Fogies," in the
Washington Post

⬛

We're a secret generation. Nobody knows what we think.

Bethany Ericson, 22,
Brighton, MA

⬛

I'm not aware of too many things
I know what I know if you know what I mean

Edie Brickell
and the New Bohemians,
"What I Am" (song)

stead, they sense that they're the clean-up crew, that their role in history could be sacrificial—that, whatever comeuppance America has to face, they'll bear more than their share of the burden. It's a new twist, and not a happy one, on the American Dream.

Are they a "generation"? Yes, with a personality that reaches across the board—rich and poor, black and white, Hispanic and Asian, male and female, celebrity and everyman. Whatever a 15- or 25-year-old's individual circumstances, he or she can sense a composite personality, a generational core. It's something each individual can help define, "slack" within, or fight against—but cannot easily ignore. The simple fact of ethnic and socioeconomic diversity (in contrast to the far greater homogeneity found in older generations) is an essential part of this persona.

If we call them a generation, we have to set birth-year boundaries—but where? Over the past quarter-century, demographers have persisted in defining the birth years of the "baby boomers" as reaching from 1946 through 1964, and the "baby busters" as starting with the 1965 birth year. But the demographers' approach crams people into a generation based on the fertility traits of their parents, not on the behavior of the people themselves. For years now, pollster Pat Caddell has been urging that the Boomer boundary be pushed forward, that young people born in the early 1960s simply don't fit that sociocultural B-word. Caddell is right. The last Boomers were born in 1960.

The 1961 birth year is a milestone identified by every sub-30 biographer of this generation who has looked closely at the matter: Doug Coupland, Bret Easton Ellis, Nancy Smith, Steven Gibb, David Gross and Sophronia Scott. (Gross and Scott's cover story about the "Twentysomething" generation appeared in July 1990, just after the first 1961 babies had celebrated their 29th birthdays.) Babies born between 1961 and 1964 are tired of hearing themselves called "baby boomers" when they know they don't carry the usual hippie-cum-yuppie baggage. Author Doug Coupland, himself a "baby boomer" if demographers are to be believed, originally suggested "Generation X" as a title for this four-year cohort of Boomer-NOTs.

Coupland is on to something. At every age, the life

RENT
THIS
SPACE

cycle story of his Camelot-era "Xer" babies has differed sharply from the story of Boomers growing older just in front of them. Trace the life cycle to date of the babes of '61. When they were born, they were the first babies people took pills not to have. When the 1967 Summer of Love marked the start of America's divorce epidemic, they were the wee kindergartners armed with latchkeys for re-entering empty homes after school. In 1974, they were the bell-bottomed seventh-graders who got their first real-life civics lesson watching Nixon resign on TV. Through the late 1970s, they were the teenage mall-hoppers who spawned the "Valley Girls" and other flagrantly non-Boom youth trends. In 1979, they were the graduating seniors of Carter-era malaise who registered record low SAT scores and record high crime and drug-abuse rates. In 1980, they cast their first votes mostly for Reagan, marched off as the high-quality 19-year-old enlistees who began surging into the military, and arrived on campus as smooth, get-it-done collegians who marked a sudden turnaround from the intellectual arrogance and social immaturity of Boomer students. In 1985, they were the M.B.A. grads who propelled the meteoric rise in job applications to Wall Street. And in 1991, they hit age 30 exactly when ABC pulled the plug on *thirtysomething*—and when young-adult viewers began flocking to Fox-TV.

If that's the first birth year, where should we put the endpoint? History shows that, on average, modern generations stretch across a little over 20 birth years. Can 31-year-olds share generational membership with 11-year-olds? Yes, although neither group might realize it until another decade has passed. Future events may draw lines that today we don't know about. But for now, mark this generation's younger edge at the 1981 birth year, and declare 1982 babies the leading edge of the fledgling "Millennial Generation."

Today's preteens—the trailing edge of the rising generation—show the same basic personality as kids now in their teens and twenties, albeit under a somewhat tougher umbrella of parental protection. Their video games stress action, acquisition, and one-on-one heroism. Save a princess, find a treasure, don't get killed. The entertainment they like best is unremittingly

> We are an impatient, quick and dirty generation.
>
> Scott Matthews, et al., *Stuck in the Seventies* (book)

> I hunt
> Therefore I am
>
> Metallica, rock group

> What looks from the outside like an inert generation whose silence should provoke contempt is actually a terrified generation whose silence should inspire compassion.
>
> Naomi Wolf, "The Coming Third Wave," in the *Next Progressive*

***crasher

>wait a minute, why do we have to be a generation at all? why can't we just peacefully take up our place on the great palette of time without people like you coming along and calling us "post-whatever" and "neo-pseudo-classical-glurb"? I take offense. I may not have the demographical skill to summon up all three trillion of you boomers into one cohesive "impulse item rack" at walmart, but I like being nice and undefinable. you're taking the fun out of everything.

> Our generation is probably the worst since the Protestant Reformation. It's barbaric.
>
> young adult, *Metropolitan* (film)

physical, in a style one TV executive calls "Indiana Jones meets a game show." Teen problems fester, and the academic improvements come distressingly slowly. Locking in our image of this younger side of the generation is the 1981-born Gregory Kingsley, recently granted a divorce from his parents by a Florida court, and such media creations as John Connor, the killer-robot's hustling young aide-de-camp in *Terminator 2*, and that bellwether brat, Bart Simpson. Bart has been allowed to start growing older, fixing the little under-achiever forever at the youngest edge of the generation he is helping to define.

America's 11- through 31-year-olds are congealing into a bona fide generation that encompasses many common personality traits, as well as a few trends from the younger to the older edge. The elder "Atari" wave—those pioneers of coin-op PacMan and Space Invaders—represents the last gasp of America's demographic "baby boom" and then a gradual decline in birth numbers. Born in the 1960s, Atari-wavers lie at the more abandoned, damaged, criticized, alienated end of their generation. These are Coupland's twentysomething "Xers," who have suffered the most from the betrayed expectations of a youth world that went from sweet to sour as they approached it. They are also the 13ers most impeded, and angered, by Boomers.

Born in the '70s and early '80s, the junior "Nintendo" wave—those Super Mario III and Tetris joystickers—represents the true "baby bust": Since World War II, 1975 marks America's record-low birth year. By then, the adult world was down on children, and there were few youthful expectations left to be betrayed. These are Coupland's "Benetton Youth," the *Shampoo Planet* kids who entered school when adults were beginning to reinvent some of the old societal shields that once protected the world of toddlers. As precursors of the wanted-baby Millennials, Nintendo-wavers are aware that adult treatment of children is improving, if mostly to the benefit of kids just a bit younger than they are.

Around 1982, when "Baby on Board" signs first appeared on car windows, social trends started shifting away from neglect and negativism, and toward protection and support. The abortion and divorce rates receded somewhat, teacher salaries gained ground, and a flurry of new books chastised parents for having treated kids so poorly in the 1970s. This abrupt shift in societal attitudes marks the beginning of the Millennial Generation. Congress endorsed this trend by

"DO YOU HAVE A CARD FOR A HALF-SISTER'S BIOLOGICAL FATHER'S PERMANENT COMPANION?"

making all children in poverty born after September 30, 1983, automatically eligible for Medicaid—but *not* those born before. As the babies of the early 1980s aged into schoolchildren, the newly positive adult attitudes began moving up the age ladder with them. *Three Men and a Baby* spawned a sequel, *Three Men and a Little Lady*. By the late '80s, a new national priority had been declared: the task of smartening up and cleaning up the primary-grade kids destined to become the high school class of 2000.

What to call this "lost" generation between Boomers and Millennials? Back in the early 70s, when they were no more than kids, adults sometimes dubbed them "Computer" babies or the "High-Tech" Generation. Such names had a soothingly modern and affluent ring to them—and just a hint of the technophilia that was beginning to distinguish them from back-to-nature Boomers.

Since then, a few commentators have tried to sustain the happy tone by coining monikers like "(P)Lucky" or "Scarce" Generation. The assumption was that the babies of the late '60s would prosper from their relatively small numbers—thanks to market-driven de-

> They are our children, and we should love them . . . . But even if we don't love them, we need them, because they are our future.
>
> Mario Cuomo, nominating Bill Clinton

> This is the "but not for me" generation—things may be tough all over, but I won't be affected. They don't make any connection between their pessimistic outlook for the overall economy and their optimism about their own well-being.
>
> *Fortune,* "The Upbeat Generation"

clines in college tuition and housing prices and increases in entry-level wages and benefits. Thus far, exactly the opposite has happened. *Fortune* magazine has tagged them the "Upbeat Generation," pointing to polls showing their personal optimism about the future. Yes, their "no problem" jauntiness does say something important about how they look at life. But according to all the polls, 13ers believe it will be much harder for them to get ahead than it was for their parents—and are overwhelmingly pessimistic about the long-term fate of their generation and nation. Imagine a gang of plunging skydivers who know they only have one parachute to share among them; you wouldn't call them "upbeat" just because each diver hopes he's the one who gets the chute.

Downbeat labels are much more common—like "Nowhere," "Boomerang," "Caretaker," "New Lost," "MTV," and "Baby Bust" Generation. The last is by far the most popular and a special favorite among demographers. But there's a problem: "Baby Buster" is at once incorrect and insulting. The Atari wave is not a birth "bust" at all, but includes some of the biggest cohorts of babies ever born in America. Even during the low-fertility '70s, the term "baby bust" says far more about adult attitudes toward children during that era than about the personality of the children themselves. Yet the worst part of this "baby bust" nomer is how it plants today's teens and twenties squarely where they do not want to be: in the shadow of the "boom," and negatively so: Bust after boom, as though wonder has been followed by disappointment.

Other suggested names similarly lock them for life in the Boomer afterglare. Coupland's "Generation X" term is derived from a '60s-era tag the British gave to their Boomer-era mods and rockers (a tag that, in the '70s, was borrowed by a rather nasty rock band of British Boomers). Shann Nix suggests "posties," presumably an abbreviation for post-yuppies. But every generation is "post-" something (Boomers were "postwar"), and being post-yuppie is not something today's young people want to dwell on any more than they absolutely must.

These eighty million Americans need a non-label label that has nothing whatsoever to do with Boomers. So take a number. Thirteen. The tag is a little Halloweenish, a little raffish, a little heavy. It's the floor where elevators don't stop, the doughnut bakers don't bother to count. In Medieval Euro-fable, the thirteenth generation is the last to suffer from a curse on the living. Counting back to the peers of Benjamin Franklin, this generation is, in point of fact, the thirteenth to know the American nation, flag, and Constitution.

More than a name, the number 13 is a gauntlet, a challenge, an obstacle to be overcome. "My generation was born on Friday the Thirteenth," Gregg Linburg insists. "That's a day you can view two ways. You can fear it, or you can face it—and try to make it a great day in spite of the label." The thirteenth card can be the ace, face down, in a game of high stakes blackjack. Kings and queens, with their pompous poses and fancy curlicues, always lose to the uncluttered ace, going over or going under. Aces—like 13ers—are nothing subtle, but can be handy to have around when you get in a jam.

***crasher

>there was this kid named wade in my first grade homeroom who could drop a loogey all the way to the floor and reswallow it at will, and every time someone writes one of these "lost generation" diatribes they lump me together with wade. I hate being lumped together with wade!

>2. Something of a National Curse

"An army of aging Bart Simpsons, armed and possibly dangerous." "A nation of dummies" with "herky-jerky brain." "A generation of animals." A quarter-century ago, kids called older people names. These days, the reverse is true.

Not since the grown-up infants of John Winthrop's Boston were condemned by elder Puritans as "the corrupt and degenerate rising generation" has any new cadre of young Americans endured such a one-sided assault from elders. For the past decade, 13ers have been bombarded with study after story after column about how bad they supposedly are. Americans in their teens and twenties, we are told, are consumed with violence, selfishness, greed, bad work habits, and civic apathy. Turn on the TV, and it's hard to see a bad-news-for-America story—from crime to welfare to schools to consumerism—in which young faces and bodies don't show up prominently in the footage. Listen to jokes about bad manners or trashy culture, and it's hard to hear many that don't target someone under 30. Peruse the dismal projections about America's future, and it's hard to miss the neg-

Our style of adolescence is something of a national curse. Americans are growing up faster, but they may not be growing up better.

Robert Samuelson, in *Newsweek*

An unprecedented proportion of today's youth lack commitment to core moral values like honesty, personal responsibility, respect for others and civic duty.

Josephson Institute for the Advancement of Ethics, "The Ethics of American Youth" (report)

CHILDREN'S WRITING
SKILLS "DEPRESSING"

STUDENTS DON'T
PROTEST OVER
VIETNAM NOW—THEY
DON'T EVEN KNOW
WHERE IT IS

STUDENTS'
COMPREHENSION OF
SCIENCE CALLED
SHALLOW

NOT ALL STUDENTS
ARE GREEDY

Washington Post
(headlines from the 1980s)

———

Their speech is turning
into what has
been termed
"McLanguage"—
verbal fast-food
consisting mainly of
inflection and gesture.
("It's like . . ." Shrug.
"You know, like . . .")
. . . WHAT'S GOING ON
IN THEIR BRAINS?

Jane Healy, author of
"Endangered Minds"

ative assumptions about how today's young people will someday behave as parents and leaders.

In particular, we hear, 13ers are DUMB. They can't find Chicago on a map. They don't know when the Civil War was fought. They watch too much TV, spend too much time shopping, seldom vote (and vote for shallow reasons when they do), cheat on tests, don't read newspapers, and care way too much about cars, clothes, shoes, and (especially) money. The arrival of such blighted minds, we are reminded, could not have come at a worse moment in global history: just when information and knowledge are playing a crucial role in determining the rise and fall of nations.

The dumbness onslaught began in 1983 with the widely-heralded report of the U.S. Department of Education, *A Nation at Risk*, which complained of "a rising tide of mediocrity" then emerging from the nation's schools. Several years earlier, after the Wirtz Commission looked into why Boom-era SAT scores kept declining year after year, the government issued a report that was unerringly gentle on test-taking Boomers, rationalizing their poor performance as a natural consequence of the social turbulence of the '60s and '70s. Not so in the '80s, with 13ers in the target scope. "For the first time in the history of our country," the *Nation at Risk* authors charged, "the educational skills of one generation will not surpass, will not equal, will not even approach, those of their parents." They went on to suggest that if 13er minds had been foisted upon the U.S. by an unfriendly power, Congress probably would have considered it "an act of war." Granted many of the report's complaints were leveled at the adult community for tolerating low teacher salaries, experimental curricula, weak discipline, declining standards, and whatnot, but according to the expert consensus, the adults weren't the dummies. The kids were.

In the decade since, one blue-ribbon report after another has officially pronounced them "disappointing" and "depressing." Various expert committees have quantified their inadequacies down to the second decimal place—ranking them way behind the Germans and Japanese, somewhere down around the Sri Lankans and Jordanians. Typically, each new report kicked off a flurry of TV stories, op-ed columns, and political speeches declaring 13ers a national embarrassment. These elder critiques were not necessarily intended to disparage young students. The purpose, more often, was to generate funding for math, history, or whatever teaching specialty the expert authors happened to represent. But the elder judgment was clear: Kids graduating in the 1980s were, as one Boomer college president put it, "junky."

Along the way, one professor-author after another has resonantly certified the stupidity of today's national student body. E. D. Hirsch, Jr. wrote *Cultural Literacy* to describe what 13ers lack, and then published another book listing 50,000 alphabetized facts they should know but supposedly don't (Descartes, René ... Des Moines, Iowa). In 1987, Chester E. Finn, Jr. and Diane Ravitch published their federally commissioned book *What Do Our Seventeen-Year-Olds Know?* Their answer: not much. "We do not contend that the 'younger generation is going to the dogs,'" they explained. "We merely conclude that it is ignorant of important things that it should know." Over the last decade, the typical 13er has encountered hundreds (maybe thousands) of scripts, songs, ads, columns, stories, reviews, and media wisecracks grinding the point home.

In the wake of this barrage, 13ers have become a symbol—to older generations, at least—of an America in decline. Back in the 1970s, social scientists looked at the American experience over the preceding half-century and observed that each new generation, compared to the last, marked another step upward on the Maslovian scale of human purpose, away from concrete needs and toward higher, more spiritual aspirations. Those due to arrive after the Boomers, they expected, would be even *more* cerebral, *more* learned, *more* idealistic than any who came before. When 13ers finally hit their twenties and reached out for a handshake, startled elders could hardly hide their dismay. After describing the hypothesis about "an ongoing trend away from material aspirations toward nonmaterialistic goals," *American Demographics* bluntly announced: "This trend is not apparent in the class of 1986. In fact, young adults seem to be turning away from intellectual and philosophical concerns."

Since disappointment leads naturally to second-guessing, 13ers have become an object lesson for the growing chorus of social critics expressing second thoughts about what has happened to America in recent decades. Whatever regrettable chapter of recent history is discussed—the rage of the '60s, the narcissism of the '70s, the greed of the '80s—the hidden question is: Whatever made today's kids turn out the way they did?

Apparently, it serves no one's purpose to make any comparison to their advantage. When the critics notice negative youth currents abroad—for instance, the vast punk culture in England or resurgent fascism in Germany—they shudder at the possibilities here at home. But when they see something positive, they ask another kind of question—like why the kids who go slam-dancing in L.A. don't show the same civic pride as the kids who storm tanks in Beijing or Moscow. When the critics look back in history, they seem incapable of finding even one comparative virtue in 13ers worth mentioning. Other generations had plenty: In the early '30s, politicians lauded youth for their collective muscle. In the early '50s, corporations bragged about brilliant young technicians. In the early '70s, the media celebrated youngsters as the pied pipers of self-discovery. But youths in the early '90s? Ask the producer, marketer, or journalist, and all you get are blank stares.

CAMPUS BESTSELLER

PRESUMED IGNORANT
PRESUMED IGNORANT
PRESUMED IGNORANT
PRESUMED IGNORANT

Maybe 13ers are just a bad bunch. Or, worse, maybe they're living symbols of the final exhaustion of civilization. That, in effect, is the thesis of Allan Bloom's best-selling 13er-bash, *The Closing of the American Mind*. After pummeling 1980s-era college students with dozens of gee-aren't-you-dumb lines ("the only common project engaging the youthful imagination is the exploration of space, which everyone knows to be empty"), Bloom went on to describe Nietzsche's nightmare vision of the future and populate it with 13er-like caricatures: anti-heroic, mind-dead, values-empty, sensation-addicted boobs. (Thus spake Zarathustra: "Alas, the time of the most despicable man is coming, he that is no longer able to despise himself. Behold I show you *the last man*.") A few years later, former Bloom student Francis Fukuyama wrote *The End of History and the Last Man* to demonstrate, by implication, that today's young are the vanguard of a new breed that will never know true belief, true beauty, true passion. To fathom this creature of pleasure and pain—this animal driven only by appetites and not by ideas—you needn't wade with Bloom or Fukuyama through centuries of philosophy. You just have to imagine a TV-glued 13er audience nodding in response to Jay Leno's line about why teenagers eat Doritos Tortilla Chips: "Hey kids! We're not talkin' brain cells here. We're talkin' taste buds."

To Boomers like Fukuyama and Leno, the image of a 13er descent into Plato's republic of pigs has a self-comforting corollary: It leaves Boomers standing forever at the apex of history, surpassing both their ancestors and successors in Maslovian consciousness. Twenty years ago, long-haired, bell-bottomed young Boomers heard themselves flattered in gushing tributes like *The Greening of America*, a 40ish professor's best-selling paean to a generation destined to transcend civilization. Today, settling into its role as modern Zarathustras, that same generation—now 40ish itself—is leading America to purge the young of a spiritual dross that threatens to *sink* civilization.

Over the last decade, the nation has begun to act on the assumption that 13ers are "lost"—reachable by Pavlovian conditioning perhaps, but closed to reason or sentiment. In the classroom, we bribe them with hamburger coupons for getting A's; after school, we instruct them in "emotional literacy"; in the military, we delouse them with "core values" training; on campus, we drill them in the vocabulary of "political correctness." The object is not so much to get them to understand, but just to get them to behave. Back in the Boomer era, when youths did things that displeased older people—when they

A 17-year-old who collects stuffed animals as well as product endorsements wakes up one morning and decides she just wants to veg out and watch MTV.

Anna Quindlen, describing tennis star Monica Seles, in the *New York Times*

———

Watching kids dive into a trunk to get a $400 CD player, watching them run through rooms picking up products and hugging them to themselves, is watching greed take over America.

Peggy Charren, President of Action for Children's Television, describing 1980s-era game shows for children

———

This news is not only shocking; it is frightening. . . . When 95 percent of college students cannot locate Vietnam on a world map, we must sound the alarm.

U.S. Senator Bill Bradley

drank beer, drove fast, didn't study, had sex, took drugs—the nation had an intergenerational dialogue which, if nasty, at least led to a fairly articulate discourse about values and social philosophy. For 13ers, the tone has shifted to monosyllables ("just say no"). The lexicon has been stripped of sentiment ("workfare" and "wedfare" in place of "welfare"). And the method has shifted to brute survival tools: prophylaxis or punishment. While state legislatures rush to remove the word "rehabilitation" from their penal codes, public spending atrophies for 13er-targeted programs, *except* for condom distribution and prison construction.

Confused about their nation's direction in a "New World Order," older Americans are using a profoundly negative image of 13ers to rekindle a sense of national community—and urgency. Some of the same resources once directed against an external "Evil Empire" are now being used against the new generation coming of age. Military bases are being retooled into prisons. Naval ships are patrolling for drugs. And, in what (Boomer) Attorney General William Barr has called a "peace dividend" from the ending of the Cold War, 300 FBI agents who once tracked foreign spies are now sleuthing around in inner-city neighborhoods. Meanwhile, most of the talk about salvation or redemption has shifted down the age ladder. "Save the chil-

THE END OF HISTORY

1,000,000 B.C.   10,000 B.C.   100 A.D.   1776 A.D.   1993 A.D.

dren" is the '90s-era political battle cry—save the tiny-tot Millennials, that is, from becoming another "lost" 13er-like generation. Youths in their twenties, even their teens, are deemed beyond repair.

This generation—more accurately, this generation's *reputation*—has become a metaphor for America's late-twentieth-century loss of purpose. Polls show that Americans of all ages have become broadly disappointed with our institutions, with our economic performance, with our sense of community, with our culture. We regret our today-fixation but are unable to shake it, and we fear for the future. Yet the caricatured image of our collective woes, the indelible icon of national decline, doesn't include most of us. It doesn't include the federally subsidized senior in a sunbelt condo or the midlife swinger skipping out on his children or the ex-hippie professor waging old ideological wars at his students' expense. No, the image is a blow-up of only one figure: an eraser-headed kid with reflective shades, a backwards ball cap, and high-top sneakers, his Walkman tuned to heavy metal, a $300 price tag dangling from his designer leather jacket. That 13er is our manchild of the '80s. He, all grown up, is the future we fear.

What's more, 13ers know it. Even when they aren't explicitly

***crasher

>honestly, guys, I hate to ruin your night, but none of us thinks about this generation stuff at all until:
a) some dork writes a column that is so myopic, froofy and condemning that even the laziest of my friends throw the paper down in disgust...
or,
b) some plastic-haired spazmoid tv reporter thrusts a mike and camera in front of our face on the way to biology class and asks us how our disenfranchised youth is going to vote. other than that, all this twentysomething angst is something we keep to ourselves. nobody likes a whiner.

***2boomers

>do you always crash bulletin boards like this just to wreak havoc?

***crasher

>only when something on the screen particularly pisses me off.

***2boomers

>so you don't like the name "13ers" either, one is to suppose?

***crasher

>I didn't say that. I don't like giving names to generations, period. it's like trying to read the song title on a record that's spinning.

***2boomers

>we're writing about it, so we have to give it a name.

***crasher

>well, do what you gotta do.

***2boomers

>who are you? where are you typing from?

***crasher

>oh and if I tell you, everyone finds out, and then I have to be like a spokesman for my generation, and do mall appearances, and it all just gets to be a big hassle....

***2boomers

>you can at least tell us how old you are.

***crasher

>I'm 23, I'm in the basement of a large house in chapel hill, and I'm sort of still in school. so how old are 2boomers?

***2boomers

>41 and 45. hey, is there some way we can get you to behave while we're dumping this program on-line?

***crasher

>not as long as our nuclear power plant keeps working.

singled out as a metaphor for national decline, they get the picture. Before they came along, America was doing great. Since they came along, America seems to have floundered. All the diagnostic experts keep pointing backward to the era of their arrival—the '60s and '70s—as the fatal hour when everything started going to hell. Like the child of divorce writ large, this generation figures there's got to be some sort of causal connection. Part of being a 13er is to wonder always: What is it that I've done to cause so many people to be angry or unhappy?

To date, 13ers have seldom either rebutted elder accusations or pressed their own countercharges. Whatever criticism 13ers can't ignore they usually internalize, giving the lie to Zarathustra's dictum that they cannot despise themselves. Polls show them mostly agreeing that, yes, Boomer kids probably *were* a better lot; that Boomers did listen to better music, pursued better causes, and generally had better times on campus; and that maybe 13ers are indeed a little (what's that word?) "junky." So why fight a rap you can't beat? Besides, as they see it, why waste time and energy arguing with elder critics who've stacked the verbal deck against them—and who neither know *nor care* about what's actually going on in their lives? Only recently have angry 13er rejoinders begun to surface, mainly against Boomers. But episodic letters-to-editors and *Newsweek* "My Turn" columns are but tiny ripples against the negative tide.

Adult Americans are by now of the settled opinion that 13ers are—front to back—a disappointing bunch. This consensus is rooted partly in fact, partly in blurry nostalgia, partly in self-serving sermonizing, but the very fact that it is a consensus has become a major problem for today's young people. No one can blame them if they feel like a demographic black hole, a "thirteenth generation" curse on American history, whose only elder-anointed mission is to somehow pass through the next three quarters of a century without causing too much damage to their nation during their time.

Maybe the most insidious effect of creeping '70sism is its viselike grip on our most precious resource: young people like Travis Knox, 20, of Los Angeles . . . . Knox now finds himself frequenting an L.A. club called 1970, where patrons unashamedly Hustle in puka-shell necklaces, platform shoes and synthetic hip-hugger bell-bottoms—a zombielike army of Leif Garretts and Farrah Fawcetts doing battle to Giorgio Moroder songs.

"Seventies Something,"
in *Newsweek*

———

They don't even seem to know how to dress, and they're almost unschooled in how to look in different settings.

Paul Hirsch, sociologist

———

Unlike yuppies, younger people are not driven from within. They need reinforcement. They prefer short-term tasks with observable results.

Penny Erikson, 40,
Young & Rubicam ad agency

———

The most progressive ideas you'll hear from the baby-busters will probably be about how they want to progress on home in good time each day.

Fortune

———

[Teenage workers] get themselves to work punctually, but once there rarely do more than the minimum that is expected of them.

Ellen Greenberger and
Laurence Steinberg,
When Teenagers Work (book)

The high-expectation, low-sweat generation . . . [has] yet to introduce a new art form or cultural movement of any significance.

Mademoiselle

———

TV is their collective dream machine, their temple . . . . TV is a release from having to think, to feel deeply. It's all about yuks and easy sentimentality.

Todd Gitlin, professor, Cal–Berkeley

———

Picture a 13-year-old boy sitting in the living room of his family home doing his math assignment while wearing his Walkman headphones or watching MTV. He enjoys the liberties hard won over centuries by the alliance of philosophic genius and political heroism, consecrated by the blood of martyrs; he is provided with comfort and leisure by the most productive economy ever known to mankind; science has penetrated the secrets of nature in order to provide him with the marvelous, lifelike electronic sound and image reproduction he is enjoying. And in what does progress culminate? A pubescent child whose body throbs with orgasmic rhythms; whose feelings are made articulate in hymns to the joys of onanism or the killing of parents; whose ambition is to win fame and wealth in imitating the drag-queen who makes the music. In short, life is made into a non-stop, commercially prepackaged masturbational fantasy.

Allan Bloom,
The Closing of the American Mind
(book)

With them, once the fizz is gone, that's it.

Josie Esquivel, analyst
for Shearson-Lehman,
describing sneaker-buying kids

———

We as a group were more educated and intellectual than they are.

Former (Grateful)
Deadhead Dean Crean, 36,
criticizing the "copycat" late-'80s
Deadheads in their twenties

———

One possible reason occurs to me as to why Scholastic Aptitude Test scores have sunk to their lowest level in years. Kids today are really, really, dumb . . . . Why learn about sines and cosines if the cash register is going to make the change for you?

Roger Simon, in the
Los Angeles Times

———

Students had great difficulty expressing even one substantive thought.

National Assessment of
Educational Progress,
in a 1988 report

———

We have at present a generation whose majority has little or no interest in reading. This one factor alone would absolutely assure us a nation of dummies . . . .

Steve Allen, *Dumbth* (book)

———

No 17-year-old, given a choice between a $50 gift certificate for Tower Records and one for Barnes & Noble, would choose the Barnes & Noble.

Erroll McDonald,
executive editor, Pantheon Books

In 1986, in a study funded by the National Endowment for the Humanities, Diane Ravitch and Chester Finn gave 8,000 17-year-olds (born in 1969) a comprehensive exam in history and literature. They graded the exams according to 29 separate categories. The results:

Grade	Number of Subjects
A	0
B	0
C	2
D	7
F	20

Ravitch and Finn, *What Do Seventeen Year Olds Know?* (book)

━━━

Just when you think America's students can't get any dumber, the government or some private think tank comes out with a report on the declining educational performance of the young.

Jack Anderson and Dale Van Atta, "Fighting the Dumbness Trend," in the *Washington Post*

━━━

I have not yet found one single student in Los Angeles, in either college or high school, who could tell me the years when World War II was fought.

Benjamin Stein, in the *Los Angeles Times*

━━━

Today's young Americans, aged 28 to 30, know less and care less about news and public affairs than any other generation of Americans in the past fifty years.

Times Mirror Center for the People and the Press, "The Age of Indifference" (report)

Forty percent of high school seniors can't name three South American countries. Will they be the right people to advise Platinum Cardmembers on a $20,000 Amazon journey? One-third of today's ninth graders can't write a brief summary of a newspaper story. Will they be able to take phone messages from important clients?

Louis Gerstner, Jr., President, American Express

━━━

Twelve to fifteen books over a fifteen-week semester used to be the rule of thumb at selective colleges. Today it is six to eight books, and they had better be short texts, written in relatively simple English.

Daniel Singal, "The Other Crisis in American Education," in *The Atlantic*

━━━

We are seeing such junky college students.

Arthur Levine, president of Bradford College

━━━

U.S. students might live on burgers and fries, but many of them don't have the math skills to add up the bill, a new study released Thursday shows. . . . Only 66 percent of eighth graders and 77 percent of twelfth graders correctly totaled the cost of soup, burger, fries, and cola on a restaurant menu.

USA Today

━━━

How sad these poor young people should make us feel with their indifference to practically everything on the planet that is interesting, infuriating, maddening, exhilarating, fascinating, amusing, and nutty. Herky-jerky brain makes them vulnerable to the 10-second sound bite, which leaves them defenseless against demagogues.

Russell Baker, in the *New York Times*

━━━

Those under thirtysomething tend to watch television, not programs.

Richard Harrington, in the *Washington Post*

━━━

Given the yawning knowledge chasm—the gap between what they minimally should, and actually do, know (in matters historical, political and economic)—on what basis is the average teen voter to make his electoral selection: the candidate's hairstyle, taste in music, number of syllables in his last name?

Don Feder, in the *Washington Times*

━━━

Recent Labor Department studies suggest that workers 30 and under are at least 25 percent less productive than their counterparts of 25 years ago.

Morris Shechtman

━━━

Young people, I want to tell you today, think. It's not illegal yet. Think! Think! Yes, God has given you gorgeous black, brown, and white bodies. Yes, but there is something that he's put in your cranial cavity that is so marvelous that you can even connect with Him. But you've got to think. You've got to think.

Johnny Ray Youngblood, pastor, New York City

It's a far cry from 20 years ago, when the legal voting age was dropped from 21 to 18. Student rallies, speeches, and petitions flooded almost every campus.... Today, hardly a whimper.

description of student apathy during the 1992 primary season, in the *Washington Post*

———

While the lagging test scores of American schoolchildren in mathematics and reading have troubled educators, a new kind of deficit, in many ways equally alarming, is becoming all too apparent: emotional illiteracy.

New York Times

———

American 13-year-olds know just a little more math than children in Jordan, about the same as children in Slovenia, and less than children in Korea and Taiwan.

U.S. Secretary of Education Lamar Alexander

———

A weak attention span, malnourished by MTV and comic books, makes students shun contemplating reading anything as long as Tom Jones.

J.C. Furnas, historian

———

I'll never forget walking through the South Bronx, doing research and seeing boys, thirteen or fourteen years old, wearing these necklaces with silvery rings hanging from them. In the rings were upside-down Y's. I thought these were peace symbols. And I said: "Isn't it interesting that these boys here in the poorest part of New York are so civic-minded that they are concerned about the threat of

nuclear destruction." Of course, when I looked more closely, I saw that they were Mercedes-Benz hood ornaments.

Tom Wolfe, commenting on *The Bonfire of the Vanities*

———

What someone should say to impressionable kids who will watch this is that we have enough poets, rappers, painters, singers, bands, models, and dancers. More than enough, in fact. You might want to think about getting a real job. You might want to think about real life. You might want to stop watching empty-headed drivel like "The Real World."

review of MTV's "The Real World," in the *Washington Post*

———

It's incredible how little they know. There's almost a total lack of knowledge.

David Warren, political science professor, University of Rhode Island

———

Teens are not reading now, and if they're not by the time they're 30, there won't be newspapers.

Larry Richardson, "Yo, Kids! Read This!" in the *Syracuse Herald-Journal*

———

The clothes and cars I see every morning are a symptom of a rampant materialism that is changing for the worse the relationships between teenagers and their school, their peers, their community, and, most important, their families.

Patrick Welsh, high school teacher, Alexandria, VA

And even if you've "majored" in business, chances are you'll be too illiterate to be good even at that.

Paul Fussell, *Bad, or, The Dumbing of America* (book)

———

Who taught our children to hate so thoroughly and so mercilessly?

David Dinkins, Mayor of New York City

———

Workforce 2000, a Hudson Institute report, predicts that the current average skill level of 21- to 25-year-olds is 40 percent lower than the skill level that will be required of the new workers needed by that year.

Source: Hudson Institute

———

Like many their age, these sodden youths habitually sneer at adults, ridicule most emotions, and twist themselves in ever-tighter circles of egomania.

review of *The Secret History* by Donna Tartt, in the *Wall Street Journal*

———

Their characters are all gorgeous androids, their lifestyles witless L.A. clichés.

review of "Melrose Place," in *Time*

———

If the characters were any dumber, they'd need fertilizer.

review of "Melrose Place," in *Newsweek*

>3. Doing the Things a Particle Can

Back in the 1980s, a New Jersey elementary school ran an experiment with two white rats. The kids fed "Nut" a balanced diet from the school cafeteria. They fed "Honey" potato chips, root beer balls, and soda pop. Nut stayed healthy-looking, while Honey's coat grew yellowish. One day, just after the science teacher had invited dignitaries into her classroom to help celebrate the moral (junk gets you nowhere), Nut choked on a saltine and dropped dead. Honey, cheerfully munching on peanut candy, stayed very much alive.

The 13th generation has so far lived, like Honey, on a social, educational, and economic diet of potato chips, root beer balls, and soda pop. And, like Honey, 13ers are damaged—but surviving. They do what they must in a world slow to help, but quick to criticize and punish, people their age. They've hardened their shells. You want what they've got? Fine! You don't? Move along, and don't block the merchandise.

Seldom moving in mass, 13ers are an atomized, dispersed, kinetic generation. Like speeding electrons in a perfect void, they ignore all barriers and whiz along separate if similar paths, leaving others to define the gravitational nucleus of the larger society. Zoom in with a microscope, and there he is: Particle Man.

This Particle Man, a proto-13er of either sex, is a go-it-alone sort who looks at life with eyes open, bracing for the worst, expecting to beat trouble on her own. A Bogartian risk-taker, she figures she has little to lose, so she goes for the big win. Don't expect her to be gentle or trusting, to revel in the nuance of human emotion, to weep at injustice, to write romantic poetry at sunset. This is no great philosopher, institution-builder, or team player. But if you need help in a hostile world, if you need something done fast and don't much care how, Particle Man is the one to call.

Within him lies an American revival of the basics of life. Like a postmodern hunter and gatherer, Particle Man prefers action over talk, facts over meanings, results over process, accountability over excuses, what he can see over what he can't. You'll find his motto written on his sneaker pumps: Just Do It.

The brain that strikes elders as noncerebral is, from her own perspective, focused and cagey. So what if she supposedly can't find Korea, Vietnam, Panama, or Kuwait on a map? What she does know is

BICYCLEXPRESS

that the first two are where older generations got bogged down for years, and that the last two are where Particle troops sliced through the enemy in a matter of days. A good poker player, she's smart but smooth, finding an edge in knowing more than others think, adept in hiding what she knows until she needs to use it. She knows her education was a joke, and that there's a lot she doesn't know but should. But she knows where to learn it if she must, what that knowledge costs, and whether it's worth the price.

Since the late 1960s, the proportion of all freshman women who won a varsity letter in high school sports rose from 13 to 42 percent, while the proportion who used sedatives fell from 15 to 2 percent.

Source: "The American Freshmen: Twenty-Five Year Trends" (UCLA, 1991–1992)

Particle Man's eyes are keen and unblinking, enabling him to see his own condition the way others do, without flinching, and to see others more clearly than they see themselves. He is quick to recognize what really motivates people, to evaluate everything from a salesman's angle to a politician's spin. He likes watching ads because, to him, ads reveal things to him that elders don't notice. He trusts people who pursue money more than those who pursue "fairness," "the public interest," or other elusive goals he thinks might be a cover for something else. For straight news, he trusts the *Wall Street Journal* more than *The Mac-Neil/Lehrer NewsHour*. While older people listen attentively to what some expert guests might be saying on *Night-*

***crasher
>hey, nice "he" and "she" stuff, boys--always pleasant to see a couple of boomers gettin' their pronouns all nice and pc. you've got all the womyn and myn covered, but why stop there? might I suggest a hybrid of "she," "he," and "it," shortened to, say, "s'h'it"?

***2boomers
>all we're saying is that half your generation is female.

"BUY A SECOND BEEMER? I CAN'T EVEN RENT OUT MY VACATION CONDO . . . HEY, IS IT ME OR IS THERE SOMETHING WRONG WITH THE SERVICE HERE?"

line, Particle Man is trying to figure out what financial interest each talking head is shilling for, what its speaking fee was before the broadcast, and what the fee will be afterwards.

In her despiritualized life, she strips billowy questions down to their real-world fundamentals. Having come of age without war but with an obsessive fear of nuclear holocaust, she sees apocalypse for what it is—just death. She sees herself as post-ideological, in some ways even post-religious. She's hesitant to impose her beliefs (on everything from school prayer to abortion) on others. Her Particle God is straightforward, prone to action. What God sells, He services; when He bills, He collects—then it's over.

Particle Man values the physical. Muscles matter, style counts, speed is crucial. To him, nothing is incontrovertibly real unless he can *touch* it, *feel* it, *do* it. He understands the chasm that separates the realm of things and deeds from the realm of words and symbols. Fighting a war or delivering a pizza, he knows talk alone gets him nowhere. What people demand—more to the point, what people pay for—are results. So Particle Man focuses on pleasing whoever's name is on the paybill, and he otherwise doesn't much care who approves or disapproves.

Beneath her hardened exterior lies a Particle heart that is soft, if selective. Friends and family matter enormously. She gets along well with her parents; she even likes their music. She despises nothing more than divorce and cruelty to children, having known too much of that herself. She celebrates unconditional love, because she hasn't known enough of that herself. She can smile readily at strangers if necessary for her job, but she reserves genuine emotion for those close to her. Beyond family, her civic virtue is intensely private. Saving the world matters less than feeding one meal to one hungry child.

His values are fixed on the bottom line. What works is good; what doesn't, isn't. He rejects the therapeutic ethos under which he was raised, in favor of an ethos of personal determinism that requires each individual to take responsibility for his own condition. His justice is all-or-nothing. He hates wrongful imprisonment. But if you do bad and get caught, don't expect mercy. He has scant sympathy for anything—a nation, an industry, a household—that just wants to "get by" by leaning on others and isn't fighting to survive on its own, as he has to do. Like the mysterious beer-ad cowboy who leaves the bar door swinging, Particle Man won't let niceties fence him into a bad situation. Helping a buddy is fine. But following "the rules" wherever they might lead? Good luck, chump.

Life moves pretty fast. You don't stop an' look around a little while, you could miss it.

Ferris Bueller, *Ferris Bueller's Day Off* (film)

All the sugar Twice the caffeine

ad slogan for Jolt Cola

I'm not afraid. Only the strong survive. I'm strong.

boy, 16, New York City

I am a member of the MTV generation to a degree. My attention span isn't terribly long.

Jeff (Dougie) Zucker, 26, *Today Show* producer

When I think of Jeff, I think of fingers snapping: Boom, boom, boom. He gets things done.

Zucker as described by (Boomer) Katie Couric

I feel the need, the need for speed.

fighter pilot and copilot, in unison as they buckle into their cockpit, *Top Gun* (film)

***crasher
>I admit, I sort of dig the particle man idea. when I was 15, I started a little makeshift company in my room to manufacture i.d.'s so that my friends and I could get into r-rated movies. we had rubber stamps, laminators, and photography equipment, the whole works--and every night we would manufacture alter egos for my pubescent friends. pretty soon, we got cigarettes, pornography, and eventually alcohol. a 7-eleven employee named elmo with no teeth needs no further convincing. when my mom found my i.d. (a french visa that made me jean-claude etoile, a 23-year-old exchange student from vichy) she just laughed and pulled it out of the dirty laundry. particle man, indeed.

She hates wasted energy, because that's a luxury she knows she can't afford. Wherever she sees useless tangles or time-wasting process, she looks for a quick bypass. When something works, she knows how to capitalize. When something doesn't work, she knows when to give it up.

His best skills lie in niches his elders don't know as well and are at times afraid to learn: telecommunications, computer technology, pop culture. His satellite dish is tuned to the latest trends among far-flung peoples, and he has a Garthlike ability to get those people what they want, quickly and cheaply. Particle Man is adept in doing (and being) what the world wants from America. If former Communist countries could choose one guy to help them build a marketplace out of social chaos—one guy to teach and train their own people—he's who they'd pick in a flash.

She excels at exactly those parts of life where she perceives older generations failing. Mainly, she does the dirty work—and gets less than fair credit for it. Again and again, she has watched older people break free of customs, laws, bureaucracies, and families which, according to some eternal law of social entropy, always seem to crumble into a state of greater uselessness just when they start becoming important to her. So she stands ready to reconstruct social barriers that, as she sees it, will bring order to chaos.

Much of what Particle Man does in these tasks bothers the elder eye. To which he says, quoting Hard Harry: "Yeah, whatever."

Others have had their little binge, their little drug-debt-and-divorce debacle, their little overconsumption party. Now it's time for history's great cleanup brigade. That's not a pretty job, but somebody's got to do it. If not Particle Man, who? What he would like from older generations, maybe hopelessly, is to lend him an unjaundiced ear. Or, failing that, just to leave him be—and stop making him the fall guy for mistakes made by others.

***crasher
>I have to tell you, though, for every cagey and crafty particle man my age, there are about 20 slowly-revolving neutrons whose only real craft is thinking up diseases so that they won't have to wait tables this weekend. I wish I could say that this whizzy, get-it-done attitude applied to all my friends, but it turned many of them toward the pursuit of doing nothing, but with a passion.

>4. A Lot of Adult Mistakes

Every day, over 2,500 American children witness the divorce or separation of their parents. Every day, 90 kids are taken from their parents' custody and committed to foster homes. Every day, thirteen Americans age 15 to 24 commit suicide, and another sixteen are murdered. Every day, the typical 14-year-old watches 3 hours of TV and does 1 hour of homework. Every day, over 2,200 kids drop out of school. Every day, 3,610 teenagers are assaulted, 630 are robbed, and 80 are raped. Every day, over 100,000 high-school students bring guns to school. Every day, 500 adolescents begin using illegal drugs and 1,000 begin drinking alcohol. Every day, 1,000 unwed teenage girls become mothers.

Assessing the harsh living environment of today's rising generation, one national commission recently concluded: "Never before has one generation of American teenagers been less healthy, less cared for, or less prepared for life than their parents were at the same age." In the 13er cult film *Heathers*, one teenager put it more bluntly: "You don't get it, do you? Society nods its head at any horror the American teenager can bring upon himself."

Thirteeners may or may not be a "bad" generation, but what is not debatable is that their *condition* is bad. Even their worst critics have to admit that whatever badness they are is a reflection of how they were raised—of what other people did to them, thought of them, and expected from them—and of what happened in the adult world throughout their childhood years.

Coming of age in an era when America hands out sympathy and entitlements to so many victims of past wrongs, 13ers might reasonably expect a little of the same. After all, the import-beaten union worker gets his unemployment compensation, the ex-hippie yuppie gets his home mortgage deduction, the stars-and-stripes retiree gets his pension COLA. Why not give 13ers

Children in Poverty*, 1979–1982:

Sweden	5%
West Germany	8%
Canada	10%
United Kingdom	11%
United States	17%

* using the official U.S. definition of cash-income "poverty"
Source: Luxembourg Income Study

Living in a world where grown-ups break the rules
Paying for a lot of adult mistakes

Janet Jackson,
"Living in a World (They Didn't Make)" (song)

▬

Turned on the TV this morning. Had this shit on about living in a violent world. Showed all these foreign places. Foreigners live in all of them. Started thinkin', man—either they don't know, don't show, or don't care about what's going on in the hood.

black youth in Los Angeles,
Boyz 'n the Hood (film)

▬

We are raising a generation . . . without a future.

Bill Clinton

▬

It is fair to assume that the United States has become the first society in history in which a person is more likely to be poor if young rather than old.

Senator Daniel Patrick Moynihan

something for a few of the minor inconveniences they too have borne over their short life spans—like disintegrating families, failed schools, and a zero-wage-growth economy? No way, Wayne. America reserves its big-bucks assistance to older age brackets, to those who grew up in "harder times."

OK, forget about the past. Why not just give 13ers a little help with their current problems—like the fact that a growing share of them don't qualify for welfare, can't afford a house, and will never get a pension. No again. Sorry, but with all that hot cash flying around in the '80s, older Americans somehow settled into the view that 13ers got more than their share—and, if a few didn't, something must have been seriously wrong with them. (I saw one just the other day—no job, but walks in and buys a twenty-dollar CD. Can you *believe* it?)

These days, 13ers bear the heaviest brunt from America's new turn toward post-therapeutic determinism. Never given much reason to feel entitled themselves, 13ers generally go along with the view that each person should take care of his own condition. In fact, with their huge voting margins in favor of federal budget-chopping, 13ers did more than any other generation during the '80s to repopularize the notion of self-sufficiency. So who are they to complain that America now cheerfully agrees with them—even if the agreement only extends to issues affecting their own age group? Confronted with sexually active teens, welfare moms, unemployed grads, or inner-city gangsters, America says, "Hey, let them hurt and learn." But when it comes to applying the same principle to older people—for example, to seniors who run up huge Medicare bills because of lifelong drinking or smoking habits—America says, "Hey, go easy on them." If government spending is perceived as producing undesirable behavior among the young (like the welfare "means test" that cuts benefits for the working poor), the public's instinct is to fix the

***crasher
>I don't hear anybody but bloated yupsters complaining about the '80s. they seem so intent on disowning that entire era, like they were completely different nasty greedy people then. really, man, you guys have got to find yourselves a decade and stick with it. all I remember from this "period of waste and excess" is that I always had enough money to play a fifteenth game of "galaga" and still buy the extended remix of "she blinded me with science."

problem by cutting funding. Yet if spending is perceived as doing the same among the old (like the Social Security "earnings test" that cuts benefits for working seniors), the public's instinct is to fix the problem by *increasing* funding.

As they watch so many older people enrich themselves (while blaming young people for, of all things, being greedy), 13ers sometimes play the blame game themselves. When they do, they look up the age ladder and see one massive, opaque population mass—Boomer yuppies—as the culprits. But Boomers are just one of three over-age-30 layers in today's constellation of living American generations. And there's plenty of blame to go around.

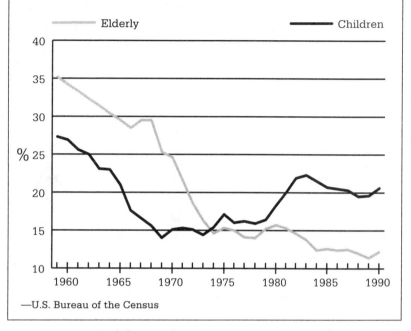

Official Poverty Rates for Children (Under Age 18) and the Elderly (Over Age 65), 1959 to 1990

—U.S. Bureau of the Census

The senior citizens of the "G.I. Generation," numbering nearly 30 million, comprise America's most politically powerful generation since Thomas Jefferson's. They deserve the tag "G.I." partly because of their war-hero hubris, but also because the two dictionary definitions for that acronym ("General Issue" and "Government Issue") aptly describe their generation's we-first collegialism and immensely beneficial lifelong relationship with government.

To G.I.s, 13ers were the kids who were born right around the time of their famous row with Boomers (the "generation gap" of the '60s and '70s). At the time, fiftyish G.I. fathers were reviled by their own children for supposedly having become spirit-dead macho men, and G.I. mothers for supposedly having wasted their lives as stay-at-home housewives or for having chosen nurturing (alias "women's") professions. Having heard others tell them how badly they had failed at building the Great Society, G.I.s gave up the argument and entered the '70s with what amounted to a "forget it" attitude toward children. (Heck, if the young don't like us, we'll pick up our marbles and leave.) Pick up a few marbles they did: From 1965 to 1979, real fed-

The neighborhood houses and community centers that helped previous generations of restless youths, white and black, are gone or struggling. The police officer who might once have turned a delinquent kid or young addict over to a minister or social worker may have little choice now but to send him to jail.

"Young Black Men," editorial in the *New York Times*

eral spending per elderly person quadrupled. And leave they did—away from their own families, often into sunscape communities that explicitly barred children and sometimes even exempted themselves from school taxes. Later on, when threatened by tax hikes, the same group whose first president exhorted the nation to "Ask not . . ." fueled revolts like California's Proposition 13 that enabled them to pay only a fraction of the tax due from younger homeowners.

In national politics, G.I.s organized themselves into A.A.R.P.-style generational lobbies to promote their own age-bracket agenda. They succeeded in shifting public and private resources, and the very definition of age-based "entitlements," away from the young and toward themselves. They became the best-insured, most leisured, and (in relation to the young) most affluent generation of elders in American history. Before the first G.I.s started to hit their 65th birthday in the mid-'60s, the elderly age bracket was the nation's most poverty-prone; in 1975, this distinction jumped to the (13er) child age bracket, where it has stayed ever since.

G.I.s occupied the White House for 32 years, far longer than any other generation in U.S. history. After coming of age as patient savers and world-conquering heroes, they spent midlife building what they expected to be an everlasting economic cornucopia. But their V-for-Victory hubris tempted them to overreach—and to overreward themselves. Bit by bit, their seven presidents from Kennedy to Bush tilted public policy toward the short-term interests of their own G.I. peers and against the long-term interests of young 13ers. They tolerated a tenfold increase in the national debt, an even larger increase in unfunded future liabilities for elder entitlements programs, a deterioration of public and private investment in infrastructure, and an accelerated depletion of groundwater, fossil fuels, atmospheric ozone, and other irreplaceable natural resources. From JFK's "Pay Any Price" to LBJ's "Guns and Butter" to the national debt-leveraging of Reaganomics, G.I.-led America has spent the entire 13er life cycle favoring consumption over invest-

***crasher

>my grandpa isn't from another generation, he's from neptune. every time we go visit him, he asks my little brother and me about "trout fishing," which is the remnant of some conversation we had with him in 1975. we both pretend to be tibetan monks who don't like girls and have never seen a beer, then we take his money and bolt out of there before we get too weirded out.

YOU'RE O.K. I'M MESSED UP

ment, living beyond current income, and raiding the future to make up the difference.

Inevitably, such raids have done best for G.I.s, whose lives are mostly in the past tense—and worst for 13ers, whose lives are mostly in the future. It is not the youngest Americans who have reaped the benefits of Social Security COLAs, runaway Medicare spending, S&L bailouts, senior saver discounts, unlimited mortgage deductions, CEO golden parachutes, and tax cuts for $100,000-plus households. And it is not the oldest Americans who must pay the price for mounting budget deficits, unfunded benefit liabilities, dwindling savings rates, lackluster R&D, crumbling highways, and deepening foreign import penetration. It's no surprise that recent polls show the over-65 age bracket with the strongest support for government as it presently operates, and the under-30 bracket with the most cynicism about it.

In effect, G.I. seniors have opted for a trade in the currencies of old age: Their economic well-being has come at the expense of the moral authority prior generations of American elders once wielded over the young. How G.I.s today appear to 13er youths could not be more different from how America's Depression-era seniors appeared to G.I.s when they were kids themselves. Back then, people in their seventies earned respect not for their economic and political clout, but for their cultural achievement and wisdom. Now, the opposite is true. The up side is that 13ers look upon G.I. seniors as builders of big things that worked well in their heyday, as natural optimists comfortable with progress, as corny parental figures who gave to their own (Boomer) children the kind of *Happy Days* '50s experience 13ers often wish they had received. The down side is that, to 13er eyes, G.I.s are nonparticipants in cultural trends, irrelevant in values debates, and advocates of the sort of endless economic pump-priming that threatens to bankrupt the future.

Average number of school days per year:	
Japan	240
West Germany	210
Great Britain	210
France	210
United States	180

Source: National Governors Association

It's hard to see why someone age 68 should automatically pay lower taxes than someone age 28 with the same income. Yet, that happens.

Robert Samuelson, *Newsweek* columnist

Over a third of the young men and women between the ages of 19 and 29 have little or no ambition ten years after their parents' divorce. They are drifting through life with no set goals, limited educations, and a sense of helplessness.

Judith Wallerstein and Sandra Blakeslee, *Second Chances: Men, Women, and Children a Decade After Divorce* (book)

Survey question asked of Americans age 15 to 24: Compared to when your parents were your age, do you think it's easier or harder to be a young person today? In roughly the same proportions for all races, 17 percent say easier and 77 percent say harder.

Source: 1991 survey by People for the American Way

```
***crasher
>man, what must those older folks be thinking? I mean, what the hell
does my grandma think when she turns on cable to watch "the golden
girls" and instead gets "dude looks like a lady" on mtv? no wonder they all
seem so glassy-eyed. they must all think they've seen the apocalypse.

***2boomers
>you ought to give them a few pop culture lessons, crasher.

***crasher
>they'd never listen anyway.
```

Grown-up 13ers are just beginning to notice how government hands out benefits and tax favors to what Coupland calls "Silver Fox" retirees who, as young eyes see it, are awash in money and nice houses. They notice how well-to-do seniors get big discounts (for plane fares, movie tickets, food, admission to National Parks) when poor 25-year-olds have to pay full price. They notice how rising FICA taxes on low-wage young workers fuel programs that help the comfortable old, and how the anti-tax crusades of affluent elders starve programs that help the struggling young. For now, 13er resentment against "entitled" G.I.s remains unfocused and inconsequential. Like most other Americans who came of age after D-Day, they'll pay their G.I. tithe. But, unlike Americans in their thirties through sixties, 13ers feel no personal connection to the struggles and victories for which this aging generation of heroes and heroines continues to claim a reward.

Next comes the generation that has had the greatest shaping influence on the 13ers' day-to-day world: the "Silent Generation," forty million strong, now mostly in their fifties and sixties. They got the tag "Silent" back in the McCarthy-era '50s, when their leading edge came of age gliding compliantly into newly built suburban society. By today's standards, that society was oversimple, conformist, and bland—if full of affordable homes, entry-level jobs, and terrific career prospects. Much like 13ers (but for very different reasons), the Silent have always felt a sense of generational inadequacy and an awkward location in U.S. history. They were born too late to be authentic G.I.-style war heroes, with all that outer-world hubris—and too soon to share fully in the Vietnam-era rage and youth rebellion, with all that inner-world smugness. The Silent timing wasn't all bad, however: Theirs is far and away the wealthiest generation in the history of America, maybe the world—making them the only living Americans who could half believe (along with Woody Allen) that "eighty percent of life is just showing up."

More than any other generation, it can be truly said that the Silent raised 13ers. For most of the 60s-born Atari-wavers, the Silent were in fact the biological mothers and fathers. Yet even for later-born Nintendo-wavers—many of whom had younger parents—the Silent personality has always exercised a profound influence over their lives. When 13ers were kids in the '70s, the Silent provided most of America's therapists and lawyers, community leaders and school principals. When 13ers began coming of age in the '80s, the Silent provided most of America's college presidents and media moguls, corporate CEOs and cabinet members, generals and legislators.

For millions of Silent parents, 13er babies were a problem from

Christmas is a time when kids tell Santa Claus what they want and adults pay for it. Deficits are when adults tell the government what they want—and their kids pay for it.

Richard Lamm,
former Governor of Colorado

———

The best marketing agent for old-fashioned values was my first-grade teacher. Miss Billard handed out our savings books every Wednesday, so we could watch our pennies grow. Now our kids watch the government deficit grow. Why should they practice self-restraint?

mother of college student whose daughter ran up huge department store credit-card charges

———

On buses, in stores, on the Metro, we should smile at them, start conversations with them, respect them . . . . We can't let a whole generation think we are afraid of them.

caller to Washington, D.C., talk-radio program

the start. The infants who arrived too soon and too often. The tiny tots who started walking, talking, and demanding real attention right around when their thirty- and fortysomething parents reached their late-'60s moment of maximum life cycle confusion, what author Gail Sheehy has described as "passages." Chafing under the new youth charge that no one over 30 was to be trusted, the Silent stopped emulating older G.I.s and redirected their antennae toward the boiling Boomers. Where little Boomers had been America's whole focus when G.I.s were hitting midlife, little 13ers were roadblocks in the path of the midlife Silent quest to recapture a lost youth. The sexual revolution hit the virgin-groom Silent dads, and women's lib the virgin-bride Silent moms, at a time that was exhilarating if inconvenient for them—but devastating for their children.

The Silent set the tone for a decade many 13ers today look upon as the most ridiculous of their young lives: the R-rated 1970s. After the tumult of the '60s had died down, the fortyish Silent sputtered into midlife with far less confidence and collective power than G.I.s had shown two decades earlier. They set off trading (up?) in real estate and marital partners, diversifying (dismantling?) their families, and pushing outward (downward?) the bounds of cultural taste in music, film, television, and art. They became the Donald Kennedy generation of do-your-own-thing school administrators who, in discipline and achievement, were no match for what the G.I.s had once been; the Ralph Nader generation of lawyers, jurors, and plaintiffs who set America off on its litigation craze; the Phil Donahue generation of TV and radio talk show hosts that vented the dark sides of the adult psyche; the Jack Nicholson generation of screen stars who fostered a new cynicism in young viewers; and the Joyce Brothers generation of therapists who counseled kids to "open up" when their families broke down.

Come the 1980s, a new ambivalence seeped into the Silent-13er relationship. Silent moms and dads watched their high-school-age kids get mediocre scores on the same SAT test they remembered having aced back in the '50s. They then watched their college-age kids display little of the nuance, romanticism, and other-directed sensitivities their own generation had always valued so highly. Silent parents began to feel a very real disappointment in their kids—and they let their kids know it.

Worse, many Silent parents came to realize that their sons and daughters would probably never match their own adult standard of living. Remembering how they themselves had shot ahead of their own parents' economic achievements while still in their twenties, the Silent watched and worried as child poverty soared and their own postgraduate children boomeranged back home. They seethed with frustration as the U.S. Congress, in their hands, reached its present-day gridlock while debt-fueled consumption

ARE YOU 13ER MATERIAL?
DO YOU HAVE THE RIGHT *GENERATIONAL* STUFF?
TAKE THIS SIMPLE SELF-QUIZ AND FIND OUT!

IF YOU PUT A QUARTER INTO A VIDEO GAME AND...

GUN
MEGA DEATH

NOTHING HAPPENED.

IT'S AN ALIEN!!
RELAX... GO WITH THE FLOW...
LIVE AND LET LIVE.
INSTRUCTIONS KILL OR BE KILLED

WHAT WOULD YOU DO?

A PURSUE PEACE PROCESS. NEGOTIATE. MEDIATE. SCORE NO POINTS.

B ORGANIZE. LOBBY CONGRESS. DEMAND FREE GAMES.

C COMPLAIN. BOYCOTT. KEEP LITTLE KIDS AWAY FROM VIDEO GAMES.

D SHOOT FIRST! START A WAR. GET THE TOP SCORE!!

ANSWER KEY: A SILENT B G.I. C BOOM D DUDE!

***crasher
>hee, hee, hee, hee...

***2boomers
>what's so funny?

***crasher
>it's just that the whole thing looks like some big generational soap opera. I half expect the silents to come home and tell the g.i.'s that they're having the 13ers' love child...while the boom is out back in the shed inventing some sort of "youth ointment"...

***2boomers
>you're missing the point. we're trying to show that all these generations have different life cycle connections with history, giving them different collective personalities and making them interact with each other in peculiar ways. that way we can explain why your age group gets dumped on all the time.

***crasher
>I just can't think of it like that, all these boundaries, cut and dried relationships, weird grudges. I don't want to be a part of this great big play. all the actors make me sick.

The adults we were supposed to respect and learn from wore T-shirts or carried mugs with slogans like "He who dies with the most toys wins."

Marci Ecker, student, Lehigh University

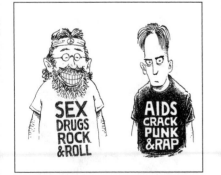

America's Living Generations		
	birthyears	age on December 31, 1992
Lost	1883–1900	over 91
G.I.	1901–1924	68 to 91
Silent	1925–1942	50 to 67
Boom	1943–1960	32 to 49
13th	1961–1981	11 to 31
Millennial	1982–?	under 11

soared ever higher. Yet unlike the more complacent elder G.I.s, the midlife Silent have felt anxiety and guilt over what America has been doing to its young on their watch. "Fiscal child abuse," Congressman John Porter has called it. Yet his generation has precious little idea how to stop it.

To be fair, we could say a lot more on behalf of these older generations. Yes, the G.I. and Silent have left positive legacies and set positive examples. G.I.s invented the big band sound, patiently endured a catastrophic depression, soldiered a global struggle against fascism that mankind couldn't afford to lose, and ultimately led the West to a lopsided victory in the Cold War. The Silent invented rock'n'roll, marched for civil rights, ushered their society into the postmodern Information Age, and generally made America a kinder. . . . OK, let's stop there. No sense spending more time praising these generations than they spend praising 13ers.

Are we forgetting someone? Boomers? Oh yes, Boomers.

>5. Woodstock—Blech!

"How can kids today be so dumb?" the *Washington Post*'s Tony Kornheiser wondered sarcastically, in an especially robust 13er-bash. "They can't even make change unless the cash register tells them exactly how much to remit. Have you seen their faces when your cheeseburger and fries comes to $1.73, and you give them $2.03? They freeze, thunderstruck. They have absolutely no comprehension what to do next."

Boom to 13th: "Shape Up!"

13th to Boom: "*SHUT* Up!"

Boomers in the media waste no occasion to describe how superior they are to the pile of demographic junk they see in their rearview mirrors. They persist in heaping insult on injury, hyperinflating their already huge collective egos with every tidbit that documents the alleged stupidity and vacuity of the young.

***crasher
>this tony kornheiser dude has got to be the biggest sack of dung I've ever heard! so us kids can't give you change for your mcwhateverburger quick enough for you? let's yank away your cushy day job, your dictaphone and your dental insurance...slip your fat butt into a pair of burgundy polyester mcpants, make you slap mayonnaise on 15,000 crudburgers until 4 in the morning, and we'll see how fast you want to make change for whiney goofballs like yourself!

The typical Boomer sees little in 13ers beyond cunning; the typical 13er sees little in Boomers beyond bombast. To self-appointed Boom defenders of culture, 13ers play the unlettered, gold-chasing Hun. But 13ers turn the analogy around. To them, it's the Boomers who play the highbrow Visigothic horde whose vast self-indulgence leaves nothing behind for those who follow. Whatever the age-bracket, 13ers always enter it just after the signposts have been trampled, the granaries emptied, the towns and farms pillaged—just when the mood of the countryside has turned ugly toward any new traveler passing through. They learn how wonderful life used to be in that territory only through the tales of others. All they ever get to see are the ruins.

Every phase-of-life has been fine, even terrific, when Boomers entered it—and a wasteland when they left. America's 70 million Boomers might prefer to think of their generation as the halcyon of social progress, but

Do the following words apply more to young people today or young people 20 years ago? Response of all adults:

Trait	Today	20 Years Ago
Selfish	82%	5%
Materialistic	79%	15%
Reckless	73%	14%
Idealistic	38%	49%
Patriotic	24%	65%

Source: 1989 Gallup Poll

the facts show otherwise. Yes, the Boom is a generation of trends, *but all those trends are negative.* The eldest Boomers (those born in the middle '40s) had relatively low rates of social pathology and high rates of academic achievement. The youngest Boomers (born in the late '50s) had precisely the opposite: high pathology, low achievement. This wasn't entirely their fault. Boomers, like 13ers, are products of their times and of older generations who nurtured them in a certain way.

The modern damage to American childhood, adolescence, and young adulthood began to afflict late-born Boomers even before

Of all college students (roughly half) who have heard of the New Age movement, 14 percent have a favorable opinion of the movement and 47 percent have an unfavorable opinion. Among students with A averages, 65 percent view it unfavorably.

Source: George H. Gallup International Institute

13ers came along. In the 1940s, the very thought of making babies propelled young soldiers and Rosie-the-Riveters to victory over fascism; in the 1950s, baby-making was just standard suburban behavior; by the 1960s, the very thought drove young couples to doctors to prevent it. A child's world was unerringly sunny in the '50s, overshadowed by adult arguments in the '60s, scarred by family chaos in the '70s. In the '50s, nearly every movie or TV show was fit for kids to watch; come the '60s, it was touch and go; come the '70s, forget it. The quality of new teacher recruits remained high through the '50s, became suspect in the draft-pressured '60s, and sank (along with teacher pay) through the '70s. Adolescent sexual discovery meant free love in 1970, herpes in 1980, AIDS in 1990.

In and after college, Boomers produced even more debris for their

Do you think that rock musicians were more creative 20 years ago, or more creative today? Do you think they were more concerned about making money back then, or more concerned about making money today?

	Age of Respondent	Today	20 Years Ago
MORE CREATIVE	18-29	35%	45%
	30-49	30%	43%
MORE CONCERNED ABOUT MONEY	18-29	75%	5%
	30-49	62%	1%

Source: 1990 Gallup Poll

High School Seniors Agreeing	in 1975	in 1988
Because of future shortages, Americans will have to learn how to be happy with fewer "things"	75%	54%
I would probably be willing to use a bicycle or mass transit (if available) rather than a car to get to work	56%	26%

Source: "Monitoring the Future: Questionnaire Responses from the Nation's High School Seniors" (University of Michigan, 1975–1988)

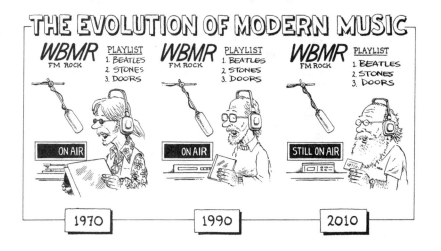

THE EVOLUTION OF MODERN MUSIC

WBMR FM ROCK — PLAYLIST 1. BEATLES 2. STONES 3. DOORS — ON AIR — 1970

WBMR FM ROCK — PLAYLIST 1. BEATLES 2. STONES 3. DOORS — ON AIR — 1990

WBMR FM ROCK — PLAYLIST 1. BEATLES 2. STONES 3. DOORS — STILL ON AIR — 2010

successors. Campuses, once sites for grand movements uniting students against enemies from without, have evolved into P.C. battlegrounds pitting students against enemies from within. Postgraduate life, once fluid with adventure and experiment, has become a mixture of *Slacker* alienation and *Blade Runner* survivalism. The entry-level job market, booming in 1970, is bone dry now. Becoming a "thirtysomething," a big yuppie deal in the 1980s, is a tired subject today.

The Boom-era damage has been particularly severe among the hardest-pressed 13ers. The gap between the young rich and the young poor, bridgeable for Boomers, has become a yawning canyon. Minority-group claims have lost much of their '60s-era luster and leadership. Inner cities, then perceived as morally solid and economically improving, are now social Dresdens of ruined families, gang crime, and sudden death. Boomer teens who got in trouble heard political leaders call for social services; 13ers who get in trouble mainly hear calls for boot-camp prisons—or swift execution.

Whatever went wrong, 13ers—not Boomers—have gotten the brunt of the backlash. Again and again, America has gotten fed up with Boom-inspired transgressions. But after taking aim at the giant collective Boomer ego and winding up with a club to bash them for all the damage they did, America has always swung late, missed, and (*POW!*) hit the next bunch of saps to come walking by.

Constantly stepping into post-Boom wastelands and getting bashed for it, 13ers see Boomers as a generation that was once given everything—from a *Happy Days* present to a Tomorrowland future—and then threw it all away. Whatever the phase of life, childhood to college to young adulthood, 13ers accuse Boomers of having used up

"Do you really think we enjoy hearing about your brand new million-dollar home when we can barely afford to eat Kraft Dinner sandwiches in our own grimy little shoe boxes and we're approaching thirty? A home you won in a genetic lottery, I might add, sheerly by dint of your having been born at the right time in history? You'd last about ten minutes if you were my age these days, Martin. And I have to endure pinheads like you rusting above me for the rest of my life, always grabbing the best piece of cake first and then putting a barbed-wire fence around the rest. You really make me sick."

Douglas Coupland, *Generation X* (book)

I like to think (God, I pray) I have learned from your generation's irresponsibility and cavalier attitude toward family, sex, drugs and the Earth. I have to clean up the mess you left behind, and if you think I should be joyous and dancing in the streets, you are dead wrong.

Jill Strass, Washington, DC

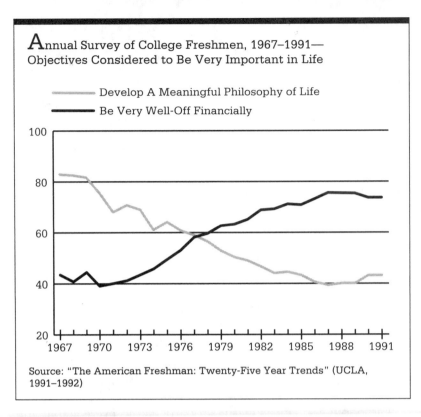

Annual Survey of College Freshmen, 1967–1991—
Objectives Considered to Be Very Important in Life

Develop A Meaningful Philosophy of Life
Be Very Well-Off Financially

Source: "The American Freshman: Twenty-Five Year Trends" (UCLA, 1991–1992)

its moral capital, squandered all its elder goodwill, and told the last exiting Boomer to turn off the lights on the way out. And so, like a generation of River Phoenixes *Running on Empty*, 13ers have to cope and survive in whatever the Boom leaves behind.

Both generations know who holds the fancier life cycle résumé. Mainline Boomers came of age during the '60s, a terrific decade to have been young, while 13ers were stamped by the '80s, a decade about which they already have a hard time manufacturing nostalgia.

Thirteeners show a mixed attitude toward the '60s. Young conservatives can't stand that decade; to them, it brings to mind intoxicating rhetoric, immoral behavior, and big mistakes leading to punishing social consequences. Young liberals miss the ethos of that era and envy Boomers for having known it first hand. Whatever their politics, 13ers widely admit that the '60s kids captured the attention of the nation in a way that '80s kids never did. Sometimes, today's young adults join in '60s nostalgia by conjuring up a stylized image of careless innocence and infinite parental indulgence. But what ruins this image beyond repair is the Boom itself—especially the juxtaposition of how Boomers behaved back then with their PC rectitude of the present day.

Many a 13er would be delighted never to read another commemorative article about Woodstock, Kent State, or the Free Speech Movement. Or to suffer through what Coupland calls "legislated nostalgia," this celebration of supposedly great events in the life cycle of people they don't especially like. Even among 13ers who admire what young people did back in the '60s, workaholic, values-fixated Boomers are an object lesson of what not to become in their thirties and forties. But, like tie-dyed Marlena Baxter, making a living selling falafel to Grateful Deadheads, or like bell-bottomed Olivia d'Abo, cast as a hippieish girl in *The Wonder Years*, 13ers know how to present a Boomerish front when it works to their advantage. They just rent *Easy Rider* and *Hair* videos, and hey, no problem.

However often 13ers outwardly mimic their next elders, inwardly they fume plenty. They fume when they hear Boomers taking credit for things Boomers didn't do (civil rights, rock'n'roll, stopping the Vietnam War) and for supposedly having been so much more creative, idealistic, morally conscious, and generally *better* than 13ers. When they watch Boomer films wallow in self-absorption over "what we did" in the '60s. When they hear fortyish professors lecture them for being sexist, racist, amoral morons. When they see Boomers out at night being their grinning yuppie selves, and then read Boomer-penned articles in the morning paper dripping with judgmentalism—like the one in the *Washington Post* about how, to today's "gilded youth," the "fiery concerns of many of their predecessors over peace and social justice are mementos from a dimming past."

They fume at the thought that Boomers are willing to let them become the bicycle messengers, video-checkout kids, and VCR repairmen of their fast-track world, but would never let the 13th Generation emerge as a cultural force to challenge the *gravitas* of The Great Boom itself. Twenty years ago, Silent 40-year-olds in the media, advertising, and public relations listened respectfully, often approvingly, to the creative ideas of kids in their twenties. Today,

So who's got the attitude problem? It's a generational conceit to look at the generation just behind one and call it trashy. It makes those old hippies feel good when they say, "young people today have no idealism". . . . But before they indulge in too much self-satisfied disappointment over how we're turning out, they might take a moment to fathom how disappointed we are in them . . . .

Steven Gibb,
Twentysomething (book)

Your summer of love is our winter of despair . . . .

Everett Tassevigen,
"The 13th Generation"
(poem)

Let the self-satisfied, self-appointed, self-righteous baby boomers be the first to practice the new austerity they have been preaching of late.

Mark Featherman,
"The '80s Party Is Over," in
the *New York Times*

Boomer 40-year-olds can't imagine hearing recent grads telling them anything they haven't already thought of. (Uh, why don't you go over there and work the phones—or, even better, what about the copy machine? I bet you know how to run that baby real well!)

Through it all, today's young adults sometimes wonder: *Can't those Boomers see how they look to us?* The 13er image of the proto-Boomer is an ugly mosaic built out of the worst figments of each Boomer phase of life. The klutzy naivete of vintage Mouseketeer preteens blends into the flaky radicalism of Woodstock hippies, into the dissolute narcissism of Travolta disco dancers, into the Sharper Image consumerism of brie-and-chablis yuppies, into the smug pomposity of today's politically correct neopuritans. Glomming this into one life cycle pastiche, 13ers see Boomers as the most colossal hypocrites in the million-year history of *Homo sapiens*. Someday, some way, 13ers would love to get those Boomers on life's equivalent of *Remote Control*, swivel their yuppie chairs around, and dump them in a vat of greenish goo.

Like two neighbors separated by a spite fence, Boomers and 13ers have grown accustomed to an uneasy adjacency. In 1989, a handful of young-adults formed a mock organization, "The National Association for the Acceleration of Time," that urged Boomers to hurry up, get old, and get out of the way. No chance, guys. Nobody's going anywhere.

America's next great generation gap—this time pitting righteous middle-aged Boomers against alienated young-adult 13ers—is heating up, on the verge of boiling over.

***crasher

>I don't see it as our generations complaining about each other. I just see an older group of people with a strangling death grip on the media, putting out movies, writing songs and dreaming up sitcoms that don't speak to anyone my age.

***2boomers

>are you saying that you don't like any movie or tv show that has come out recently?

***crasher

>no, I like them all okay...but it stops there. there's so much whining over "the lost dream" these days that I would rather stay inside and throw darts with my housemates.

***2boomers

>at some picture of a yuppie, no doubt.

***crasher

>personally, all I want from you is an admission.

***2boomers

>an admission of what?

***crasher

>an admission that your generation wasn't as spiritually fantabulous as you would have us believe. rock and roll, civil rights and vietnam protests were movements that you were not responsible for yet you guys take credit every chance you get. and crap like drugs, crime, sexual diseases and family stress is all stuff you blame us for, when you are the ones that raised them all to an art form. you blame young folks for having no concept of the higher ideals in life, when you're the ones who trashed most of them. you delved into this selfish, flaky, hippie drug philosophy when it was hip, then did a 180, and then accuse us of having a short attention span!

***2boomers

>o.k. you've got a point.

***crasher

>you guys seem to have completely lost sight of the emotional work ethic. you spend all your money on every 2-second varnish remover, baldness cure or instant religious salvation that comes on cable after midnight. you are always looking for the easy way out, figuring that it's much simpler to stick a vacuum cleaner in your love handles than to eat right in the first place. your gnatlike attention span has produced a culture of ideas that is far junkier than any video game we could ever waste an hour playing, and the voracity with which you go through self-help books, celebrity diets and unauthorized biographies shows how little soul you had to start with. you were given everything, and then somehow started to confuse your quest for ideological perfection with self-indulgent laziness.

someone famous once said that "some people are born great, and others have greatness thrust upon them," but you guys seem hell-bent on having greatness surgically implanted.

***2boomers

>any surgery we can do to ease your pain?

***crasher

>okay, one wish. can you slice the song "woodstock" by crosby, stills, and nash out of every radio station playlist in the nation? it has that line "by the time we got to woodstock, we were half a million strong..." there were only 300,000 people there! that sounds picky, but it really makes me angry.

***2boomers

>we'll see what we can do.

>6. Born a Little Late

In 1979, a new breed of college frosh slipped into American campuses and started calming them down. For years, faculty members had obligingly lined up to introduce themselves. Suddenly, as Georgetown's campus minister put it, "students began lining up to introduce themselves to us." Two months later, America's 444 days of hostage humiliation began. Just after the Iranian mob swarmed into the U.S. Embassy, a University of Georgia student center gave a special screening of the movie *Patton*. The students gave the film a standing ovation, hanged an effigy of the Ayatollah, and marched through the streets chanting anti-Iran slogans. In 1980, with American campuses split between two generations, a national survey found half again more freshmen than seniors agreeing with the statement "my country right or wrong." These USA!-chanting kids struck tenured '60s-style radicals as precisely what they thought they'd never see: a reactive, revanchist generation. A decade earlier, college kids wore flowers in their hair and were proudly "greening" America. Now they dressed in black and were busy tracking down jobs.

The frosh of 1979 marked the leading edge of a new generation. They had been the babies of JFK's inauguration, the 3-year-olds of Tonkin Gulf, the 8-year-olds of Woodstock and Chappaquiddick, the 13-year-olds of Watergate, and now the 18-year-olds of national humiliation. Over the next decade, they would age into the 20-year-olds of Reagan's "Morning in America," the 22-year-olds in caps and gowns when *A Nation at Risk* derided American education, the 26-year-old Wall Street neophytes of the 1987 crash, the 29-year-olds of Desert Storm, and the thirtyzeroes of the 1991 recession.

Like father, like son? Like mother, like daughter? Everyone agreed these kids were unBoomlike—but were they a flashback to what their parents had been, '50s-style College Joes and Betty Coeds? Hardly. Silent and 13th both belong to "sandwich" generations, stuck for life between others of greater power and reputation. But where the postadolescent Silent had been awkward naifs, mawkish and sentimental, these 13er kids were canny cynics, hard and smooth. Small wonder. When you revisit contemporary history as these two generations separately experienced it, it's hard to avoid the conclusion that the life cycle experience of the college class of '83 has been much the *opposite* of their Silent moms' and dads'.

The Silent Generation children of the 1930s were the most homogeneous, least immigrant American kids of the twentieth century. They were nurtured on *The Little Engine That Could*, network radio, and six teams to a sports league. By today's standards, life was slow, simple, conformist, lacking in nuance—but strong on the fundamentals. There was poverty (yes, the Great Depression left quite an impression on a child), but even most poor kids had intact families and felt part of a mainstream culture. By contrast, 13ers are the *most* diverse, *most* immigrant young generation this century. Nurtured on zoom-a-zoom-a-zoom-a-zoom, 78-channel cable, and 24-hour-a-day TV sports, they see life as fast, complex, entertaining—but weak on the fundamentals. And, in their world, being poor often means no father at home and a life of constant danger.

Born in the middle 1930s, today's sixtyish Silent passed through childhood in an era of parental overprotection and reached their thirties just as barriers to youth freedom were beginning to break. The adult world held lots of well-guarded secrets. Adolescent innocence gave sexual discovery a rapturous and weepy *Summer of '42* quality. Teen life was a simple conformist treadmill—date, steady, pin, marry, have a baby. In high school, scholastic aptitudes hovered at record levels. The rare "juvenile delinquent" was a Lonely Crowd outcast, tormented but with an aura of romance. Growing up in a world of blunt, scolding adults, the young Silent developed a taste for subtlety, gentility, communication, feelings.

The 13er experience could not have been more different. Born in the early 1960s, the first 13ers passed through childhood in an era of

A war he can't forget
In a time I can't remember

Poison, describing a Vietnam veteran, in "Something to Believe In" (song)

My first memory was when Nixon resigned. It was in first grade at Immaculate Conception grade school here. They brought all the classes together and we watched him fly away in a helicopter. Obviously, we didn't understand much. It was just Nixon. Bad. Nixon. Disgrace.

Dennis Cleary, student, Ohio State

> The era that we look back on with the misty fond nostalgia of childhood and early adulthood is a cultural wasteland devoid of any and all redeeming qualities. We are a generation of blunted wits dulled at the hands of Mike and Carol Brady. We are societal mutants weaned on "Zoom," the Fonz, and Pop Rocks. We are evolution's greatest practical joke.
>
> Scott Matthews, et al.,
> *Stuck in the Seventies* (book)

> I can't remember a time when Americans weren't into "Me."
>
> Steven Gibb,
> *Twentysomething* (book)

> All the great themes have been used up, been turned into theme parks.
>
> Hard Harry,
> *Pump Up the Volume* (film)

parental underprotection and are now approaching 30 just as new safeguards are being added to the youth world. Adults hid little from them, and their early access to wild goings-on stripped them of much of the pleasure of discovery. The symbolic meanings—of sex, drugs, politics, feminism, whatever—had all faded. Romance? Forget it. (Sinatra's crooning "Love and Marriage" became the sarcastic theme song for a Fox-TV family sitcom featuring two nasty 13ers.) What 13ers found instead were the harsh realities of social pathology. In school, they were mired in disappointing levels of achievement, and young criminals were perceived as purely bad, even evil. No child generation in world history has taken more trips to see therapists, yet 13ers are growing up as probably the least emotionally demonstrative of all American generations this century.

Looking through a child's window on the world during the '40s

```
***crasher
>that's because we got dragged to the therapist during soccer practice! none of those
guys ever gave me any advice that applied to the physical world as I saw it. dr. waxcraft
just gave me some hypertension pills and told me not to be such a drain on the family unit.
my old girlfriend's therapist hit on her. a whole group of children can't be demonstrative
when nobody speaks their language!
```

and '50s, the Silent grew up in awe of the power of elders. When they were small, America was in the skids of depression. As they reached adolescence, national confidence, community life, and families were all strong. Adults focused on the future, planned for it, and invested in it. In the childhood memory of today's 60-year-old midlifer, the crowning memories of the outer world are probably of events like D-Day and V-J Day, when heroic young adults were conquering continents and making the greatest of personal sacrifices to create a brighter world for everyone. Back then, everything seemed possible; as the popular saying warbled, "the best is yet to come." Kids got ready to climb on board the great Up Escalator of postwar America.

As America's true "children of the '60s" (and '70s), by contrast, 13ers grew up cynical about the *powerlessness* of elders. When they were small, the nation was riding high. When they reached adolescence, national confidence weakened, and community and family life splintered. Older people focused less on the future, planned less for it, and invested less in it. To child 13ers, the midsummer of 1969 produced three events—the Apollo moon landing, Ted Kennedy's extramarital misadventure at Chappaquiddick, and Woodstock—that many of them would later look back on as (1) a final apogee of national achievement, after which everything seemed to go downhill, (2) the beginning of a new era of sexual freedom, which later translated into an epidemic of parental divorce and disappearing dads, and (3) the heralding of a youth culture that, by the time 13ers stepped into it, became a desertscape of drugs and disease. A Consciousness Revolution that seemed euphoric to young adults was, to 13ers, the beginning of their ride on a down escalator.

"IT'S DISCO FEVER, MA'AM. THERE'S NO KNOWN CURE, BUT AT LEAST YOUR SON IS STAYIN' ALIVE, STAYIN' ALIVE!"

The twin debacles of the early '70s—the collapse of Vietnam, and Watergate—also represented something very different to these two generations. To the Silent (surging into Congress as the "Watergate Baby" winners of the 1974 election), these events brought hope, a fresh turn at power, a chance to "open up" American politics and culture. To 13ers, Viet/Gate fostered the view that adults were not particularly virtuous or competent—that, in a pinch, kids couldn't count on adults to protect them from danger.

***crasher
>"starsky and hutch" were on at 8 pm on wednesdays, which was past my little brother's bedtime, but not mine. this one episode contained lots of people getting shot, especially those bad-guy goons who guard doorways, the ones who say stuff like "sure thing, boss" and always have to go get the sandwiches. those guys always get popped in the skull right away by the good guys, and their time on-screen is somewhere below 5 seconds, so I never paid much attention to them. that night, I got into the bunk bed and was about to have lusty 4th grade dreams when my little brother poked the mattress under me. "what about those guards' mothers? don't all those guard guys got mothers and stuff?" he had watched the show hiding behind the couch in pajamas, as usual. "I suppose they do." "well," he continued, "what do they tell all their mothers when they die?" I yelled at him to go to sleep, but the question made me really uncomfortable. after a half an hour I peeked down at him, and he was asleep, but he had a terrible grimace, and he was clutching the sheets hard. I don't know, I've always remembered that.

At Troutwood-Madison Junior High in Dayton we used to have this little thing on the blackboard where every day we'd put up how many days the hostages have been in Iran. I can remember so clearly the 444 days, and it finally stopped the day Reagan came in.

Beth Griese, student, Ohio State

Ronald Reagan was around longer than some of my friends' fathers.

Rachel Stevens, senior, University of Michigan

I could tell you where I was the night we bombed Libya, if you really want to know.

Julie Phillips, in the *Seattle Weekly*

He places the Walkman in the case alongside a Panasonic wallet-size cordless portable folding Easaphone (he used to own the NEC 9000 Porta portable) and pulls out today's newspaper. "In one issue—in one issue—let's see here . . . strangled models, babies thrown from tenement rooftops, kids killed in the subway . . ." —he flips through the pages excitedly— "baseball players with AIDS, more Mafia shit, gridlock, the homeless, various maniacs, faggots dropping like flies in the streets, surrogate mothers, the cancellation of a soap opera, kids who broke into a zoo and tortured and burned various animals alive . . . ."

Bret Easton Ellis,
American Psycho (book)

Unlike our Sixties counterparts, we had very little to worry about in the Seventies. There was no war, no Civil Rights Movement, no new drugs. All the great battles had already been fought; we were left only to languish in the boring aftermath, uttering, "Okay, now what?"

Scott Matthews, et al.,
Stuck in the Seventies (book)

Similarly, the Carter-era hostility to powerful institutions had one meaning for a 50-year-old seeking a "mature" view of a "complicated" world, quite another for a 10-year-old busy building dreams. Having been nurtured as youths to dream about big houses and big rocket ships, Thinking Small was a Silent midlife tonic, a statement of moral conscience and refined sensitivity. But never having had their own chance to Think Big, a preadolescent 13er heard the drumbeat of a new message: that America's best days had passed. Later, the '80s-era binge of debt-fueled consumption once again meant one thing to a 55-year-old at the peak of his earning years, and quite another to a 13er teen whose adult-subsidized spending brought momentary pleasure coupled with worries that he wouldn't be able to maintain that consumption later on in life when all the bills came due.

None of today's older generation ever had to absorb such bleak themes at like age. When young, the Silent blithely eased into an adult world that, as they then saw it, very much *did* have its act together. Two decades after entering that gray-flannel world, most who had played by its rules were prospering nicely. What about 13ers? Many of them "dis" (-respect) a society that, as they see it, does *not* have its act together—a society in which, if you're young and play by the rules, you lose.

In the Silent child era, kids asked questions that adults never answered. In the 13er child era, as Neil Postman wrote in *The Disappearance of Childhood*, adults gave kids "answers to questions they never asked." Back in the early '70s, Norman Lear produced television shows like *All in the Family* that bred child skepticism. Thirteeners watched and learned. Then, two decades later, his People for the American Way savaged the grown-up kids thus nurtured for their "apathy and disengagement from the political process." Like Tatum

O'Neal learning to be a hustler in *Paper Moon*, the most important life cycle lessons 13ers have absorbed were not always what older generations put in the lesson plan.

Yes, history does play tricks. A generation that came of age yearning to take everything out of the closet never dreamed it would someday raise a generation that wouldn't mind putting a few things back in. A generation of parents suffering from claustrophobia never imagined that its own children would someday suffer from agoraphobia—a fear of openness. The Silent peers of Redford and Streisand still have trouble facing the fact that their 13er kids are turning out so unlike *The Way We Were*.

>7. Parents' Things Are Always More Important

In *Ourselves and Our Children*, a 1978 book whose priorities reveal themselves in the title's word order, a committee of Silent Generation authors insisted that "consider yourself" be the first principle of parenting. "Benefiting our children," they staunchly asserted, was "not necessarily our first motivation." Through most of the 13er childhood years, a great many public spokespersons of parenting age discouraged childbirth—and even those who advocated it reminded parents that their duty to serve *themselves* was at least as great, if not greater, than their duty to serve their children. By the mid-1970s, bookstores were loaded with popular books (also mostly by Silent authors) warning against the marital resentment, financial distress, and physical discomfort that supposedly resulted from the bearing and raising of children.

Thirteeners started out as, by any measure, the least wanted of twentieth-century American baby generations. They were born to Silent and Boom parents in roughly equal measure—the Atari wave ('60s babies) mostly to Silent, the Nintendo wave ('70s babies) mostly to the Boom. Among the Silent, birthings *stopped* being fashionable after the early 1960s; among Boomers, birthings did not *become* fashionable until the early 1980s. The 13ers born in between included unprecedented numbers of contraceptive errors, dad's draft

My parents. Their things are always more important than my things. I'll just have to accept that.

teenager, on returning home from Girls' Probation House in Fairfax, VA

Bless this highly nutritious microwave macaroni and cheese dinner and the people who sold it on sale. Amen.

child, *Home Alone* (film)

In 1948, the child exemption in the U.S. income tax code was equivalent to 19 percent of the median family income. Afterwards, it fell steadily. By 1984, it was equivalent to only 2 percent of the median family income.

Source: U.S. Bureau of the Census

***crasher
>the very notion of "birthings" being fashionable is kinda disgusting. I feel compelled to tell you about one of my best friends in the world, elyse. long before she was born, her oldest brother was killed in a traffic accident--it shattered the family, naturally, but her parents set hard to work to have other children. first came helen, then stephanie, then dana, then brigitte. by that point, they were prepared to do anything to get a boy. when elyse's mother got pregnant with her, they had a sound-scan done, and the doctor told them that they were finally going to have a boy--so with celebrations and vasectomies, they anticipated the arrival of their new baby with unprecedented publicity. his name was to be joshua, and a whole new room was built on the house covered with blue wallpaper, trucks and indians on horseback.

when elyse was born, they were in shock--and her dad sued the doctor for punitive damages. there is a picture in their scrapbook, an actual photograph of the parents at the hospital, holding the newborn baby. her mom is smiling the happiest smile ever, but damned if her dad isn't actually frowning, in obvious misery at this child he has created. elyse and I joke about it a lot, but every time I go over there I want to take that scrapbook and jam it down the garbage disposal.

avoidance devices, and mom's tickets to welfare money. Even those who were truly wanted by their parents had to confront an outer world that was unusually hostile to the interests of children.

Whatever went wrong with the 13er childhood happened on the Silent parental watch. This—not the rising Boom—was the generation in its thirties and forties during the Consciousness Revolution that marked the 13ers' growing-up years. The Silent were the ones best situated to do something about the harms then being done to children—but they didn't. To the contrary: By the 1964 end of the demographic "baby boom," a typical thirtyish Silent couple felt truly bogged down by babies they had parented so young (younger, in fact, than any other generation in American history). Just as the 13ers reached middle childhood, a cutting edge of Silent feminists began vocalizing frustrations with their lives, their husbands, their children. And the

"OH YEAH!? MY MOM'S SHRINK COULD WHIP BOTH YOUR STEP-DADS ANY DAY!"

cutting edge of Silent playboys began regretting their straight-arrow youth and acting out the Bob Dylan lyric: "I was so much older then, I'm younger than that now."

At their best, Silent parents of that era were gentle, other-directed, communicative, appreciative of the special qualities within each child, respectful of a child's privacy, and forgiving of a child's setbacks. But at their worst, they expressed moral ambivalence where a child sought clear answers, expected a child to respond too young to real-world problems, hesitated to impose structure on a child's behavior, and demonstrated an amazing (even stupefying) tolerance for the rising torrent of pathology and negativism that engulfed a child's world. As Silent author Benita Eisler wrote at the time, "We love them more 'wisely' than we were loved, with more honesty, attentiveness, and respect. Yet we are able to protect them less well."

> ***crasher
> >yeah, that and you couldn't stay married for shit...

Where the G.I.s had parented Boomers with confident, can-do control, the Silent emphasized why-to-do's more than what-to-do's. Where Dr. Spock had reassured American parents of the 1950s that they knew more than they thought they did, the gurus to whom the Silent turned for guidance appealed to their innate insecurity as parents, warning them about the many things they supposedly didn't know. For example, Selma Fraiberg urged the parents of the '60s to instill in children a superego-driven sense of consequence and guilt, rather than fear of authority, as a basis for behavior. Doing the right thing, said Fraiberg, mattered less than a parent and child each *feeling* the right thing. And, so the logic went, if a parent felt the right thing, then the child would become a more feeling person too. Thus would American society forever be spared the institutional heartlessness against which the young-adult Silent were then busy singing folk songs and marching nonviolently.

The title of Fraiberg's book, *The Magic Years*, reflected the uncommon attention Silent parents in their twenties attached to infancy and toddlerdom. Through the 1960s and early '70s, several other well-received books (like Burton White's *The First Three Years of Life*) described infant typologies that reflected a strong belief in early childhood determinism. In *Stability and Change in Human Characteristics*, Benjamin Bloom stressed that IQ scores in early childhood correlated closely with adult IQ ratings, meaning a child's lifetime in-

When I was a child, everything was always supposedly done for my good. But today we're much more honest with our kids. I told my eight-year-old, "I'm not sending you to bed at eight for your good. I'm doing this for me! You need to be in bed by eight because I need the space. I need the privacy."

mother, Denver (1983)

Let's assume you had some other industry. The industry made shoes, and then you took a large chunk of the labor force out, something like 40 percent, and you changed nothing much else—you wanted to make the same amount of shoes of the same quality with the same technology. Everybody in the world would think you'd lost your mind. That's basically what we did to parenting.

Amitai Etzioni, sociologist, George Washington University

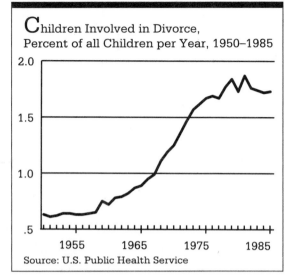

Children Involved in Divorce,
Percent of all Children per Year, 1950–1985

Source: U.S. Public Health Service

tellectual fate might be sealed by the time he entered school, for better or worse.

When the feminist and sexual revolutions struck in earnest, the Fraiberg/White/Bloom emphasis on early childhood was made-to-order for any parent seeking a scholarly justification for behavior that a decade earlier would have been considered selfish. Parents of kids over age three or four could feel liberated from child-focused priorities. As Marie Winn noted in *Children Without Childhood*, "For those beleaguered parents ... trying to save their marriages or recover from their divorces, struggling to keep their heads above water economically, pursuing their demanding new careers, hopelessly attempting to control their children's television viewing, early-childhood determinism appeared to be a gift from the gods." Applying this logic, a Silent couple with a yen for sexual adventure could conclude that a six-year-old kid would have no problem coping with family disintegration, given how carefully that kid had been tended in infancy.

The emerging Silent view, from the late '60s through the '70s, was that parental love did not require parental sacrifice—indeed, that it could be *harmed* by too much sacrifice. If parents did too much for kids, so the new thinking went, then the resentment parents would later feel would result in false or destructive parent-child relationships. The consensus among psychologists of that time was that away-from-home day-care was beneficial for small children, that working moms (or absent dads) might be *better* parents than the frustrated, homebound variety.

Working Mothers as a Percent of All Mothers	1960	1970	1980	1990
with children under age 6	20%	32%	47%	60%
with children age 6–17 only	43%	51%	64%	76%

Source: U.S. Bureau of Labor Statistics

Circa-1970 polls and social statistics showed a negative shift in public attitudes toward (and treatment of) children. As millions of mothers flocked into the work force, the proportion of preschoolers cared for in their own homes fell by half. For the first time, adults ranked autos ahead of children as necessary for "the good life." The cost of raising a child, never much at issue when Boomers were little, suddenly became a hot topic. Adults of fertile age doubled their rate of surgical sterilization. The legal abortion rate grew from next to nothing to the point where one of every three fetuses was terminated. In 1962, half of all adults believed that parents in bad marriages should stay together for the sake of the children. By 1980, less than one fifth of all adults felt that way. America's great divorce epidemic was underway.

Divorce. The fact of it, the calculations influencing it, the openness about it, the child's anxiety about it, the harms from it, the guilt after it: Here lay the core symptom of Silent nurture of the 13th. America's divorce rate doubled between 1965 and 1975, just as Atari-wave 13ers passed through middle childhood. At every age, a 13er child born in 1968 faced three times the risk of parental break-up faced by a Boomer child born in 1948. Silent parents, authors, and screenwriters addressed divorce as though it were an episodic childhood disease like the chicken pox: something you catch, get sick from, and then get over. In *It's Not the End of the World*, Silent author Judy Blume told the tale of a once-happy family suddenly disintegrating amidst shouting, slapping, and crying. The

***crasher

>jesus, if I'd known back then about all these dime-store philosophers telling our parents that it was okay to forget to pick us up from piano practice, my brother and I would have burned down a couple of bookstores.

***2boomers

>if you don't mind us asking, are your parents still together?

***crasher

>of course not. in fact, of the ten of us who live here in this house, six of us have different parents than we started out with.

***2boomers

>is it a sensitive subject?

***crasher

>are you kidding? we all know each other's gruesome stories. we could play "truth or dare" with our parents' sex lives if we wanted to.

***2boomers

>when did it happen in your family?

***crasher

>I was a freshman in high school. at the time, I could barely care less. I felt a lot more sorry for my younger brother and sister, because I'm not sure if they've ever been shown how to have a steady romantic partner. my dad once asked me, "would you have wanted me to stay, even though I would have been completely miserable?" of course, this was long after the fact, and I didn't feel like arguing, but every time I think of my little sister, a chorus of "hell, yes!" bubbles to the surface.

book's purpose was to comfort the child victims of divorce. Yet her book had the unintended effect of provoking children of secure families to reflect on the fragility of their world.

The Silent-led culture tried to reassure divorcing dads and moms that new and more sincere kinds of parent-child relationships could emerge from the family trauma then wracking millions of children and scaring many millions more. In *The Nurturing Father*, Kyle Pruett described the time spent between divorced father and child as potentially "better time, since it is usually less constricted by the depleting, conflicted misery of a painful marriage. Thus freed, father and children may embark on new explorations of the territory of their lives and relationships." Dustin Hoffman discovered his nurturing side in *Kramer vs. Kramer* only after his wife fled the family.

But if parents liked to stress the "positive" side of divorce, children were left staring at the dark side. According to one major survey of 1970s-era marital disruptions, only one-fifth of the children of divorce professed being happier afterward—versus four-fifths of the divorced parents. Half the kids of divorce recall having felt unwelcome in their new pieced-together families. At best, divorce brought kids complicated new relationships with moms, dads, and unfamiliar adults—and new time-consuming hassles shuttling back and forth between parents trying to schedule in a little "quality time" under awkward circumstances. At worst, divorce meant violent quarrels, split loyalties, estrangement from one parent (usually the father), maybe even a move away from one's house and friends. And, for most 13er kids, divorce had brutal economic side effects: moms gone all

1988 Living Arrangements of American Youths, Age 15–17	
with birth-mother and birth-father	50.9 %
with formerly-married birth-mother and no father	15.4 %
with birth-mother and step-father	13.5 %
with never-married birth-mother and no father	4.7 %
with birth-father and step-mother	3.2 %
with birth-father and no mother	2.7 %
with adult female relative and no adult male	1.6 %
with adoptive mother and father	1.1 %
with grandmother and grandfather	0.9 %
with step-mother and no father	0.8 %
all other arrangements	5.2 %

Source: U.S. Public Health Service

day, less money, homes sold. As divorces became more frequent, a child's chance of receiving support payments from the noncustodial parent declined, with only one in three getting the full amounts set by an agreement or ordered by a court.

From Boom to 13th, America's children went from a family culture of *My Three Sons* to one of *My Two Dads*. Of all child generations in U.S. history, 13er kids are the "onliest," their families the smallest, their houses the emptiest after school, and their parents the most divorced. Three of five 13ers have zero or one sibling, versus less than two in five Boomers at like age. Over the span of this one generation, the proportion of children living with less than two parents increased by half, and the proportion of working mothers of preschool children doubled. Fewer than half of all 13ers are now reaching age 16 in households with two once-married biological parents. One 13er in five has half-siblings. If the proliferation of half-thises and step-thats was a challenge for the greeting-card industry, it was devastating to the kids themselves.

In these complex new families, children often grew up in mutual-support systems where adults, notwithstanding their self-indulgence, remained painfully aware of their own capacity for error. Parental advice author Thomas Gordon warned "how parents inadvertently yet inexorably hurt children and youth—damage their self-esteem, chip away their self-confidence, stifle their creativity, break their spirit, lose their love." How can "Father Know Best" when father might actually know least? "Fathering is always a roll of the dice," Bill Cosby admitted in *Fatherhood*. "Was I making a mis-

"Timmy's—" Peg laughs. "Well, you know how he is. Always writing letters to invisible Dad and making paper airplanes out of them."

Jill Eisenstadt, *From Rockaway* (book)

"Your step-mom is cute, though. You remember when I asked her to the prom?" "Shut up, Ted!"

Bill and Ted, *Bill & Ted's Excellent Adventure* (film)

Through the 1970s, the number of "latchkey" children under age 14 left alone after school roughly doubled. A 1987 survey indicated that 12 percent of elementary, 30 percent of middle school, and 38 percent of high school students were left to care for themselves after school "almost every day."

Sources: Lynette and Thomas Long, *The Handbook for Latchkey Children and Their Parents* (book); U.S. Bureau of the Census

"TAKE *MY* PARENTS—*PLEASE!*"

take now? If so, it would just be mistake number nine thousand, seven hundred, and sixty-three." The *Ourselves and Our Children* writers urged parents to "feel freer to reveal ourselves . . . as developing, many-dimensioned, imperfect human beings . . . ." The dominant cultural image of '70s-era parents became that of a "pal" who, remarked Cosby's Silent psychologist-advisor, Alvin Poussaint, is "overly permissive, always understanding; they never get very angry. There are no boundaries or limits set. Parents are shown as bungling, not in charge, floundering as much as the children."

During the years the Silent passed through parenthood and 13ers through childhood, parent-child relationships became less authoritarian and judgmental, and more egalitarian. In what author Benita Eisler termed relationships of "uneasy equality," Silent parents began looking upon children as sources of help and solace. "You and Me Against the World," sang Helen Reddy to a fatherless child in *Pete's Dragon*. Like dad and son in *Close Encounters of the Third Kind*, Silent adults became more childlike and 13er children more adultlike.

***crasher

>so whaddya do? it's really rather simple; you can choose to be another weak-kneed historical statistic and end up being as much of a confused, self-absorbed dork as your parents were, and go ahead and marry someone you don't particularly like, have kids, eke out an existence and get a messy divorce that shatters your children's concepts of the higher, more beautiful ideals in life. or...you could choose to be a real adult, wait until you find someone who is your emotional complement, take a vow to stick around until you die, and mean it. I ain't come close yet, but at least I know what runway I'm on.

>8. Way Big Into Raisins at the Time

The year was 1968—not exactly the Year of the Baby. But amidst the assassinations, riots, student strikes, Vietnam buildup, and rise of Richard Nixon, one of the highest-grossing movies of the year featured a baby. *Rosemary's Baby*. Daddy had sold a soon-to-be-born child to a witch's coven. *Please* don't have this baby, many in the audience had to be wishing. In the end, Rosemary stunned the audience by bearing the hideous witch-babe and wanting to raise it.

Through the 1970s, the moviegoing public showed an unquenchable thirst for a new cinematic genre: the bad-baby horror film. In 1973, *The Exorcist* cast 13er Linda Blair as a vomiting, screaming, demonic imp in the first-ever R-rated film about a child. The film drew such a wide audience its studio reissued it in 1975, followed in a three-year span by a spinoff (*The Omen*), a sequel (*Exorcist II: The Heretic*), the spinoff's sequel (*Damien—Omen II*), second and third spinoffs (*The Demon Seed, It's Alive!*), the first spinoff's second sequel (*Omen III*), and the third spinoff's sequel (*It Lives Again*). In *It's Alive!*, a baby was born with claws and teeth. "It" murdered everyone in the delivery room except its mother, before escaping to gouge the necks of innocent Los Angelenos. (A baby born in 1974, the year *It's Alive!* was released, would have been 18 during the 1992 L.A. riot.) These witch-baby films stretched on until the early '80s, when audiences stopped flocking to them, and Hollywood stopped making them.

Even outside this genre, America's '70s-era film industry broadly echoed the anti-child sentiment of *Rosemary's Baby*. Movies made for and about child 13ers seldom celebrated them the way '50s movies had with little Boomers. Back then, *Shaggy Dog* movies featured bright little kids who any moviegoer figured would grow up into interesting, creative people. But by the '70s, moviegoers left the theater worried about what kids might grow up to be. Would they be hucksters (*Paper Moon*)? Prostitutes (*Taxi Driver*)? Molls and racketeers (*Bugsy Malone*)? Emotional misfits (*Ordinary People*)? Spoiled brats (*Willie Wonka*)? Even those few cinematic kids who behaved well were just bit players in family dramas about parental self-discovery (*Kramer vs. Kramer*). Meanwhile, as the Disney studios laid off cartoonists and started dabbling in sex-charged movies, the proportion of G-rated films fell from 41 percent to just 13 percent.

I was four years old
in 1969
When everybody had
their thing and I
had mine
There were some people
smokin' weed
There were some others
doin' speed
But I was way big into
raisins at the time

Susan Werner,
"Born a Little Late" (song)

I remember wallpapering my younger brother's room with *Playboy* centerfolds . . . . I remember bongs and pipes and art and music among my parents' greatest artifacts and my mother's vibrator and reading my father's *Penthouse* Forums. . . . Sometimes I wonder if their experiment backfired.

Adriene Jenik, "Family Ties," in the *L.A. Weekly*

Unofficially, federal experts put the actual number of "runaways" at roughly one million annually since 1976. Runaways comprise 40 percent of all incarcerated youths.

Source: William T. Grant Foundation

———

***crasher
>but even I hated veruca in "willie wonka" as much as any red-blooded american. that horrible song she sang about wanting one of the geese that laid golden eggs--i cringed every time she started it up. she was, in the words of grandpa joe, "a bad egg," and all us kids knew it!

The new "R" rating drove home the point that kids were no longer welcome in cinemas.

Throughout the pop culture, little kids and (by 1980) teenagers heard a recurring message from the adult world: that they weren't wanted, and maybe even weren't liked, by grown-ups. Nothing thundered this message home more than television. Thirteeners are not America's first generation to have grown up with TV; that distinction belongs to Boomers. But 13ers are the first to have grown up with a "mature" medium that bombarded children with the harsh realities and dark desires of adult life. Hour after hour, day after day, 13er eyes gazed upon countless images of a sort Boomers never had to confront at the same age.

Contrast the very different television experiences of a typical Boomer born in the late 1940s with a typical 13er born two decades later. By age five, the Boomer had seen little or no television; the 13er had seen 5,000 hours worth, thanks to a parent who probably used TV as a babysitter. A preschool 13er would have watched *Sesame Street*, *The Electric Company*, the superkinetic *Zoom*, and other child fare that turned education into fast-paced entertainment, social conscience into a double-dose of Oscar-the-Grouch realism. At age ten, the Boomer saw the likes of *The Mickey Mouse Club*, *Lassie*, and *The Ed Sullivan Show*; the 13er tuned in to the sarcastic social humor of *All in the Family*, the revelations of adult weakness in *Dallas*, and the gradual spread of suggestive sitcoms, violent cop serials, and taboo-breaking documentaries. In her teenage years, the Boomer saw *Bonanza*, *Ozzie and Harriet*, and *Dobie Gillis*; the 13er watched frenetic MTV videos, living-room dramas about splintered families, and children behaving first as Gary Colemanish non-kids, later as Bart Simpsonish bad kids.

Families with Children in 1988		
Percent of children in each household type who . . .	biological mother & biological father	biological mother & no father or step-father
live in poverty	11%	38%
show some health vulnerability	38%	45%
show any antisocial behavior	24%	40%
have ever repeated a grade	12%	24%
have ever been expelled or suspended	4%	11%
have ever had emotional counseling	3%	7%

Source: U.S. Public Health Service

Unlike a Boomer in the old days, a 13er was armed with remote control and could zap-zap-zap his way through 78 channels of self-edited hyperspeed entertainment in which images mattered far more than words. He could tune in to soaps and social dramas and talk shows that depicted adults in various states of ennui and vacuity, exaggerating their psychosexual flaws. And he could watch his TV set spew out PG-rated words on prime-time network shows, R-rated violence on cable, and X-rated sex if he had a VCR and a few bucks for a rental.

As the Silent Generation matured into civic and cultural prominence, its members intentionally set a tone that was in many ways the exact opposite of what they remembered adults having set in depression- and war-era America. They recalled how they had come of age as smothered conformists who had accepted the adult world at face value and had made big mistakes as a consequence—like having had too many (13er) kids too soon. They refused to let their own children repeat those mistakes. "I hate the idea that you should always protect children," insisted Judy Blume. "They live in the same world we do." *Mad* magazine's Al Feldstein put it more bluntly: "We told them there's a lot of garbage out in the world and you've got to be aware of it."

Each year since 1984, between 72 and 79 percent of teenagers have believed that "divorce laws are too lax"—up from 55 percent in 1977.

Source: The Gallup Organization, *America's Youth, 1977–1988* (book)

These are the toys of our generation. The childhood of our whole generation is represented here, and they're just throwing it out.

young graduate, on seeing a box of toys discarded by a friend's divorced father, *Metropolitan* (film)

This chapter will teach you many ways of knowing whether or not you are sick enough to need a doctor . . . . Carefully pick your time to talk with your parents. Remember, parents are usually exhausted when they first come home from work. Make lists, including "Things I Can Do When I'm Lonely" and "Things I Can Do When I'm Scared."

excerpts from *Alone After School, a Self-Care Guide for Latchkey Children and Their Parents* (book)

Part of this "garbage" was a growing (and justified) sense of danger in the child's world itself, spurred in part by social critics who resisted the prevailing cultural gale winds. Academic journals suddenly abounded with articles about a brand new topic: family violence. Over the 13er child era, the homicide rate for infants and children under four rose by half, the number of reported cases of child abuse jumped fourfold, and the number of vulnerable "latchkey" children fending for themselves after school more than doubled.

Cognizant of the dangers of leaving 13er kids unattended in what came to be euphemistically called "selfcare," adults removed shields that previously had protected children from the harsh truths of life. A litany of books and pamphlets urged little kids to watch out, to protect themselves, to dress and carry themselves more maturely, to handle adultlike problems on their own. The kaleidoscope of this "New Realism" movement grew darker by the year. Consider the thematic U-turn taken over the decades by scouting and national kids' clubs. In the '50s, they had emphasized the positive elements of a Boomer child's own world (nature, libraries, schools, families). Then, in the '60s, they began offering older kids a positive view of the adult world (the New Frontier and Great Society, trips to the moon, the United Nations). By the '70s, they shifted the focus from positive to *negative* aspects of adult society (poverty, racism, sexism, pollution, energy shortages). Come the '80s, and scouting wrapped new negative messages around the child's own world (with special warnings about drugs, sex, child abuse, and other crimes against kids).

A Brief Chronology of the Evil-Child Movie Era

1964	Children of the Damned
1968	Rosemary's Baby
1973	The Exorcist
1974	It's Alive!
1976	Look What's Happened to Rosemary's Baby
1976	The Omen
1976	Carrie
1977	Exorcist II: The Heretic
1978	It Lives Again
1978	Damien—Omen II
1978	Halloween
1980	The Children
1981	The Final Conflict
1981	Halloween II
1984	Firestarter
1984	Children of the Corn

An identical trend appeared in children's literature. Publishers began churning out "Breakthrough" books in a new "Young Adult" category that quickly seeped down to the elementary grades. In *Are You There God? It's Me, Margaret*, Judy Blume gave preteen girls a comforting picture of someone just like them facing a passage—menstruation—very real to all girls that age. Later, Blume introduced young

"AND *THAT* IS WHERE BABIES COME FROM."

readers to more hypothetical real-life problems: parental divorce, casual high school sex, even the violent death of a parent. In the years 1977-1981, the New Realism movement reached its apogee with books about abortion, adolescent cohabitation, teen lesbianism, child abuse, family-friend rapists, and suicide. Guiding kids through the afterwash of the divorce epidemic and sexual revolution, Norma Klein's *It's Okay If You Don't Love Me* depicted a young girl juggling her own sex life with two boyfriends while sorting through relationships with her mother's lover, her mother's former second husband, and her father's second wife and their two children.

From the late 1960s until the early '80s, America's preadolescents grasped what nurture they could through the most virulently

I came back as a bag of groceries
Accidentally taken off the shelf
Before the date stamped on myself

They Might Be Giants, "Dead" (song)

***crasher
>now you can say what you want about tv shows, r ratings and willie wonka, but I refuse to accept the notion that judy blume was in some small way bad for me. when you're 13 and your whole life consists of school, girls and masturbating, judy blume is the messiah. "then again, maybe I won't" saved my life just as "tales of a 4th grade nothing" had done four years earlier. you can't harsh on my main woman judy blume without expecting zeppelinfuls of hate mail.

***2boomers
>maybe her books were useful to you, but many kids found that her books dilated their eyes and made them stare into the glare of a nightmare day. like her book about divorce, in which a young girl lost her father and her house and was left with only a stuffed animal. one of us has a daughter who told us how, when she was reading that book late at night, she sneaked out to the garage to make sure her dad's car was still there.

"My p's were hippies. They got home movies of me being born. Lotsa trippin people sittin around my living room."
"Cool." And even weirder than Ohio and tornadoes.
"Cool? They sent me to this communist school and named my sister Goldenrod."
"No."
"She changed it to Gloria last year."

Jill Eisenstadt,
From Rockaway (book)

anti-child period in modern American history. Back in the '50s, being a good adult did not necessarily mean smiling at children; it meant doing well by them. By the '70s, a smile from a Mean Joe Greene to a Coke-drinking kid lost in a stadium—or just a smiley-face button—was supposed to compensate for the hard fact that kids from fragmenting families were getting lost all across America. Adults of all ages warbled with anti-institutional cynicism, let-it-all-hang-out realism, do-your-own-thing pluralism, and *I'm OK, You're OK* value neutralism.

Whatever harms parents rationalized themselves into letting their own children suffer, the national treatment of *other people's* kids was, if anything, worse. The English language doesn't have a word to describe this kind of adult behavior. The Germans do: *Kinderfeindlichkeit*. Translation: a society-wide hostility toward children.

America's '70s-era *Kinderfeindlichkeit* reached across all adult generations, deep into daily family life. With older G.I.s still smarting from attacks from their own kids (and busy fueling the federal revenue machine for their own ends), with the Silent now bidding adieu to their earlier child-focused conjugal and career sacrifices, and with fertile (yet still single) Boomers denigrating babies as surgically-removable barriers to their own self-exploration, the mere sight of a tiny 13er was enough to provoke waves of adult revulsion. In the '70s—quite unlike the '50s or '90s—a parent who brought little kids into a restaurant was commonly met with no high chairs, no children's menu, and disapproving glances from waiters and patrons alike. Many rental apartments that had tolerated children during the Boom era banned them during the 13er era. The ascendant Zero Population Growth movement declared the creation of each additional child to be a bad thing for Planet Earth. America's priorities lay elsewhere, as millions of kids sank into poverty, schools deteriorated, and a congeries of elected politicians set a new and distinctly child-hostile course of national overconsumption and debt.

From daily discipline to sex education, from moms and dads to

***crasher
>jeez, you guys--being a kid in the '70s wasn't that bad. as long as you could endure mini-leisure suits, velour shirts and tony orlando, you could still have fun on your big wheel!

***2boomers
>crasher, you can't imagine what it was like to cart around a baby in the '70s. take it from somebody who did. especially in a place like cambridge, massachusetts, everyone looked at you and your baby like you were wasting global resources. a decade later, with another baby, you got nothing but smiles and lollipops.

authors and scriptwriters—in all elements of life that touched a child's world—'70s-era adults spelled out the cold hard facts. Seldom did anyone make any clear distinction between right and wrong. Instead, the adult role was limited to warning kids of dangers while letting them make their own choices. It was basically the same every-person-is-a-consenting-adult approach that regulatory agencies were assuming toward risk throughout American life: Paste on a warning label listing every possible consequence—and whatever happens, happens. Older generations thereby stripped 13er children of adult protection, denied them a positive vision of the future, turned them cynical, and set them up like clay pigeons for the volley of criticism those same elders would shoot their way a decade later.

***crasher
>so you can imagine how sickened my friends are, after having been dealt the straight dope for 20 years, at the new stab for censorship in everything we do. we were witness to violence, wild deviant sexual acts, drug use and every other sick thing there was...and then the minute one of us tries to rap about it (or even buy an album with somebody rapping on it) along comes this cascade of do-goody goggleboxes in their forties, toting "family values" signs, suing artists, censoring tv shows, and arresting record shop owners. they really make me want to vomit. if they were so concerned about family values, they should have stopped reading "men who love the women who love to hate them" in their bedrooms and come downstairs to play scrabble with us while they had the chance.

>9. Are We Being Tested On This?

Luisa Rebull of Arlington, Virginia, sat with her exhibit at a high school science fair, when an adult stranger came by her table. "I talked to him for fifteen or twenty minutes, teaching him about right ascension, declination, and longitude of the ascending node, among

Are we being tested on this?

high school student, after a teacher hands out a copy of a classmate's suicide note, *Heathers* (film)

———

I think they paid Dickens by the word.

Jennifer Benitez, 9th grade, San Francisco

other things. At the end, he seemed genuinely surprised that a student would know more than he did." When that man was a student himself, adults routinely expected kids to know more than they did about academic subjects. Not anymore. Today, the consensus of older generations is that 13ers got an inferior education and are equipped with inferior skills. For a 25-year-old who did her lessons, worked at odd jobs to help pay college tuition, and is still paying off college loans bigger than her annual salary, this is a very bitter pill.

As with so much else in their lives, 13er schooling fell into the Boomer backwash. In the 1950s and early '60s, Boomers attended schools that may have been the best in U.S. history. They were staffed with the brightest and most literate members of a generation of women (G.I.s) who had few job opportunities elsewhere. Those teachers had the respect and backing of parents. Taxpayer revolts against school funding were unthinkable. Students were expected to give "right" answers and compete hard for grades and college admissions. Schools confidently performed their educational mission and were criticized only when they fell below prevailing standards of excellence. Social turmoil stayed outside the schoolhouse doors.

With 13ers, that all changed. As question-raising Silent educators and parents gradually supplanted the more socially disciplined G.I.s, the level of teacher-parent cooperation deteriorated. As America's image of its national future began to darken, the association between "child" and "future" that had once worked to the advantage of quality schooling began to work against it. The résumés of entry-level teachers changed dramatically: The Vietnam War sucked in tens of thousands of vocally anti-Establishment Boomer men into the profession (who, through 1969, could avoid the draft by entering teaching), while advances in women's rights prompted bright young

In high school did you . . .	College Freshmen circa 1966	College Freshmen circa 1990	Change
sometimes stay up all night?	60%	79%	+ 19%
frequently win a letter in sports?	32%	50%	+ 18%
sometimes argue with a teacher?	52%	42%	− 10%
sometimes discuss religion?	33%	21%	− 12%
sometimes visit a museum or gallery?	71%	53%	− 18%
frequently borrow from a library?	52%	22%	− 30%

Source: "The American Freshman: Twenty-Five Year Trends" (UCLA, 1991–1992)

women to enter other fields, making teacher salaries suddenly uncompetitive. Boom-era campus turmoil seeped down to the lower grades, stripping public schools of their old status as sanctuaries against the troubles of the outside world.

The topic of education was hardly neglected in the late '60s. To the contrary, when coming-of-age Boomers set out to "liberate" America from various G.I. Generation institutions, schools were among the first and biggest targets. What *did* happen is that the Consciousness Revolution brought to educational theory much the same battering ram it brought to child-raising theory: a rationale for a leave-'em-alone nurture, for constructive neglect by the adults important to a child's life.

Schools stood accused of having been dehumanizing instruments of social oppression, capable of turning kids into machine-like robots. Even the harshest critics of '60s-era schools, of course, seldom described their Boomer products as dehumanized robots. Instead, the critics' primary purpose was to nurture an even more moral and intellectually competent student generation, one that would out-Boom Boomers and thereby push civilization to new heights (and, most assuredly, into no more Vietnams). Yet there were a few areas where the quality of American youth did seem improvable: Compared to the Boomer article (it was thought), the new kids could learn better work skills, show more respect for the value of a dollar, get along better with their parents, and display greater maturity in their day-to-day dealings with older people. Thus were born the reforms that would mark 13ers as a very unBoomlike generation.

The operational catalyst of circa-1970 school reforms was the "open education" movement launched by English schoolmaster A.S. Neill. In *Summerhill*, Neill took the Rousseauian model of education to its modern frontier. Accordingly, every child would be seen as "innately wise and realistic. If left to himself without adult suggestion of any kind, he will develop as far as he is capable of developing . . . . Parents are slow in realizing how unimportant the learning side of school is . . . . All that any child needs is the three R's; the rest should be tools and clay and sports and theater and paint and freedom." As the cognoscenti of American education flocked to England to study Summerhillian methods, popular books joined the growing chorus for "person-centered" and "experience-centered" education in titles like *Compulsory Mis-Education, Death at an Early Age, Edu-*

I sn't that something they make criminals do?

Maryland high school student, on a state decision making 75 hours of community service a requirement for high school graduation

■■■

I understand the critics who say the message is "Get an A and we'll give you a hamburger," but there has to be some way to motivate some students other than self-satisfaction.

Patrick Herrity, advocate of giving consumer coupons to high-achieving students in Virginia high schools

■■■

It's fair to say that secondary education once was considered substantially more demanding. Students knew there was such a thing as failure, . . . but the system has become much more compromising. Teachers and students tend to negotiate themselves out of requirements, and students know that except in the grossest of circumstances, they will make it through.

Ernest Boyer, Executive Director, Carnegie Foundation for the Advancement of Teaching

When you get home from school, you are like, no more books. You are like, I'll watch videos and I'll eat something, and you're like, I'll let the books rest for a while.

high school student,
Bethesda, MD

At many campuses today the political relation between undergraduates and the faculty has shifted in important ways since the late sixties and seventies. Increasingly, what one sees is . . . a more traditionalist student body resisting the exhortations of a markedly more radical faculty. Often, the resistance expresses itself as simple indifference to the humanities; if studying the humanities has come to be an exercise in intellectual obscurantism and political sloganeering, well, there are other subjects worth pursuing. Is it any wonder that humanities enrollments have fallen off so precipitously in recent years?

Roger Kimball,
Tenured Radicals (book)

1991 Survey Question: How would you rate the educational preparation of high school graduates?

	"Excellent" or "Very Good"	"Only Fair" or "Poor"
Recent graduates going to college, asked about themselves	70%	30%
College educators, asked about incoming students	36%	62%
Recent graduates with jobs, asked about themselves	70%	29%
Employers, asked about newly hired employees	30%	66%

Source: The Harris Education Research Center

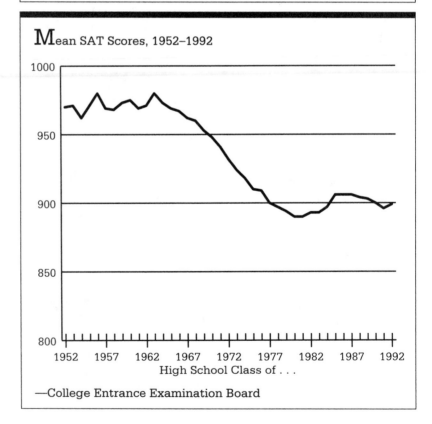

Mean SAT Scores, 1952–1992

—College Entrance Examination Board

cation and Ecstasy, and Charles Silberman's best-selling *Crisis in the Classroom*.

Open education was defined less in terms of what it was than in terms of what it was *not*: facts, subjects, rules, grades, bells, walls. Schools offered kids freedom to choose when and what to learn among various "learning tools" provided for them—often with no fixed schedule, sometimes without books, nearly always amid disruptive noise. As author John Holt put it, "the teacher was like a travel agent, helping the child go where the child wants to go." Existing curricula were suspect: Grammar was downplayed, basic readers were frowned upon, a "new math" deemphasized the traditional ten's place, and civics lessons were taught with catchy jingles. Textbooks shifted their emphasis from accuracy and graduated difficulty to user "sensitivity" and "accessibility"—in other words, niceness and easiness.

> Percent change in U.S. college enrollment in foreign languages, from 1960 to 1986:
>
> | | |
> |---|---|
> | Japanese | + 1,282 % |
> | Chinese | + 839 % |
> | Spanish | + 130 % |
>
> Source: Association of Departments of Foreign Languages

The reformers tried to promote self-esteem by attuning students to their own (and other people's) inner selves. They exalted feeling over reason, empirical experience over logical deduction. Rather than ask students to evaluate a book's literary quality or interpret its universal message, for example, a new-style teacher probed students to explain how that book made them *feel*, and how people different from themselves might feel differently about it.

After many a wall came down (and many a ribbon cut on new schools that didn't have them), the pluses and minuses of open education became apparent. On the plus side, it helped affluent kids become more sensitive to people who didn't share their own advantages, and it could provide a very exciting education in the hands of a teacher with unusual creativity, a superhuman energy level, and a knack for bringing order to chaos. On the minus side, open education sapped discipline, encouraged kids to shun difficult subjects, discouraged student preparation, left teachers exhausted at day's end, and hampered effective grading of student performance. (How could anyone not give an A to a kid whose analysis of *King Lear* was that reading it made her feel bad?) With teachers busy praising more than prodding, grade inflation ran rampant. All the em-

When college educators were asked in 1991 whether "the caliber of recent high school graduates is better or worse than it was ten years ago," 52 percent said worse and 34 percent said better. When employers were asked the same question, 56 percent said worse and 29 percent said better.

Source: Harris Education Research Center

These days, U.S. classrooms increasingly reflect an autonomous approach . . . . But some people fear that Americans' enchantment with autonomy may go too far. Parents may be inadvertently creating a generation of aggressive, competitive, cutthroat adults.

Psychology Today magazine

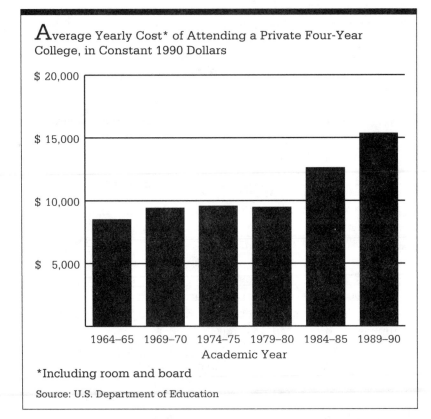

Average Yearly Cost* of Attending a Private Four-Year College, in Constant 1990 Dollars

*Including room and board

Source: U.S. Department of Education

***crasher
>you know, I found my diary from fourth grade last week. like to hear an entry? I'm not making this up.

***2boomers
>we'd be delighted.

***crasher
>"dear diary, today we had a substitute teacher named miss marsh. she has horn-rim glasses and a mole. during social studies gary kline went up to the potted plant and peed in the plant. miss marsh told him to please stop and that there were proper places to relieve oneself. during arts and crafts gary kline poured rubber cement on my model of the acropolis and then lit it on fire. I never knew rubber cement burned like that. so I hit him and then the principal came and put the fire out and took me to the guidance counselor. I told miss stern what he did, and she said that there were things about gary kline that I didn't know and that he was just expressing himself and that if we stop him from expressing himself then he'll only get worse."

phasis on child self-esteem fostered a "Lake Wobegon Effect" in which every kid had reason to believe himself above average. And so 13ers widely basked in the aura of what might be called "premature excellence."

From kindergarten to college, standards were allowed to weaken or disappear altogether. In 1970, reformer Roland Barthes insisted "there is no minimum body of knowledge which is essential for everyone to know." Nor was there any one set of values that was necessarily better than any other. From sex ed to civics classes, teachers applied the SIECUS mode of laying out the facts, offering a minimum of guidance, and encouraging kids to base their values not on some adult definition of right and wrong, but rather on their own feelings and experiences. In *Deschooling Society*, Ivan Illich argued that children shouldn't be required to attend school, that even the most open of classrooms kept them from participating fully in community life. Natural child would thus grow up as natural man, untainted by the wrongs of the Vietnam- and Watergate-stained adult society.

Educators who refused to embrace open education faced the embarrassing circa-1970 charge of being the scholastic equivalent of LBJ and Nixon. As the '70s progressed, these traditionalists usually had to make compromises. Schools published legalistic codes of student rights, softened discipline, and generally allowed teenagers to do as they pleased with their publications and student clubs. By the late '70s, school administrators constantly had to confront rowdy students, meddling parents, fractious school boards, and Prop 13-style revolts against school taxes. Teachers no longer figured that, in a crunch, they could count on much support from anybody. They reduced demands on students (and parents), and the average time spent on homework dropped to only half what it had been fifteen years before.

Then, in the 1980s, the first 13ers thus taught found themselves caught in a guru warp. Just as they started graduating from college, the 1983 *Nation at Risk* report marked the end of the reform era that had spanned their entire school careers. As the cutting edge of educational philosophy suddenly swung back the other way, the college classes of the middle '80s became the target of a searing academic whiplash. Ever since elementary school, they had constantly been told that there weren't any standards, that they were doing well, and that they had to listen to their feelings. Now, after all those years, they heard that there had indeed been standards, that they had failed to meet them, and that no one much cared how they felt about that failure.

Since the early 1980s, most 13er college students have continued to confront the consequences of reforms that, to their eye, have mainly worsened the learning environment. On today's campuses, adults seem only thinly in charge, crime festers, students are left to fend for themselves, and any concept of core curriculum (like the "core" anything else in their lives) is either unmentioned or controversial. All

You know it's gonna be like this all day, man. Teachers lecturing us about what kind of monsters we are.

high-school student, *River's Edge* (film)

■

Lake Wobegon Effect

phrase coined by John Cornell, after his 1987 survey showing that 32 states using national tests reported "above average" scores at every grade level and in every subject

■

Since the late 1960s, the share of all incoming college freshmen expecting to get at least a B average has grown from 33 to 41 percent; and the share expecting to graduate with honors has grown from 4 to 14 percent.

Source: "The American Freshman: Twenty-Five Year Trends" (UCLA, 1991–1992)

this leaves 13ers with a feeling of *déjà vu*—that what they didn't like about grade school still haunts them in higher academe.

In the humanities, "deconstruction" theorists instruct them that the intrinsic meaning of a word doesn't matter—while "remedial" teaching assistants tell them that all the meanings they never learned matter a lot. Thus do 13ers learn that everything is relative, except their own ignorance. In the sciences and professions, professors urge their charges to pay more attention to ethics, to real people, to social responsibility—and then grade them all anonymously according to multiple-choice exams with scant attention to who cheats. Thus do 13ers learn to distinguish between the pleasant talk and the unforgiving bottom line. Meanwhile, the number of older (and foreign) students keeps swelling, student-aid programs atrophy, and the competition for scholarships and term-time jobs grows ever more fierce. Finding little guidance from a faculty that would rather be authoring learned articles than tutoring unlearned students, 13ers are often confused about what courses they should take and what academic preparation they need to enter an uncertain economy. Finally, upon graduation, they hear their generation called dumb, unfit, inferior.

Are they?

The data documenting 13er academic failings are in many ways powerful and persuasive. Aptitude test scores remain well below the record levels of the Silent and early Boom years. Overall college completion rates (among men especially) are below what Boomers achieved. Traditional writing skills have atrophied badly. Today's most gifted collegians cannot match what faculty members recall of the most gifted Boomers. Math and science ability lags well behind global rivals. Most alarmingly, the skills, behavior, and work habits of many of today's

high school dropouts are at or below what one would find in the sorriest of Third World schools.

No one is more aware of this generation's academic deficiencies than 13er young adults are themselves. They thirst for continuing education, buy self-help books, and catch up on what their "relevant" courses neglected to teach. Many look back with regret on their school experiences—on how little they got back for the time and money they put in.

Yet whatever went wrong with the 13ers' education, the scholastic rot arrived before they did. It was Boomer, not 13er, students who rang up 14 of those 17 consecutive years of SAT score decline (1946 babies scored the highest, 1963 the lowest). Indeed, the '60s-baby Atari-wavers deserve credit for putting the brakes on the Boom-era skid. And the '70s-baby Nintendo-wavers, now in the fifth through twelfth grades, show signs of reversing some negative Boomer trends. Already, they are scoring better than the 1930s-born Silents in identical IQ tests.

Even this generation's worst critics, moreover, cannot accuse 13ers of having failed to learn what was in the curriculum. While 13ers are notably weak analysts and logicians, they are notably good diarists, good at describing their feelings and observations. (That's precisely what open education taught them to do.) A '90s-era math study that showed Americans scoring far worse than the Japanese asked all the students from both countries whether they had ever been taught the material tested in the exam. Nine of ten Japanese said yes—versus barely half the Americans. (Had the test been in the "base five" of the now-discarded New Math, these results might have been different.) An '80s-era survey of student knowledge of U.S. history blasted 13ers for being unable to identify American presidents, yet gave them no credit for their ability to identify prominent blacks and women. As many knew about Harriet Tubman as knew about Thomas Jefferson or Abraham Lincoln. (Again, that's a reflection of the emphasis schools have lately given Black History Month, which in some schools is the only month of the year when students are assigned to write biographies.)

The expert conclusion that 13ers are dumb often says more about the tester than it does about the tested. Nearly all the blue-ribbon international comparisons, for instance, evaluate students near the end of that portion of the American educational system considered weak

At San Diego State University, where 550 part-time instructors have been let go and 662 classes canceled, more than 1,300 students got none of their requested courses when the semester began. Some have perfected the process known as "crashing," by which they attend classes to which they have not been assigned and beg overloaded professors to admit them. And many are "freeway flying," madly dashing by car between the campus and various junior colleges trying to gain the credits they need to graduate.

Robert Rheinhold,
in the *New York Times*

⸻

I don't mean to brag when I tell you my schedule: In addition to carrying a full load of classes, I had two jobs that added up to full-time work. During the week, I went to school (11 a.m. to 8 p.m.) two days and to work at one job (8 a.m. to 7 p.m.) on the other three. On Sundays I worked at my second job (4 p.m. to 12:20 a.m.). Sometimes I wonder if I got an early look at what "real life" is going to be like . . . .

Sharyn Wizda, George Washington University, Class of 1991, in the *Washington Post*

by global standards (elementary through high school), and not near the end of the portion still considered the best in the world (college and graduate school). Also, these studies tend to evaluate American students by criteria where they can't measure up, and undertest or ignore criteria where they excel.

Take social studies. The Council on Learning labeled college students "unenlightened" for how they answered a global quiz whose questions read like a stack of State Department memos and whose graders marked as wrong any answer suggesting that the U.S. should act in its self-interest. (The supposedly correct answer was that the U.S. should defer to multinational decision-making bodies.) For 13ers weaned on Vietnam, Iranian hostage-taking, and a U.S. trade imbalance, that answer didn't necessarily make sense. Had the Council on Learning tested global survival skills (like how to raise capital in Poland, where to locate video outlets in Russia, how to ship food inside Somalia), 13ers might well have scored leagues higher than the Council on Learning's own graders.

Take writing. The National Assessment of Educational Progress published a survey showing only 2.6 percent of all high school students able to write "a really good letter." What's *that*? Each generation has its own standards about what constitutes effective personal communication. Compared to older generations, 13ers are poor at Palmer penmanship and lit-critty essays, but excel at other ways of getting ideas across: Computer mail. Videos. Desktop publishing. Ad copy. Press releases. *USA Today*-style journalism. Thirteeners might be far more likely than the National Assessment's own experts to know how to send "really good E-mail," produce "a really good

"VERY GOOD TIMMY! NOT DRAWING ON THE PAPER IS A VERY BOLD PERSONAL STATEMENT!'

***crasher
>now I feel like everyone's gonna stare at my writing to see if I step into any grammatical cow patties.

***2boomers
>you seem to know a noun from a verb. how did you get so smart?

***crasher
>well, boys, not all of us are remote-control-totin', lazy-ass slackmeisters chewin' on bite size doritos with a 15-watt cerebrum. some of us are waiting for demographers like you to wither, so that we can run the world.

***2boomers
>you've got a long wait, crasher.

***crasher
>tell me about it. personally, I got beat up every day after school for six years. being the class reject during grade school did wonders for my patience. I spent the entire time reading and plotting revenge.

video," or write "a really good ad." Since today's public opinion is more easily swayed by a politician's sound-bite or a CNN video-bite than by the most brilliant of essays, who can say that 13ers are somehow off track? And how come no blue-ribbon commission has ever ranked them in these skills against their foreign rivals—or (more to the point) against Boomers?

Just how *do* 13ers match up against Boomers, not just in calculus and sonnets, but also in the daily skills needed in modern life? Pepperdine's Michael Gose asked long-time teachers who had taught Boomers in the '60's and 13ers in the '80's to compare the two student generations in 43 measures of aptitude and achievement. At first glance, the result was a Boomer rout: 38 to 4, with one tie. The teachers rated Boomers much higher in all the fundamental skills, academic inclination, personal responsibility, task orientation, morals and ethics, communication skills, and willingness to work hard for the purpose of learning. But the few realms where 13ers outscored Boomers were telling: "skills in negotiation," "defenses to prevent extreme dependency on parents or authorities," "skill in interacting with adults on an equitable basis," and "information about . . . where to go for business, consumer, or personal wants and needs." The students of the 1980s, Gose concluded, were "more aware of what's going on, how institutions work, how to manage social relations, how to cope with adults, and how to get things done in the community," and were "sharper than ever, even if not in quite the same ways I, as one of their teachers, would like them to be."

Despite (maybe *because of*) the flaws in their schooling, 13ers have

Given the yawning knowledge chasm—the gap between what they minimally should, and actually do, know (in matters historical, political and economic)—on what basis is the average teen voter to make his electoral selection: the candidate's hairstyle, taste in music, number of syllables in his last name?

Don Feder, in the *Washington Times*

These kids are winners. They wake up winning every morning.

Paul Cain, math teacher in a violence-prone El Paso high school, describing five students in the class of '92 who were accepted to MIT

learned enough savvy, if not Hirsch's 50,000 facts, to help them solve life's practical problems. Given that their education fell short on teaching them basic knowledge, it at least gave them tools and taught them how and where to prospect for knowledge—a truly useful skill in an era of information overload. Even one of their harshest critics, Lynne Cheney of the National Endowment for the Humanities, concedes that they "know how to look it up." And not just look it up, but also organize it, check it, reference it, and print it with a computer-aided speed and accuracy that leave elders awestruck. Cheney's (Silent) peers ought to know. It's getting hard these days to find a 55-year-old journalist or professor or lawyer who wouldn't be informationally deaf, blind, and dumb without the techie 25-year-old who shares the office.

At root, the blue-ribbon 13er-bashing reflects a social reaction against the relativism of 13er-era schooling. Yet today's much-touted search for absolutist "standards" begs the question of what those standards should be. Does fourth-grade penmanship matter as much as keyboarding? Does eighth-grade error-free spelling matter as much in the Spell-Check 1990s as it did in the 1950s? Does a high-school senior's longhand letter-writing matter as much as his being able to use word-processing software to edit? Does immediate recall of 50,000 facts matter so much to a college senior with instant fiber-optic access to billions of facts? How do watercolors rank against VGA graphics? Were 13ers to set the standards, you'd better believe DOS would rank right up there with grammar as something kids would be required to learn, with test results published yearly.

Visit a top-quality '90s-era high school, and all it takes is one open mind and two open eyes to come away impressed, even thrillingly so, by 13er students' grasp of difficult subjects. By their up-to-the-minute grasp of what they need to learn to compete in a global marketplace (knowledge of Asian and Slavic languages, for starters). By their can-do attitude, in the face of more social problems in one week than older people had to face in a full school year or more. And by that uniquely 13er (and, dare to say it, uniquely *American*) intelligence that is at once efficient and practical, a special blend of savvy and salesmanship.

Certainly, the reformers failed in turning 13ers into a higher form of Boomer. All the emphasis on feelings somehow lost its way with a generation turned hard. All the stress on self-esteem helped spawn a generation with huge collective ego problems. All the effort to deracinate the curriculum left 13ers not only less burdened by memorized "facts," but also less united as a generation by any common assumptions about their nation's cultural moorings or social ideals. To be sure, the reformers did succeed in smoothing out a few Boomer flaws: They reduced the level of student argument, injected a new pragmatism in American youth, and crafted this into a highly street-smart and tech-smart (if not traditionally literate) generation. Yet, on balance, one suspects that grown-up 13ers are a very far cry from what all those Summerhillian disciples had in mind when they traipsed back home from England and started knocking down classroom walls.

Thirteeners are unlikely ever to impress elders with their academic prowess, and they know it. Instead, they will always take special pride in what they picked up on their own and in their ability to succeed in life despite what happened (or failed to happen) in the classroom. They'll use the word "excellent"—that prefix to "dude" in Bill and Ted slang—to describe a lot of adventures they'll have along the way. But as they party on, they'll never use that word to describe the education that was supposed to prepare them for the journey.

>10. Heavy Thoughts Tonight

THE SCENE: A street in small-town Ohio. THE SOUND: An enormous thump-thump-thump, audible from half a mile away, coming from a minivan with 25 speakers playing at full volume, more than enough to do severe ear damage to anybody inside the van. THE LEAD ROLE: Scott, age 20, the driver. THE DIALOGUE: "They tell me it will hurt me down the line, but I don't care. I'm young and stupid, I guess."

Shocking elders is nothing new. Kids have always flaunted words and songs and mannerisms that come across a bit garbagey to the outside world. They have always dared to engage in fun that strikes

Something wrong, shut the light
Heavy thoughts tonight
And they aren't of Snow White

Metallica,
"Enter Sandman" (song)

◾

From 1976 to 1988, the proportion of high school seniors saying they "get a kick out of doing dangerous things" rose from 30 to 38 percent. The proportion saying they "like to test myself every now and then by doing something a little risky" rose from 38 to 48 percent.

Source: "Monitoring the Future: Questionnaire Responses from the Nation's High School Students" (University of Michigan, 1976–1988)

others as a bit dangerous. But what is new, what goes beyond garbagey fun, is how so many of today's kids twist the dial up, up, up until their "fun" reaches a point of perverse catharsis and self-destruction. Then, when asked about it, they get blasé and cheerfully say something like, "Yeah, the weather's nice, and I'm obliterating myself. How about you?"

THE SCENE: A townhouse in a wealthy Maryland suburb. A basement, ringed with exercise equipment and posters of greased hunks. THE SOUND: Clanging metal, hard breathing, a reporter asking questions. THE LEAD ROLE: Larry, age 18, described by the reporter as having "a hard, smooth surface, physically and emotionally." THE DIALOGUE: "I want to be big, big, big. I'm nowhere near the size I want to be."

A year earlier, Larry had been a teenage publicist, a champion promoter whose clients ranged from Reebok to Pictionary. He had written a book in which he boasted of his plans to be rich and famous and retire by age 21. Then Larry hired a friend to take his SAT test for him. He got caught, was charged with perjury, and turned into a notorious local example of what elders so dislike about today's kids. Amidst all the debris of his ruined plans, Larry decided to pump up and add a quick 40 to his 170-pound frame.

These days, many a kid who feels at life's edge seizes upon some physical ideal and tries to push, push, push a body way beyond it. Boys beef up, often to ridiculous and hazardous extremes. Girls waste away with anorexia and binge-and-purge bulimia—eating disorders nearly unheard of before the 1970s whose victims are nearly all female, white, and young. In an era otherwise marked by unprecedented focus on good health, adolescent obesity is on the rise, and teens of both sexes are increasingly piercing, tattooing, or otherwise disfiguring their bodies. Where the old Boomer drugs-of-choice lifted mind over body, heightened sensory awareness, and enabled comfortable young people to open themselves up to new feelings (pain included), the 13er drugs-of-choice put body over mind, dim the senses, and enable anxious young people to vanquish social or athletic competitors.

Thirteeners have absorbed the modern cultural message that their worth is not intrinsic, that they are only what others can see. Where

"*SPANDEX SATAN* HAS BEEN A PILLAR OF THE HEAVY METAL COMMUNITY SINCE 1970, SENATOR. WE'RE NOT A CULT. WE DON'T ADVOCATE TEEN SUICIDE . . . WE SING ABOUT IT BECAUSE WE LOVE THE KIDS."

Boomers viewed (and prided) themselves from the inside out, 13ers do so from the outside in. When, like Larry, a kid suffers a huge personal downer and reacts by pushing his body beyond normal limits, the typical adult response is unsympathetic. In Larry's case, all he got was a sarcastic feature story in the *Washington Post*.

THE SCENE: A tidy house in a middle-income New Jersey suburb. A closed garage door. THE SOUND: A car engine idling behind the door. Footsteps. A worried parent opening the door. THE LEAD ROLES: Four dead teenagers. THE DIALOGUE: None.

Each year through the 1980s, five thousand youths between the ages of 15 and 25 killed themselves. In 1976, the suicide rate for that age bracket broke an old record, set way back in 1908. Today, for the first time ever recorded, Americans in their late teens and early 20s are more suicide prone than older Americans. Surveys show that 10 percent of adolescent boys and 18 percent of adolescent girls are willing to admit that they attempted suicide.

What can one say about a generation 1,000,000 of whom have tried (or will try) to kill themselves before age 30—and 100,000 of whom

Father: "I'm very disappointed in you." Daughter: "Join the club."

Maid to Order (film)

———

You young people are a disgrace to the human race, to plants even. You shouldn't even be seen in the same room as a cactus.

teenager to his buddies, *River's Edge* (film)

———

From 1971 through 1989, the number of adolescents admitted to private psychiatric hospitals increased fifteenfold—even though the overall youth population declined. During the 1980s, psychiatric care for adolescents was one of the fastest-growing (and most profitable) branches of medicine.

Source: *Chicago Tribune*

have succeeded (or will succeed) in their final effort? About a generation *Esquire* writer Lynn Darling describes as full of "experts on the dark side, on hedging bets and lowering expectations, too familiar with sadness"? The four kids in the New Jersey garage were like a lot of 13er teens who toy with themes of death. They were run-of-the-mill punkers, maybe a little bigger on heavy metal than most. But they went a bit further. They signed a death pact. Then they did the job. Why? Parents and neighbors were clueless. "They had bad lives," a journalist later reported. Both before and afterwards, the tears that got shed were not their own.

In *Pump Up the Volume*, Hard Harry tells this generation how "uncomplicated" suicide can be: "There you are, you got all these problems swarming around in your brain, you know, and here is one simple, one incredibly simple solution." Kids pour into theaters to absorb messages from Hard Harry, or *Heathers*, or *River's Edge*. They listen to death-metal lyrics, they rent videotapes about casual self-destruction, they play video games that invariably "terminate" with the player's electronic death, they dabble in Satan worship, they plead with the bungee-operator to lengthen the line just a tad. Where does the "fun" stop, and where do the serious cries for help begin? Old-

"I GUESS WHAT YOUR MOTHER AND I ARE TRYING TO SAY IS HEY, YOU'RE AT THE AGE WHEN YOU'RE GOING TO WANT TO START EXPERIMENTING . . . AND WE'RE COOL WITH THAT BECAUSE DRUGS CAN BE A BEAUTIFUL MIND-EXPANDING TRIP . . ."

er people have a terrible time deciphering such tearless teen agony.

And then there is the color black. It started with punk in the early '80s; today, the hottest-selling pro sports logos (Los Angeles Raiders and Kings, Chicago White Sox, San Jose Sharks, and Miami Heat) are black. Ditto the logos for everything from *Batman* to *Wayne's World*. True, both Boomers and 13ers have together made *noir* the *haut couleur* of the early '90s, the equivalent of what hippie rainbow colors were two decades ago. But for each of the two generations, black has a very different meaning. For Boomers (with their black suits, gowns, appliances, and cars), the color expresses a post-yuppie, judgmental, neopuritanical mood of severe spirituality. For 13ers (with their black T-shirts, leather jackets, logo caps, and lingerie), it reflects a post-punk, condemned mood of pessimism. Kids who regularly wear the color advertise yet another wordless message about their own social role and their own expectations—or lack thereof.

Thirteeners are cursed with the lowest collective self-esteem of any youth generation in living memory. Every new crop of Americans comes of age facing its share of family problems, adolescent agonies, and spoiled dreams. But none other this century has felt anything like the 13ers' collective sense of missionlessness—of feeling worthless, wasted, even despised as a group. Of wondering why they were even born.

For the individual, to be sure, low collective self-esteem can translate into opportunity. Weak peer competition means anybody with moxie stands a better-than-average chance of winning at America's real-life game of king of the mountain. This is why gestures of intimidation—the sharp tongue of a Charles Barkley or the end zone taunt of a Deion Sanders—play such an important role in 13-on-13 competition: Just get the other guy to face the truth—that he's a loser—and he'll cave. This is also why surveys show today's youngster to be so upbeat about his own personal future even though he's so downbeat on everyone else his age: When you talk to the pollster, you're also reassuring yourself that you've *got* to be the exception. Knowing that a pose of suicidal abandon can itself communicate confidence, 13ers excel at playing each style, each side of their generational personality, off against the other. The popular image of today's young winner is of the guy who's "dead certain" he's champ—and lets everyone know that he'd gladly forfeit his life trying to prove it. He's someone who's got the end zone taunt *and* the black jersey.

Unfortunately, when the world turns into a giant gladiatorial arena, failure becomes inexcusable. When life is do or die, it's hard for those who can't do to console themselves or gloss over their shortcomings. Sure, people in all generations have to cope with personal failure. But some generations find it easier than others. Unlike their G.I. grandparents, 13ers can't take refuge in collective youth accomplishments. Unlike their Silent parents, they're not growing up in a robust economy that offers a fresh start to a kid who makes a mistake. And unlike their Boomer bosses and professors, 13ers don't have hugely inflated egos that allow them to sublimate failure into some personal growth experience. To them, life is about individuals trying to get somewhere in an upward journey that's for keeps. And once the putative mountain kings start getting pushed off the slope, that's when the problem comes. That's when the low self-esteem transfers from the group to the individual. That's when life starts feeling hopeless.

As the children of distracted adults, 13ers learned young to be survivors, to confront problems on their own, to sort themselves out into winners and losers. Adults expected them to be smooth, to grow up quickly, to learn to make their own choices before they could cultivate a deeply-rooted sense of self-worth. By necessity, many 13ers have developed what psychologist David Elkind calls a "patchwork self," having been "denied the time needed to put together a workable theory of self." Lacking the ego-strength to try setting agendas for others, they instead react to the world as they find it. As the Atari wave joined adult society in the 1980s, what it found was that the trappings of money and power constituted the prevailing measure of success. Most older Americans at least pretended not to take this measure too seriously. But 13ers took it very seriously—while brushing off the fatuous elder dictum that "everyone's a winner." (If so, why do some people die young in shootouts while others retire young to Bermuda?)

The big problems come when something happens to keep a teenage 13er's life from going as scripted. Maybe her family life is falling apart. Maybe she's washing out of school. Maybe she is simply losing hope of ever being as rich, as smart, or as civilized as her parents. If she's lucky, she discovers a reservoir of inner strength, happens upon some great cause, finds a supportive group of friends, or even just taps into some adult-approved excuse that gives her comfort. If she's unlucky, she doesn't. Then she begins to feel like a loser—not just your momentary garden-variety loser, but a totally wasted lifelong loser, the kind who stops hoping for another chance.

BASIC BLACK

"MAYBE IT'S TIME FOR SOME *COLOR* IN YOUR WARDROBE, DEAR."

When something goes badly wrong, a 13er's first instinct is to blame himself. That makes some sense, given the world he inhabits. Consider how the public health risks of American teens have changed since the 1950s: Compared to teenagers a third of a century ago, 13ers face a sharply lower risk of dying from accidents or conventional diseases, but this advantage has been almost entirely offset by what elders look upon as "self-inflicted" risks. In the '50s, the worst threats to youth were random diseases like influenza and polio that attacked good and bad kids with equal cruelty—afflictions that have been mostly conquered. Now, the worst dangers are behavioral. AIDS. Drug and alcohol abuse. Eating disorders. Homicide. And, of course, suicide. Almost by definition, "good" kids are the ones who avoid these dangers, and "bad" kids are the ones who get plastered. Forty years ago, when a teenager landed in the hospital, the typical adult reaction was "What's he have?" Now, it's "What did he do to himself?" Thirteeners themselves have absorbed the message. Using the word "do" as a prefix to any activity—"do sex," "do 'roids," "do hard drugs"—they emphasize the freely-chosen (and instrumental) nature of whatever behavior gets them in trouble.

It's like smoking. You think it's cool. You know it's wrong. You do it anyway.

Claudia Hernandez, 15, on trying to get deep suntans at the beach

Come on baby Don't fear the reaper

Blue Oyster Cult, "Don't Fear the Reaper" (song)

So many things have already happened in the world that we can't possibly come up with anything else. So why even live?

David Peters, fast-food worker

And "do" it they have—a lot. By almost any measure, the first Atari-wave 13ers, born from 1961 through 1964, mark an extreme for the sociopathology of American youth. They set the all-time U.S. youth records for drunk driving, illicit drug consumption, and suicide. They have been among the most violent, criminal, and heavily-incarcerated youth cohorts in U.S. history. Among later-born 13ers, the picture is brightening some—but not much. Many more

***crasher

>yep, and tonight I'm going to put on some smiths, sit in the corner with some piano wire and gargle motor oil and thumbtacks with the gas stove on "high"...

***2boomers

>collect yourself, crasher. this is serious stuff.

***crasher

>it's all very well for you to sit back and wax poetic about the problems of young people today, but you just don't understand what it is like. there's a reason we don't write generational histories like you do--it's way too depressing to deal with, and we'd all rather rent a movie instead. I don't like reading this--it makes me feel like shit.

***2boomers

>13ers don't have a lock on teen angst, but you guys seem to do everything painful in greater amounts. while your elders may have sung or written poetry about death, you go ahead with it a whole lot more. we write this stuff because there may be many of you who don't know that this is not just a tiny little trend, but a generational affliction.

***crasher

>I could tell you stories, you know, times on the highway when I've turned off the ignition in my volkswagen and just coasted silently in the dark. standing on the edge of a roof just to see how far out I could go before my survival mechanism kicks in. doing one more tequila shot and letting out a deafening roar. just one flick of the wrist, that's all it takes, and I could splatter somewhere, die violently. anything to take the edge off the boredom and the doom that seems to coat everything. I could tell you about all the private moments I have, wrestling my horrible thoughts to the floor, and you can write a damn fine article about it, but don't pretend that any of you know what it's like to be young, getting old right now.

***2boomers

>agreed. try not to be so cynical, though.

***crasher

>as mr. buffett so eloquently explained, "if we couldn't laugh, we would all go insane."

kids than a quarter-century ago continue to inflict upon themselves (and others) the most violent forms of adolescent trauma.

Usually, the trauma manifests itself in the Scott or Larry forms— doing "stupid" things, getting marginally self-destructive. How close they are to the abyss of suicide, no one can guess. Depressed kids may not know themselves—until, like the New Jersey four, they try Hard Harry's "simple" solution and end up dead.

Thirteeners in pain have never quite learned how to weep, how to cry out for help and get heard. America's other twentieth-century teen generations found ways to call adult attention to their troubles. Not this one. What an irony it is: The "with it" adults of the '70s expected their tots to grow up to be totally "authentic" persons, but somehow 13ers don't feel nearly as authentic, and can't express their darker feelings nearly as well, as Boomers raised by those old unliberated Bob Hopeish G.I.s.

Recall "Particle Man," that proto-13er electron whizzing around society's periphery. In the same song lyric, They Might Be Giants wrote of another player in the same survivalist world: the socially denuded "Person Man" who, "Hit on the head with a frying pan,/ Lives his life in a garbage can." Person Man is a weak warrior who gets creamed in his first battle, a failed player in a world that tolerates everything but losers. "Is he depressed or is he a mess?/ Does he feel totally worthless?" The answer is yes. Person Man knows real pain. He shows it, too, if only his elders were looking.

***End of file. Upload completed.

***Select: (D)ownload, (U)pload, (M)enu, (Q)uit? q

***Exit USA-TALK.

***Log off at 2:55:32am, 11/29/92.

Number of NFL players reporting to training camps in 1981 who weighed more than 280 pounds: 23. Number in 1991: 370

Source: Harper's Index

Three-quarters of American college seniors say it will be harder for their generation to achieve the American Dream than it was for the last generation.

Source: Roper CollegeTrack, based on interviews at 100 campuses

C:> ph-bill

 ATDT 1(703)555-0991 . . . Phone number being dialed . . . Connection made . . .

<TRAN> what do you think?

<RECV> about the text?

<TRAN> no, about crasher.

<RECV> crasher's kind of like "honey," the rat in that new jersey schoolhouse experiment. maybe he's had a few too many pop culture mars bars, but he's surviving.

<TRAN> i can picture him sitting there in some hi-tech wayne's world basement with the dead kennedys blasting out of eight dolbys.

<RECV> probably a lot more wholesome environment than we had when we were his age.

<TRAN> no comment. at least we're getting some response.

<RECV> do you think he's the only one out there?

<TRAN> the next upload will tell. money sex violence race politics. it's got it all.

<RECV> even if they're up and watching, most 13ers aren't gonna be bothered. 99 percent of 'em are totally at home with the dark side of life, and the other 1 percent live in beverly hills 90210.

<TRAN> crasher would pull your plug if he read that.

<RECV> then it'll run on batteries. shall we dump?

<TRAN> it's late. how about tomorrow, same bat time, same bat channel?

<RECV> okeedoke.

———————————————————————— end of session ————————————————————————
———————————————— computer log OFF at 3:04:03am, 11/29/92 ————————————————

PART 2

THE AMERICAN DREAM HAS NO 13TH FLOOR

————————————— computer log ON at 9:44:50pm, 11/29/92 —————————————

C:>usa.talk

ATDT 1(202)555-3850 . . . Phone number being dialed . . . Connection made . . .

*** Welcome to USA-TALK On-Line Bulletin Board.
*** Your handle is: 2boomers
*** Log on at 9:45:23 pm, 11/29/92.
*** Messages to/from other current USA-TALK users will appear in upper-right cb box. At any time press alt-e to enter cb box.
*** SELECT: (D)ownload, (U)pload, (M)enu, (Q)uit? u
*** Upload channel currently open. Specify file at prompt:

> C:\13th-gen\part-2.doc

*** USA-TALK uploading 13TH-GEN\PART-2.DOC by 2BOOMERS at 9:45:51 pm: stand by . . .

>11. Is It All Downhill?

It seemed like such a sure bet.

When 13er babies first appeared in a nation bursting all over with worldly marvels, from 8-track stereos to Apollo moon launches, adults figured these kids would be nothing if not affluent. The flip side of the late-1960s devil-child image was the sci-fi image of the juvenile moneymaker building lunar oil derricks out of Lego blocks. A decade later, parents smiled approvingly at tykes who arbitraged baseball cards for cash, sold Day-Glo T-shirts at rock concerts, and teleshopped with mom's credit card number. Come the '80s, and adults were relieved their 20-year-old children had no wars or crusades to distract them from the flowerless-and-beadless business of getting on in life. There was reason to believe that "Morning in America" would bring plenty of sunshine for the younger generation.

At the time, the declining birth rate of the late '60s and '70s was interpreted as another ace up their generational sleeve. According to a popular theory then advanced by demographer Richard Easterlin, small numbers would work powerfully in their favor, pushing up the earnings of entry-level workers and pushing down the cost of colleges and housing. Yes, whatever else might go wrong, these grown-up hi-tech "Computer Babies" were a sure bet never to lack for material abundance.

But like most sure bets, this one rode on blind confidence more than on any special care to ensure the outcome. And, as often happens, this one crashed. Whatever happened to Easterlin's theory of rising 13er earnings? Ever since the first 13ers reached their teens, the inflation-adjusted income of all men under age 35 has sunk like a lump of coal in Santa's bag—dropping by 20 percent since as recently as

I keep hearing this is the best time of our lives. And I wonder—is it all downhill?

Mandy Silber, high school senior, San Mateo, CA

In 1979, 74 percent of working Americans under age 25 were earning an hourly wage which—if received full-time and year-round—exceeded the cash poverty level for a family of three. By 1991, that share had fallen to 47 percent.

Source: Children's Defense Fund

Dude, we gotta win that contest . . . . There's no way we can raise a family on the money we make at Pretzels 'n' Cheese.

Bill, *Bill and Ted's Bogus Journey* (film)

Real Median Income of U.S. Families, 1973 and 1990 (in 1990 dollars)

	1973	1990	Percent Change 1973–90
Family head age 65 and over	$ 17,977	$ 25,049	+ 39%
Family head age 30 to 64	$ 38,861	$ 40,441	+ 4%
Family head under age 30	$ 27,980	$ 23,600	− 16%

Source: U.S. Bureau of the Census

1979. Counting only full-time, year-round workers, the 1980s saw a 15 percent earnings drop for all men under age 25 and a 10 percent wage drop for non-college men in their late twenties. In relative terms, young whites did better than blacks, women better than men, college graduates better than dropouts, *but every one of those categories lost at least some ground.* Adjusted for inflation, today's late-twentyish person would have to be a single woman working full-time with at least a college B.A. to have a good chance of outearning a demographically identical Boomer of twenty years ago. So where is this frenzied wage auction that would make "Baby Busters" rich right out of the box? Thirteeners haven't seen it happen.

What about that other reputed boon of being a "buster"? Weren't small numbers supposedly going to pull down the costs of setting out in life? Here too, the sure-bet pony got caught on the rail. College costs were never "bid down." In fact, since the first 13ers became freshmen in 1979, the average tuition-plus-fees for a four-year private university has shot up by over 10 percent per year, more than twice the annual inflation rate. The cost of an Ivy League degree (around $15,000 for Boomer students in the late '60s) has soared to over $100,000 for today's 13er underclassmen. At public universities, fees have skyrocketed during the recent recession—a time when most prices and wages have been

Cash Poverty Rates of Families With Children

	1973	1979	1990
Family head is age 30 to 64	9%	10%	12%
Family head is under age 30	16%	20%	33%
Family head is under age 30 and Black	38%	43%	58%

Source: U.S. Bureau of the Census

stable or falling. Boomers in their heyday treated college as a long screaming summer vacation; 13ers keep one careful eye on the professor, another on a mental image of a giant money meter, ticking away at the rate of over fifty dollars an hour per student, plus interest, for classroom time.

Did small numbers help "Busters" get cheap housing? Wrong again. In the early '70s, for a typical married couple under age thirty, the after-tax cost of owning a first home consumed just 12 percent of income. Following the feverish real estate market of the '80s, and despite the rush of dual-income young households, the after-tax cost of owning the same home has risen to 29 percent of income. Way back when the Everly Brothers were singing "All I have to do is dream," it was still common to see couples in their 20s buy freshly minted suburban homes while their parents stayed put in urban apartments or toiletless farmhouses. Today, it's the couple in their 20s who rent the urban apartment, which may be no bigger than the suburban master bedroom (excluding the sauna and walk-in closet) of the renters' parents.

Home Ownership Rates by Age of Household Head			
	1973	1990	Percent Change 1973-90
Under Age 25	23%	15%	– 8%
Age 25-34	51%	44%	– 7%
Age 35-44	71%	67%	– 4%
Age 45-64	76%	78%	+ 2%
Age 65 and over	70%	76%	+ 6%

Source: Joint Center for Housing Studies of Harvard University

WELCOME TO TOMORROWLAND, 13ERS! By the way, the monorail stops here. From now on you have to get out and walk. Unless your brain is Mensa-grade, your body is Olympic-class, your luck is infallible, or your parents bank in Switzerland—or unless you don't mind incurring a ton of debt to enter some cozy profession—you face a very hazardous economic future. And welcome, 13ers, to that best-kept secret of contemporary American life: While older age brackets are getting richer, yours is getting poorer. That certainly didn't happen to any of today's older generations when they were young.

LISTEN UP, DUDES! Where earlier twentieth-century generations could comfortably look forward to outpacing mom and dad, you'll be lucky just to keep up. When you marry, you and your spouse will both work—not for some Boomerish self-fulfillment, but because you *need* to, just to make ends meet. If you want children, you'll have to bravely defy statistics showing that, since 1973, the median

They're scared. It's like reality is setting in.

Marva Gumbs, director of career services, George Washington University, commenting on the graduating class of 1991

The poor stay poor, the rich get rich
That's how it goes, everybody knows

Concrete Blonde, "Everybody Knows" (song)

The hole in my pocketbook is growing.

10,000 Maniacs, "Dust Bowl" (song)

***crasher
>h2498r238qs8dp28720ruwidh[04r[0e9[2iohskch[09u[pj'sljvspcj[3-04

***2boomers
>you again! what is this, some code or the name of the welsh village where your ancestors grew up?

***crasher
>that's me banging my fist on the keyboard, venting my electronic frustration at the constant barrage of hideous news you have about our financial situation. and I'm assuming that you guys live in comparative splendor, while I rust down in this basement, yes?

***2boomers
>define "splendor."

***crasher
> 8wefjhwiwehfn04ruwekdj34].f,093498xuehbdsfbn48yrcndihfq]iil

real income has fallen by 30 percent for families with children headed by persons under thirty. Counting only couples that stay married, the dip has still been nearly 10 percent.

And you'd better not slip up. Over the last twenty years, the poverty rate among under-30 households has more than doubled. Your generation, in fact, has a weaker middle class than any other born in this century—which means that the distance is widening between those of you who are beating the average and those who are sinking beneath it. Who among you *is* beating it? College-degreed DINKs (dual-income, no kids) are a good bet. High-school grads, maybe. Anybody with children, getting dicey. Dropouts, slim chance. Single dropouts with kids, forget it.

What went wrong, and why? It's a simple formula, really. Take a generation of kids, give them crumbly families that don't allow them much time to learn skills that aren't immediately useful; give them inferior schooling to tarnish their reputation for competence; surround them with media that teach them to distrust any

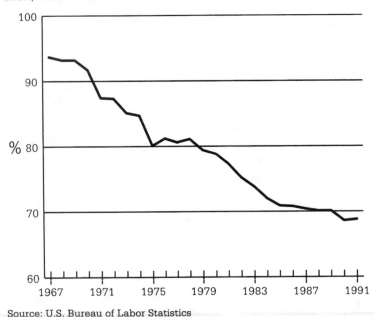

Median Weekly Earnings of Full-Time Working Men, Age 16–24, as a Percent of the Median for All Older Working Men, 1967 to 1990

Source: U.S. Bureau of Labor Statistics

	Age 18–29	Age 50+
Have there been times in the last 12 months when you did not have enough money to pay for health care?	36%	17%
Have you ever put off going to a doctor because of the cost?	46%	30%

Source: 1991 Gallup Poll

institutional avenue to career success. Then, when they're all ready to enter the adult labor force, push every policy lever conceivable—tax codes, entitlements, public debt, unfunded liabilities, labor laws, hiring practices—to tilt the economic playing field away from the young and toward the old.

***crasher
>during some particularly gruesome western civics class in 9th grade, our burly teacher mr. simmons showed us a plastic pull-down population graph of the united states. when he got to our birth years (the late '60s and early '70s), he showed how few of us there were, and how it was gonna be just so easy for us to get into college and get jobs and stuff. I remember we all cheered and told everyone else at lunch.

"THANKS SONNY, AND DON'T FORGET MY SENIOR CITIZEN DISCOUNT . . ."

I'd rather be home with my daughter. But they're paying $6.75 an hour. I couldn't pass that up.

Dave Marina, a Desert Storm veteran who landed a job fighting forest fires in Oregon

There really is a hell of a difference between this class and that of their parents. The good jobs are moving farther away from the poor jobs, and there aren't any jobs in between.

Harry Wilcox, principal, Lincoln High School, Philadelphia

It's a well-known complaint that American living standards, on average, have flattened out ever since American productivity began stagnating in the early 1970s. What's less well known is how this leveling of the national average has concealed vastly unequal changes in living standards by phase-of-life, and how the interests of older Americans have been protected at the expense of young people. Consider the following core indicators of economic well-being: worker pay, total household income, household wealth, home ownership, and the likelihood of poverty. From the late 1930s to the early 1970s, all these indicators improved briskly for every age group. Since then, they have diverged markedly across different age brackets. For households headed by persons over age 65, these indicators have continued to improve as though nothing had gone wrong. For age 35 to 65, most of them have just held steady. But for households headed by persons under age 35—the age bracket 13ers have been entering ever since the 1970s—every one of these indicators has gotten worse. Some have fallen off a cliff.

Combined with each generation's different memory of world events, this age-related spread in personal experience has created an enormous gulf between the economic perspective of 13ers and that of their elders. Unlike older Americans who grew up believing in the growing might and indomitable power of the American economy, 13ers recall economic warnings and dirgelike jeremiads dating back to the first time they stayed up to watch news stories about stagflation and gas lines. From childhood on, they've been inclined to believe the dire economic forecasts that most elders would rather shrug off—for example, that Americans will soon be working in sweatshops run by affluent foreigners.

Like Michael J. Fox in *Back to the Future II*, most 13ers would be unfazed to learn that the boss who fires them twenty years from now will be a Japanese businessman wearing a thousand-dollar suit. For that matter, they have no trouble looking forward to fantasies of impoverished decay, as portrayed in post-apocalyptic *Mad Max* videos that few older Americans can bear to watch. Nor do they imagine that they are about to inherit much in the way of social equality. A world in which a yawning social chasm separates the rich and free from the immiserated and robotic is another standard motif in the *Blade Runner* genre of sci-fi cinema.

***crasher

>there's something worse than all of this. judging from all the old movies I've ingested, poor people here used to be seen as just unlucky folks who were basically the same as us. now I see in my friends an underlying belief that the poor aren't just unlucky--they are a different kind of people, like they're missing some kind of important chromosome. it's subtle, and no one would dare say it, but it's a kind of prejudice I have to fight in myself. I think we're all so desperate not to end up like them that the only way we keep from being scared shitless is to believe that the people who sleep in front of the bathroom at the train station are from another planet.

By painful twists and turns, 13ers are beginning to catch on to the game. As $4-an-hour teenagers during the late Carter years, Atari-wavers shuddered at the chic negativism that envisioned them pedaling bikes to tiny geodesic dome-homes at the same age their parents had been polishing V-8 autos in front of spacious split-levels. And nothing suited them more, when casting their first votes in 1980, than an anti-government revolution that (they figured) would allow the young and energetic to prosper.

Yet as the decade wore on, 13ers came to realize that they bore most of the burden for the Reagan-era prosperity that so enriched their elders. They watched the drawbridge slam shut on most of the lucrative professional monopolies dominated by older age groups. They watched U.S. manufacturers respond to efficient global rivals by downsizing through attrition, letting their high-wage older work force age in place. They watched the total number of Fortune 500 jobs (cushy benefits and all) reach its historic peak in 1979—just when they first came to the job market—and then head south ever afterwards. Those paths blocked, millions of 13ers wedded their future to the one economic sector in which real pay declined, fringe benefits evaporated, and investment and output per worker showed literally no growth at all: the unskilled service sector. Ronald Mc-Donaldland.

During the Bush years, most of today's 40 million 13ers living on their own hit their first recession. And behold: This was the only cyclical downturn ever recorded in which all the net job loss landed on the under-30 age bracket. Not on Boomer post-yuppies, not on Silent prime-of-lifers, certainly not on G.I. retirees. Subtract 13ers from the employment tally, and presto: No recession!

As a group, 13ers remain faithful to the self-help spirit of the Rea-

Given the way things are, it will be much harder for people in my generation to live as comfortably as previous generations.

Agree: 65%.
Disagree: 33%.

Time magazine poll of Americans under 30 (1990)

"I think that we are all in a sense doomed." "What are you talking about?" "Downward social mobility. We hear a lot about the great social mobility in America— with the focus usually on the comparative ease of moving upwards. What's less discussed is how easy it is to go down. And I think that's the direction we're all heading in. And I think the downward fall is going to be very fast, not just for us as individuals, but for the whole preppy class."

two recent college graduates, *Metropolitan* (film)

———

———

gan Revolution. But those still in college, looking forward to the desperate job searches of today's new graduates, are beginning to ask harder questions about the policy gridlock over most of the issues vital to their economic future. Like why the college class of '92 faces the most difficult job search of any class since the Great Depression, with nearly a third of entry-level jobs disappearing and average pay falling for those who remain. Or why the proportion of college grads taking jobs that don't require college degrees has doubled over the last decade. Or why the federal deficit keeps growing on their tab. Or why the income tax rates on billion-dollar investments are held down while FICA tax rates on the first dollar of wage income keep rising. Or why unemployment benefits are extended for households already receiving checks, but nothing is done for most younger households that can't qualify. Or why senior citizens get to clamor for yet a third layer of health insurance when one-fourth of all 13ers have no insurance at all. Or why a skimpy urban youth bill, drafted in the wake of the L.A. riots, is allowed to grow into a giant Christmas tree of goodies for affluent older people.

Whatever may happen to the meek, 13ers know it's not their gen-

"AND AS YOU LEAVE OUR IVY HALLS, KNOW THAT YOU WILL NEVER FORGET THESE CAREFREE DAYS AND THE GREAT DEBT YOU WILL ALWAYS OWE TO YOUR ALMA MATER . . ."

eration that's about to inherit the earth. So where does that leave them?

Since the early 1970s, say many economists, America has been undergoing a "quiet depression" in living standards. A bit more pointedly, columnist Robert Kuttner describes 13ers as suffering from a "remarkable generational disease . . . a depression of the young" which makes them feel "uniquely thirsty in a sea of affluence." From 1929 to 1933, the bust years we call the "Great Depression," real household income fell by 25 percent all across America. Now once again: What was that dip in age-bracket income that 13ers have suffered since replacing Boomers? Twenty percent for young men? Thirty percent for young parents with children? Thirteeners get the message, even if others don't, about a "quiet" trauma today's older people would regard as a history-shattering catastrophe if it fell mostly on their heads.

>12. Tell Me When They're Moving Out

TVs. VCRs. Boomboxes. Five-disk CD players. PCs hooked to speakers and stuffed with games. Porta-phones with caller ID and answering machines. Pushbutton remote controls lying around everywhere. That's the pop image of the 13er teenage bedroom, crowded like a movie-set condo with hi-tech amenities. During the day, that image rides to high school in convertible sports cars with space-age sound systems. On weekends, it lingers around the mall where 15-year-olds pull out credit cards to buy $100 Keds or $500 aviator jackets or $1,000 IBM clones with VGA color monitors. On prom nights, it rents a fortune in sleek clothes and travels by stretch limo. And when parents are away, it capitalizes on that magic moment (like the opening scene in *Risky Business*) when everything mom and dad own—five bedrooms, bar, luxury sedan, stuffed fridge, large-screen TV with HBO—becomes the personal fief of some teenage suburban prince.

The icons of 13er affluence reach well beyond their teen years. Check out the student union of a large university: There it is, a

R*eally*, We Love Our Brand New Grads, But Please Tell Me When They're Moving Out

title of article by
Mary Fay Bourgoin, writing
of "the fear that many of us
have—our adult children will
never be able to afford to live
on their own," in the
Washington Post

R*egardless* of your current financial situation, do you remain firmly aware that the most fleeting whim of the economy could have you living back at Mom and Dad's in a nanosecond?

Douglas Coupland,
in *Details*

O*k*, so I'm still living with my parents. How bogus. How unoriginal.

Wayne,
Wayne's World (film)

mini-mall unimaginable twenty years ago, full of sports shops, restaurants, ice cream parlors, computer stores, fashion boutiques, banks, and travel agencies. Check out the juniors planning spring break: There they are, booking flights to Cancún and the Caribbean. Check out an inner-city crack house: There it is, full of young gangsters with gold chains and pocket beepers.

If older Americans have thus far shown little sympathy for the 13ers' economic plight, the reason lies largely in the sights and sounds of personal luxury that have surrounded 13ers since birth. Economic disease? Generational depression? How is that possible for kids whose teen bedrooms, college dorms, and gang houses are so decked out with lavish ornaments? Youth advertising, once reserved for cereal boxes or inside bubble gum wrappers, is now blazing away on prime-time TV, national newsweeklies, FM radio, public buses, rented videos, and highway billboards. Given that somebody's running all these ads—and given that what kids mostly buy are fancy shoes, pricey gadgets, and other discretionary stuff they want but don't really need—how could this generation be in such deep economic trouble?

***crasher
>cheesedog guys with lots of hair care products caught in a wondrous whirl of large-breasted girls white water rafting down the colorado. slick, pouty belgian male models with $7000 suits courting aryan-lookin' blondes at the bar, flicking off bottle tops with their thumbs, smiling shocking white teeth and dancing to industrial groove music, obviously about to get laid. now I ain't no social recluse or anything, but any adult who thinks that these beer ads are any way close to the way we live needs electro-convulsive shock therapy. these ads are made by evil ad execs. I buy the beer I think tastes good.

***2boomers
>why ask why?

Rarely does it occur to elders that juvenile wealth—what sociologist Jerald Bachman calls "premature affluence"—is in fact both a cause and a symptom of the 13ers' own impoverishment.

Much of this "premature affluence" is, of course, just image. Very few 13ers really do cruise to school in Land Rovers or vacation in Bermuda. But the image has a force of its own. Corporate marketers, no longer prevented by law or social stigma from targeting today's "proto-adult" youngsters, hype the fantasy of high-living kids so that everyone (including disapproving elders) can't help but notice. Thirteeners reinforce the image with their own lifestyle attitudes. Sensing their own economic vulnerability, most prefer to idealize themselves as possessing the power and security and confidence they associate with wealth. Young people with cash tend to flaunt it. Those without much find ways to show off what little they have. To admit to poverty in circa-1990 America is to admit to all the individual incompetence, family ruin, and cultural dysfunction the public now associates with it.

Even where this affluence is real, moreover, the bustling youth economy masks four harsh truths about the 13ers' economic condition. First, much of it is not really "theirs" in the sense that it reflects any ability to provide for themselves. Instead, this 13er affluence is the mall and grocery shopping kids do for working moms and dads who don't have the time. Or it's the summer house-sitting kids do for globe-trotting neighbors. Or it's the cash or clothes or car that busy, well-off parents give their kids as a "reward" for time they have to spend alone. For reasons of convenience, elder Americans do leave a significant share of their national wealth to be handled, watched over, or wasted by dependent youths. But little of this wealth serves any long-term interest of the kids themselves—such as helping them to become future wealth producers. Instead, it can make teenagers feel like bored retainers milling around in some opulent palace, having momentary, hopeless fun with whatever baubles the Rajah leaves lying around.

True, 13er teens do earn a vast amount of money (over $60 billion a year) from their own jobs. In fact, theirs is the biggest child labor generation since the days of turn-of-the-century newsboys and garment girls. The high school students of the '80s and '90s are working longer hours for pay (after school and during summers) than any previous generation of high-schoolers in American history. Yet the second harsh truth is that all this labor represents, in life cycle terms, a miserable return on youth energy and youth time. The typical teen job is a low-skill service slot offering little training and no chance for advancement, generating nothing but short-term cash. And once that cash is gone, the countless hours that might have been invested in skilled training or academic study are gone forever. The traditional youth jobs that once prepared earlier youth generations for adult careers—in farms, family-owned businesses, skilled crafts, heavy industry—have mostly vanished. Instead, the typical teenage 13er can

In 1968, 7 percent of driving-age teens owned cars; in 1990, 35 percent owned them (61 percent, among 18- and 19-year-olds).

Source: Rand Youth Poll (1988)

I spent a lot. Yeah, I got a lot of goodies.

Mike Tyson, explaining what happened to all his boxing winnings

From 1981 to 1991, the proportion of teenagers who owned their own TV set rose from 35 to 43 percent; their own telephone, from 16 to 25 percent. Of today's college students, three-quarters own a TV, two-thirds use automatic tellers, and half have all-purpose credit cards.

Sources: Rand Youth Poll (1991); American Demographics

This is my mom's house. I don't have any say-so here. I just have input.

Sonji Stewart, 26,
living with her baby in her
parents' home

I've seen kids with $50,000 to $70,000 in debt. . . . They spend the money on clothes, pizza, tuition, books, fun travel, presents for girlfriends, shoes, watches, engagement presents, proms, formals. Kids just go haywire.

Kathleen Hennessey,
professor,
Texas Tech University

work her heart out for years and still find herself no more employable than the day she started.

Third, the earnings of dependent youths ordinarily buy a level of affluence that still reflects a massive parental subsidy. In most American homes, after all, these earnings are linked to a perverse quid pro quo: Parents, wanting their kids to learn the value of money and become self-reliant individuals, typically allow them to do whatever they want with whatever they make. Thirteeners are thus far less likely than prior generations to help pay for their own room and board or to help fund their own future education and training. Bearing few living expenses and not expected to save, a generation of teenagers has become accustomed to a subsidized level of consumption they could not possibly afford on their own. Once in college, many continue to cultivate expensive tastes—the safe and secluded dorm, the squash court, the dessert tray—oblivious to the real estate nightmare and Hamburger Helper that await them after graduation.

The fourth harsh fact about youth affluence is that it's strictly temporary: It comes with a Cinderella clock. Usually, crunch time comes soon after a 13er leaves home or leaves school. This is the period, say opinion surveys, when today's young adults start getting dissatisfied with their living standards. College loans shift from payout to payback time, at rates of interest way above the three percent charged Boomers back in the '60s. Child support payments dry up from divorced dads. Dentists and doctors have to be paid with wallet cash. Jobs take longer than expected to land. Salaries are painfully small, especially by the standard of the prematurely affluent teen's own inflated expectations.

How small? To begin with, take a look at polls showing that most teenagers (of both sexes) expect to earn $30,000 or more by age 30. Then, take a look at Census surveys reporting what American men age 25 through 29 really earn. In 1990, there were *eight* with total annual incomes of under $30,000 for every one making over that amount. (And there were fifty making less than $15,000 for every one making over $75,000.) Even these earnings don't go as far as many 13ers once imagined they would. Money that used to go toward the discretionary consumer goods of a leisured lifestyle now has to go into rent, food, commuting, and other necessities—if it can stretch that far. Within a year or two, the phone call is made, the bags are packed, the surrender is declared, and another graduate heads home with head bowed.

Meet the 13er "boomerang child"—yet another addition (along with "latchkey child" and "throwaway child") to the sad lexicon of the 13er youth era. Among those who leave home with a high school degree or more, fully 40 percent (and well over half of the men) "boomerang" back to their parents' home—and kitchen and laundry—at least once. Today, more unmarried children under age 30 are living with their parents than at any time since the Great Depression.

The good news is that home-again 13ers get along far better with parents than most Boomers ever did; mom (and stepdad?) are "cool" about their music, eating habits, and overnight guests. The bad news is that the boomerang event is not always just a temporary breather. It can drag on indefinitely as these dependent grownup children pass time slacking around coffee shops, health clubs, colleges, resorts, or wherever else the smell of comfortable money is in the air. By leaning on parents, they're able to keep up (or revive) the old spending habits—buying clothes, CDs, cars, and the like.

Looking for encouragement, boomerangers find precious little in the media-created fantasy of unreal youth images: the action-show cops in designer clothes they couldn't possibly afford on a cop's salary; the hip twentysomethings on MTV's ironically-named *Real Life*, who swim around in a luxurious fishbowl; the moneyed,

They are little Drexel Burnhams, little S&Ls: free-spending in the '80s, when they got their first taste of plastic; broke now . . . . Their parents are like ATMs, hit up regularly to pay for plane tickets and help tame credit-card debt.

Anne Gowen, 25, and Sean Piccoli, 28, "A Generation Lost in Time," in the *Washington Times*

A lot of parents will give credit cards to teach their kids responsibility about handling money. It always backfires. The kids usually end up sucking the parents dry.

Ryan Kula, high school senior, Alexandria, VA

do-or-die hustlers in the *Boyz* films, who—on camera—vastly outnumber the inner-city kids struggling to keep a regular job. Aside from a handful of entertainment superstars, the media take slim interest in young people who are legitimately supporting themselves. A 13er can read the newspaper or flip the TV dial, all the way from PBS documentaries to Fox fantasies. It's seldom there.

Back when these kids were little, their parents often enjoyed setting them loose with the sort of expensive toys that the parents themselves never had at like age. But what was cute at age 16 pleases neither party at age 26. Parent and child both feel a sense of life cycle failure—the child for not being able to leave home as a grownup, the parent for not raising a son or daughter to life's ultimate postpartum. Both realize that behind the 13er's adultlike familiarity with affluence lies the emptiness of childlike economic dependence. And both wonder whether the boomerang child will grow old drafting ré-

***crasher
>my housemate just told me that kitty litter scared her into grad school. she was back home in the fall after graduation, and her mom told her to clean the cat box one night. she got halfway outside with it, until she had some flashback of doing the same thing when she was seven. she freaked, threw the litter in the street, and was calling admissions offices the next morning.
***2boomers
>and who paid for it?
***crasher
>why, her mother did, thanks for asking. where did you find all these quotes from credit card complainers? if they're so anal about their kids' bills, they shouldn't have given them the damn card in the first place! perhaps if life didn't suck so bad once you get out of college, a few of us would show a little more discretion in our shopping!

sumés in his childhood bedroom.

Taken as a whole, the 13er experience with affluence has been the direct inverse of the experience of the parents, teachers, and community leaders who raised them. In the 1930s and '40s, the Silent Generation grew up as cashless kids in a world that emphasized education and training under tight parental supervision, but offered kids few opportunities either to make or spend money on their own. As soon as they left home to get jobs, the Silent rocketed past the living standards of their parents and never looked back. In the 1970s and '80s, 13ers grew up as moneyed kids in a world that celebrated after-school earnings more than after-school study, the art of shopping hi-tech over the skill of making hi-tech. Now, many of these grown-up kids are still looking up at their parents and wondering if they'll ever just pull even.

As twentysomethings, 13ers are haunted by both the image and the reality of teen affluence. The image attracts incessant criticism mixed with troubling reminders of an extravagant standard of consumption they cannot afford on their own. The reality tempts them with a sumptuous appetizer in youth, followed by a main course that gets snatched away as soon as they arrive at the adult banquet table.

>13. Room to Move as a Frycook

The "yes sir, no sir" voice, the face that betrays no emotion, the fast-moving hands, the all-business body hustle: Sometime just before Reagan entered the White House, older Americans began to notice a very different sort of youngster pumping the gas, scooping the ice cream, and ringing the register. No longer did the customer notice those "meaningful" Boomer gestures and outbursts. That's when Americans first met 13ers on the job.

Back in the late 1960s, young Boomers yearned to find a higher calling in whatever occupation they deigned to fill. That was an era in which Kenneth Keniston, after interviewing hundreds of Boomer collegians, observed that he had "yet to find one who was worried about finding a job" and "relatively few who were worried about finding a *good* job." But 13ers look at work differently—as a means of survival, as an opportunity to prosper, as something that doesn't mean anything but just has to get done if anybody's going to get paid. And, unlike Boomers, today's 13ers are very worried about finding jobs. Many talk about little else.

Thirteeners entering the labor market have no illusions that the system welcomes what they have to offer. Experience at part-time after-school jobs? Forget it. Unskilled labor puts cash in their pockets, but two of every three 13ers consider it useless as a stepping-stone

There's room to move as a frycook, man. I could be manager in two years' time.

young fast-food worker,
Repo Man (film)

During the 1980s, the number of minors found to be illegally employed nearly tripled nationwide.

Source: *Washington Post*

From 1975 to 1988, the proportion of high school seniors who like "the kind of work you can forget about after the work day is over" rose from 48 to 57 percent. The proportion who believed that "to me, work is nothing more than making a living" rose from 19 to 25 percent.

Source: "Monitoring the Future: Questionnaire Responses from the Nation's High School Seniors" (University of Michigan, 1975–1988)

to later employment. High school degree? Maybe that's enough, if your mom owns the store or your uncle's a union steward, or if you don't mind competing in the global wage market against nimble fingers in Bangladesh. Apprenticeships? Shyeeaah riiight, provided you can still find one of the 3,500 slots available across the entire United States. Armed forces? Great for a couple years, but then what? The big heroes of Desert Storm got laid off, and the Cold War's over. College degree? That doesn't impress big corporate employers like it once did. Professional degree? Maybe, but good luck breaking into a partnership full of older careerists with oversized egos, endless credentials, and nowhere else to go. Today's economy offers its biggest rewards to an aging class of winners whom economist Robert Reich calls "symbolic analysts" and offers the least to everybody else. By preparation and reputation, 13ers understand that they fall into the "everybody else" category.

Where Boomers came of age despising a system which they knew would take care of them, 13ers struggle to game a system from which they expect a whole lot less. These days, a young job-seeker will stand in line all night to be the first inside the recruiter's door when it opens. Maybe he'll send up a self-advertising video, or volunteer his own corporate acquisition memo, or do a Michael J. Fox and crash the boss's party (where, a quarter-century ago, *The Graduate*'s Dustin Hoffman smugly submerged himself after just one mention of the word "plastics"). One way or another, he'll try to beat the odds and pull down a glittering prize, maybe one of those Fortune 500 managerial slots that Boomers once found so offensive.

Most of the rest—and those who dare, but fail—typically end up with the low-wage keyboard, phone, counter, delivery, and cleaning jobs Boomers have always found demeaning: the service-sector "McJobs" that sociologist Amitai Etzioni describes as "more time-consuming, less character building" than what talented youths used to expect. Even here, the typical 13er attitude is to wait for a break, prove themselves, and squeeze their way up, from cashier to stock clerk to night manager. They're especially attracted to working

Number and proportion of persons not covered by health insurance at any time during 1990, by age bracket		
Under Age 18	8.4 million	(24.3%)
Age 18 to 34	14.8 million	(42.8%)
Age 35 to 64	11.1 million	(32.1%)
Age 65 & Over	0.3 million	(0.8%)
Source: U.S. Bureau of the Census		

arrangements (dealer franchises, sales commissions, piecework, temping, and performance bonuses) that reward initiative and offer at least some hope of striking it big. They devour rags-to-riches stories wherever they can find them—like the one about the thousand 13er programmers at Microsoft's Seattle-area headquarters who've become stock-option millionaires.

Along the way, 13ers are emerging into a consummate generation of entrepreneurs. Few ever expect to talk themselves into cushy sinecures. They know instead that the only way they can advance is to fix a problem no one has yet found, to do a job no one has yet named. These are the guys who can get your package across town within the hour—you don't want to know how—or fix your computer and get it back on your desk within the day, or market your product in Singapore within the week. In a system that puts a premium on slow-moving (Silent) process and celebrates assertive (Boomer) egos, 13ers see speed and invisibility as their points of advantage. The suc-

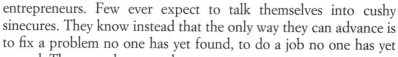

***crasher
>maybe it seems as though the kids slicing the fudge at the mall are all business and no nonsense, but just wait until the supervisor isn't there, and you have anarchy of the cro-magnon sort. during my illustrious two-year career at dr. freeze's ice cream emporium, I gave away approximately 2.4 million dollars of free product. my roommate permanently borrowed 13 cubic tons of chocolate chip cookie dough from the pastry shack, my best friend charged us 5¢ per pepperoni slice, and my girlfriend let us rent "return of the jedi" from the video store for forever. we all got fired eventually, but that was usually the best part of it. people with a death wish don't mind getting hit on the head with a crowbar!

cessful 13er does not follow the system, but the market; he doesn't look at what people say they need, but what people will pay real money to get.

In their opportunistic, contrarian, risk-taking approach to work, 13ers are breathing new life and location into the American frontier spirit. They find their frontier in financial centers, where even the

Increasing numbers of private-sector companies are discovering the efficiency of hiring bright undergraduates or recent graduates and paying them next to nothing.

Washingtonian magazine

youngest trader can make a million if he can just get the right two people on the phone at the right moment. In companies serving a niche others have overlooked—maybe she can start a folding-bicycle business, a shopping service, a bungee-jumping company, or a mail-order computer firm. (Michael Dell, the CEO of the billion-dollar Dell Computer Corporation, is a 13er.) On midnight shifts, when a multiplying number of young guards, clerks, nurses, and haulers can work full-time at extra pay before moonlighting (sunlighting?) during the day. Overseas—in Japan, Mexico, Eastern Europe, Russia—where companies and governments care more about language skills and an instinct for fast action than about fancy degrees or impressive salary histories. And outside the law, in profitable crimes like auto theft, for which there is an expanding export market and for which the odds of being caught and sent to jail are barely one in 100.

Whatever the frontier, 13ers are pushing the envelope of energy and reflex-time. They look for the main chance and jump fast if the moment is right, moving quickly into good opportunities and just as quickly out of dead ends. Come of age in the hard-charging '80s, they work as hard as they need to—but when work's over, it's *over*. They're not workaholics and don't labor needlessly on weekends (like Boomers) for the perverse joy of it. Possessed of a purely instrumental view of employment, they can distance themselves from corporate cultures and can relax without guilt when the "job" is done. As 13ers see it, they can't afford to grow attached to any line of work that doesn't pay off somehow, either in cash, promotion, or free time. And they know that employers care less about who they are than about what they can do.

Frontier or not, the 13er "just do it" on-the-job attitude often rubs older people wrong. Noticing the common 13er tendency to strip jobs of deeper meanings, and their disinterest in work for its own sake, many elders interpret the youth work ethic as shallow, unrooted, unpromising. Watching 13ers work faster, later, and at more dangerous jobs (often in violation of traffic, child labor, and occupational health and safety laws) than kids did when they were young, elders wonder what can possibly be worth that to them. Hearing them say that the future is never and the present is now, elders wonder why so many of these young nomads just don't care about building a long-term stake in anything. Reading about postmodern buccaneers caught for piracy (software), copying trademarks (T-shirts), fraud (mail-order), and cheating (bar exams), elders question whether 13ers behave with any conscience at all. Despairing over this do-any-thing-for-a-buck behavior, high schools, colleges, and professional schools scramble to inject "ethics" into the formal curriculum, some-thing they wouldn't have dared to impose on young holier-than-thou Boomers.

Thirteeners see right through these critiques. All their lives, they've listened to a media-driven culture declare that the establish-ment is bad and the individual is good. But whenever they've seen their elders apply this liberationist theology, they've noticed that the application is selective—and that the interests of the liberators are always somehow safeguarded.

As 13ers view it, the families, schools, and training programs that could have prepared them for worthwhile careers have been allowed to rot, but the institutions that safeguard the occupational livelihood of mature workers have been maintained with full vigor. Trade quo-tas protect decaying industries. Immigration quotas protect dinosaur unions. Price subsidies protect inefficient farmers. Federal labor reg-ulations protect outmoded skills. State credential laws protect over-priced professions. Huge FICA taxes take away 13er money that they never expect to see again. If you're an adult who neglects kids, soci-ety either says O.K. or gives you a wrist slap. But if you're a neglect-ed kid who tries to go one-on-one against an adult, the law comes down on you like a ton of bricks.

All around them, 13ers see how the workplace "system" is rigged against them—and how the bias against youth is so blatant that no one bothers mentioning it. All they can do is watch as the safety net for aging retirees gets new reinforcements while their own safety net gets ripped to tatters. In the private sector, the shift toward temping, short-term employment, and service-sector jobs has left today's un-der-30 work force without most of the health-and-pension cushions other living generations took for granted at the same age. In the pub-lic sector, welfare and Medicaid are getting stingier toward their age bracket, while unemployment compensation and disability coverage don't keep up with their fast, job-shifting pace. Graying unions like the UAW care a lot more about pay and benefits going to current card-carrying members (average age, 47) than to future ones. Notic-ing that geriatric health is the one field that's booming with entry-lev-

Some guy in our church at home came up to my parents and said, "What in God's name are you doing, allowing your son to sell America to the Japanese?"

Dwight Poier, 23, an American "baby banker" in Tokyo

We're like get ahead, get ahead, we're like, just get by, get by. I wouldn't do something I didn't like, and that's another thing about our generation. If they don't like it, they're out of it.

Robert Meehan, Towson State University

They're much more interested in having a personal life, but they're having trouble figuring out how because they see the people ahead of them working 60 to 80 hours a week.

Margaret Regan, Towers Perrin, commenting on corporate recruits under age 25

Only 15 percent of employed 13ers consider themselves "workaholics"—versus 27 percent for all Americans over age 30.

Source: Gallup Poll (1991)

***crasher

>compared to the job market you guys had, we definitely got the smelly end of the plunger. back in your day, the great questions in life were, "how can I become more self-actualized?" or "why is there evil when an omnipotent god is good?" for us, they are "paper or plastic?" or "would you like fries with that?"

el jobs, 13ers can put two and two together to figure out where the real public benefits are going. From where 13ers sit, even federal discrimination laws are a stacked deck. They prohibit employers from firing someone over forty because he lacks energy (the natural advantage of youth), but say nothing about firing someone under forty because she lacks experience (the natural advantage of age).

Nothing exemplifies this age-graded inequality more than the two-tier wage ladder. In the 1980s, battered by foreign rivals, many a Fortune 500 company negotiated a union contract that protected elders while making the new hires bear the full burden of market competition. Entirely new wage-and-benefit ladders were established, the new ones lower than the old ones at every pay step. These two-tier contracts "grandfathered in" older workers at noncompetitive high wage and benefit levels—and "grandsonned out" all new young hires. Trapped in two-tier shops within a productivity-flat economy, 13er employees know from the get-go that they'll never match what Boomer and Silent employees got at the same point in their careers.

Understandably, 13ers are turning against the bureaucrats, lawyers, and lobbies whom they see propping up an antiquated workplace system run by and for older generations. And they show little enthusiasm for the politicians, unions, and trade associations who shed crocodile tears over the plight of young workers while writing rules that supposedly "protect" kids against exploitation. They write so many rules, in fact, that an estimated half of all teenage 13ers now start their working lives in some job deemed illegal according to federal codes promulgated by DOL, OSHA, EEOC, DOE, HHS, and ITA, or according to the numberless regulations of state and local authorities. If you're a 13er, you've learned that these are

the caring folks who tell you to stay in school (whether or not it prepares you for work); who tell you to be responsible and pay into those benefit funds ("rock solid," like the S&Ls); who tell you not to cut in line (their early retirement comes first); and who warn you not to do anything dangerous (to their own job security).

Desperate for a break, 13er workers are coming to realize their own interests are usually best served by anything that means less system and more marketplace chaos—that is, more "creative destruction." Except around the edges, 13ers won't feel the hurt if the Seawolf submarine is canceled, Medicare is means-tested, pension COLAs are frozen, tobacco farmers are zeroed out, and taxes are raised on the rich (or middle class). And, mostly, it's 13ers who would reap the rewards if the federal budget gets balanced, the economic status quo gets scrambled, new capital gets scattered around, new exports and imports fly across borders, and a myriad new businesses get started.

Most of today's hottest marketplace rivalries involve new challenges to big companies that continue (says Michael Dell) "to do things which are effectively not necessary today." Cable TV versus the networks. Mail-order computers versus IBM. Overnight package delivery versus the Postal Service. On-line marketing versus newspaper want-ads. Foreign-owned U.S. car factories versus General Motors. Temp services versus the Fortune 500 bureaucracy. Every time, it's the challenger who is building the younger work force. And every time—thanks to the lower pay, lower benefits, and greater entrepreneurial energy of younger employees— it's the challenger who's getting the edge.

So 13ers are turning toward leaders who promise to dissolve that system in favor of the self-starter and self-server. Forget the rules. These youngsters will gladly take their chances on something new and risky. Anything's better than joining the lower caste of some stodgy, noncompeting entity that won't give them the same entry-level breaks it once gave the generations who came before. This attitude makes it harder for 13ers to appeal to the system when they hurt, but that's OK with them. The old '70s-era image of the 10-year-old hustler still controls their generational mindset. The hippie's little brother who once bragged about how he could turn a buck can hardly come back now begging for special favors.

> I'd say 75 percent of the available jobs for new college graduates are in the field of marketing by telephone.
>
> Bryan Burkert,
> recent graduate,
> St. Bonaventure University

> In 1987, Colgate-Palmolive started a program to groom recent college graduates for overseas managerial careers. By the early 1990s, more than 15,000 young people were vying for the 15 slots available each year.
>
> Source: *Wall Street Journal*

```
***2boomers
>well, crasher?

***crasher
>well, what?

***2boomers
>any biting sarcasm to throw our way? bet you're an
expert on this subject.

***crasher
>no way, boys--I'm horrible with money. I only bitch
about things I understand.

***2boomers
>that makes you a little unusual for someone your age.
besides, we're mostly talking about jobs, not money.

***crasher
>is there a difference?
```

>14. We Trust Ourselves, and Money—Period

In 1988, Swarthmore College made a daring move: At a time of hot competition among colleges in its sub-Ivy class, Swarthmore sharply increased its tuition, bringing it right up to the level of Harvard and Yale. The result? Not a decline, but a surge in new applications for admission. Four years later, a new style hit teen fashion: At the start of the worst recession in a decade, kids began leaving the price tags dangling from their new clothes. The point was not to show how little they paid, but how much. Is this crazy, or what?

Since the late '70s days of Valley Girls and teen disco junkies, the most vivid hues of 13ers have always seemed (to elder eyes) to include the color of money. Malls full of "material girl" Madonna wannabees. The *Details* magazine fashion look. The M.B.A. power-tool. Raps about hustling for cash. Cover stories about the splendorous wealth of sports, rock, and film superstars. Sitcom jokes about how today's teens come with designer genes.

Twenty years ago, young people dressed down and slummed. Today, they dress up for what appears to be a real life game of *Monopoly*. (Roll the dice: Will You Take a Walk on the Boardwalk, or Go Directly to Jail?) Twenty years ago, the biggest fights between adolescents and their parents were over global "values" involving politics, war, and religion. Today, surveys show their biggest quarrels are over "how they spend their money" and "what they do with their leisure time." Thirteeners willingly admit that money plays a central role in how they see the world: Four out of five agree that people their age are both "more materialistic" and "more selfish" today than they were twenty years ago.

Sure, a lot of this money fixation can be attributed to this generation's premature affluence and its poor economic prospects down the road. Anyone who can't obtain at age 30 the same amenities he enjoyed at age 15 has plenty of reason to obsess over dollars and cents. But that doesn't explain why so many 13ers developed the fixation so early in life, nor why the Boomers born in the 1950s (who are also disappointed with their economic lot) don't focus on money to nearly the same degree. Thirteeners trust hard green because their earliest life experiences taught them that you can't trust anything else. Having grown up in a childhood world that stressed private rights and liberties, they learned that families may leave you, neighbors may

Is it "extremely" or "quite" important for you to . . .	high school seniors in 1976	in 1988	difference
have lots of money	15%	31%	+ 16%
have clothes in the latest style	13%	24%	+ 11%
be able to find steady work	63%	73%	+ 10%
have at least two cars	5%	12%	+ 7%
find purpose and meaning in life	64%	57%	− 7%

Source: "Monitoring the Future: Questionnaire Responses from the Nation's High School Seniors" (University of Michigan, 1975–1988)

rob you, government may cheat you—but money is always faithful. Like your body (another 13er obsession), it is a pure extension of your personal will. It depends on no one else. In sufficient amounts, it can vanquish any foe or deter any predator. Money isn't everything—but for a generation uninvited to most other avenues of social approval, it's the best thing within reach.

At an early age, 13ers have developed a remarkable precocity in knowing how to get maximum leverage out of whatever cash they have. As kids, they eke the most consumption they can out of each dollar they earn at Hardee's. They take over the grocery and clothes budget when mom hits the workplace. They help divorced moms stretch dimes in deadbeat-dad households. In college, they're constantly weighing dollar trade-offs. (Should I take these course credits here at State U. or across town at the community college where tuition is $90 less a credit, not including the $1.25 a gallon I'd have to pay for gas?) On the job, they heavily populate the nation's retail cash registers and dominate companies that help older people consume (mail order, catering, shopping services, landscaping, interior design, travel agencies, resorts, tours).

Their easy familiarity with money—like their grasp of so many other undiscussed bottom lines of life—reflects a genuine 13er edge over their elders. Attuned to the realities of the market, 13ers are used to figuring out what people around them really want, and to taking careful notice of how much things cost and how much jobs pay. They make clear-headed tradeoffs between pleasure and pain, businesslike

Survey question: "How much do you enjoy shopping for Christmas gifts?" Among people age 18 to 29, 40 percent said "very much"; among everyone 30 and over, only 26 percent said so.

Source: Gallup Poll (1989)

Any time you can make $400 or $500 in an hour, you can't go back to $5 or $6. It's like the value system. I like the Gucci, the Fendi. Till the day I die, I gotta have that stuff.

Washington, DC, prison inmate

A sixteen-year study of 600 college students found that economic concerns have risen dramatically in importance among young people considering marriage.

Source: "Marrying for Money," in *Self* magazine

I wouldn't want to work alongside some of my fellow students. They're so intense in here, you wonder what they'll be like in the big bad world. Even now, it's just bucks, bucks, bucks, the talk. And nobody cares what they do.

Ron Falcone, student, Virginia Tech

choices about how best to put scarce resources to use. Seldom do they diddle with symbols that don't work, or allow something to be damaged for the sake of some abstraction, or tolerate hurt without any compensating benefit for themselves or for somebody they know. While this attitude leads some 13ers to crime, it instills in most of them an abundance of personal generosity and a resistance to waste and stupidity.

As a credo, however, this money fixation can also make life's journey immeasurably more difficult. It tempts many into wrongly believing that the best way to possess riches is to pursue them directly. In youth, today's older generations were taught to focus themselves on adult-approved incremental goals that had nothing to do with money (good grades, eagle badges, blue ribbons). Thus nurtured and thus rewarded, kids were guided along a pattern of behavior that led them into grownup situations where money naturally gravitated toward them. By contrast, 13ers were nurtured to distrust incremental and nonpecuniary goals. They suspect, often rightly, that adults have rendered such goals far less relevant than they used to be to ultimate success in life. Why plod through humdrum home-

***crasher
>jesus, do you really think we're that rotten? it seems to me that money has always been everyone's reason for waking up in the morning, no matter what generation you slid yourself into. you make it sound like we have absolutely no grasp on the higher ideals in life.

***2boomers
>well, a lot of you trust money more than you trust anything else.

***crasher
>I have friends who would egg your house for saying something like that.

***2boomers
>egg away. that doesn't make it less true.

***crasher
>you get to a point in the way of thinking when you say to yourself either "okay, I'm going to be famous and therefore rich, until which I will starve without heat and inhale easy cheese until the landlord bolts the door" or "okay, I'm never going to be rich, but I'm going to make damn sure that I help out a few people and take as many road trips to seattle as possible." you think money is the basis for our existence, when it's really much simpler. fun is.

***2boomers
>easy, crasher. good times in seattle cost money. as somebody said in "top gun," "your ego's writing checks your body can't cash."

A BRIEF HISTORY OF RIPPED BLUE JEANS

1960: OH NO! NOW YOU'LL HAVE TO GET A NEW PAIR!

1975: WOW MAN! DIDN'T YOU JUST BUY THOSE SEVEN YEARS AGO? — I CAN'T THROW 'EM OUT... THEY'RE LIKE OLD FRIENDS!

1990: PRE-RIPPED DESIGNER JEANS ONLY $69.95 — TOTALLY RADICAL!

work when mere competence is worthless—when you look around and notice that, in entertainment or law or sports or politics, you are either a superstar or a nobody? And why care about grades if everyone can get into college, if even a high-achieving McLean, Virginia, high school can post a hallway billboard touting M&M candies as "Better Than Straight A's"?

For all the self-help fire that burns within their hearts, 13ers collectively lack that strong attachment to the familial, educational, and economic institutions that once helped move older generations from here to there on the ladder of adult success. Despite all the hype about self-reliant whiz-kid tycoons, adults did not teach 13ers about the patience and other self-denying building blocks they need to achieve lasting personal prosperity. Instead, each day, 13ers by the millions ponder how to leap the gap to genuine adulthood without embarking on all those endless and complicated and officially marked paths that seemingly don't lead anywhere.

This all-or-nothing perspective explains this generation's unusual enthusiasm for taking risks. The standard argument against betting

> In a lot of ways, they are entrepreneurship at its best. They are not graduates of the school of business at Harvard. But damn if those SOBs don't know how to make money. Straightforward capitalists. No question about it. We tend to play these suckers cheap. But it's a business.
>
> Isaac Fulwood, police chief, Washington, DC, describing local drug dealers

on long odds is that, on average, you'll end up somewhat worse off than when you started. But many 13ers perceive no difference at all between a small step backward and where they are already. So citing the averages is no argument against the slim possibility of winning the jackpot. Yes, the slow-but-steady "young fogey" image does hold for some: mainly young professionals who have managed to enter the system and don't dare upset their fragile prospects of promotion. But for countless harder-pressed 13ers, especially the "forgotten half" of non-college youths who are traditionally the most risk-averse, betting against the odds has become a way of life.

Older Americans notice this way of life in the large numbers of 13ers who are making routine and rapid changes in their jobs, careers, and geographical location—who are, according to an article in the *Wall Street Journal*, "more willing to gamble their careers . . . than earlier generations." Go into any city and take a look at what they're up to. Check out their penchant for setting up new businesses or for requesting a profit share in lieu of regular pay. Check out their disinterest in insurance or future pension income. Check out the high-school dropouts, gambling their bodies as daredevil bicycle messengers and gambling their meager paychecks on lotto tickets. A few blocks away, check out the burgeoning volume of extreme-risk criminal activity in an inner-city youth culture that recognizes no middle ground between abject poverty and pimp-and-dealer splendor.

To many, the only way to cross the void and reach prosperity is with the assistance of some enormous slingshot. This is why gambling for money is reaching epidemic proportions among Americans under 30, in and out of school. Though she believes in hard work, the typical 13er also respects the power of sheer luck. Though she knows that nothing compensates for going broke, she also knows that most of them are broke to begin with—which makes it easier to accept the prospect of losing on a long shot. Statistics say that most people lose

How optimistic are you about your career and financial prospects in the next ten years?

Optimistic	89%	Pessimistic	11%

How optimistic are you about the nation's economic prospects in the next ten years?

Optimistic	45%	Pessimistic	55%

Source: 1992 *Fortune* poll of employed Americans, ages 21–29

PLAY THE
WHEEL OF
CAREER
FORTUNE

CENTRAL HIGH

MINIMUM BET
$50,000⁰⁰+

PICK COLLEGE HERE

"YOU CAN'T WIN IF YOU DON'T PLAY"

at gambling. But statistics also tell 13ers that most of their generation cannot possibly attain the material rewards they all desire. So why not take a shot?

Like warriors on the eve of battle, 13ers face their economic future with a mixture of playfulness and fatalism. Squared off competitively against each other, this melange of scared city kids, suburban slackers, hungry immigrants, boomerang grads, and shameless hustlers is collectively coming to realize that America can only afford to offer its Dream to a select set of winners. And that America cares little about its anonymous losers.

So this generation finds itself playing not *Monopoly*, but a real-life game of *Chutes and* (No) *Ladders*. Facing the economic future, each 13er finds himself essentially alone, to an extent that most elders would have difficulty comprehending. Between his own relative poverty and the affluence he desires, he sees no intermediary signposts, no sure, step-by-step path along which society will help him,

You still got the gall, to
try to rule . . .
But you failed the New
Jack School.

Queen Latifah, rapper

———

The young male
residents of Harlem are
less likely to live to age
40 than the young male
residents of
Bangladesh—and face a
higher risk of being
killed by age 25 than the
risk faced by U.S. troops
during a full combat tour
in Vietnam.

Sources: U.S. Public Health
Service; New England
Journal of Medicine

———

I put the gun up to his
head and go, bam bam
bam bam.

Delroy Ross, 20, Harlem,
who set $10,000 as his price
for a hired killing

———

I know people who'll be
dead before I go to
college. That's just a
fact of life.

Kenji Jasper, 15,
Washington, DC

urge him, congratulate him. Instead, all he sees is an enormous chasm, with him on one side and everything he wants sitting on the other.

>15. New Jack School

Try an experiment. Put yourself in a closed environment in which the 13er childhood experience is pushed to its logical extreme. Instead of merely weak families and frequent divorces, let's assume teen mothers and no in-house fathers at all. Instead of merely ineffective and chaotic schools, let's assume schools whose major tasks are to screen for lethal weapons, provide life support to teenage mothers, and prevent the spread of deadly diseases. And instead of merely dimming career opportunities, let's assume a moonscape economy in which the very word "career" seems like a cruel joke.

The result? Time horizons shrink from years to days. Life goals are redefined in terms of pleasure and pain. Adult autonomy becomes possible at puberty—boys as gun-toting warriors, girls as heads of households. No wealth is created, just begged or ripped off others. Human connections are fleeting, life expectancy measured in months, even days. Quick wits mean the difference between riches and death. One wrong move can bring a hail of bullets in a world where the victim you forgive today may knife you in the back tomorrow.

What is this, some nightmare? Some *Tron*-like gladiator video game? No, it's the world of many 13ers coming of age in Watts, Anacostia, the South Bronx, Oakland, the Chicago projects, Memphis's Beale Street, or any of a hundred urban wilderness areas scattered across America. A world that's

Number of Arrests per 1,000 Persons, by Age		
	age 14–17	age 18–25
1950	4	13
1960	47	42
1970	104	74
1980	126	114
1988	117	117

Source: U.S. Federal Bureau of Investigation

an asphalt state of nature where only the strong survive. A world where young people harden themselves to daily suffering and hopelessness in a brutal, nomadic, pre(or post-?)civilized lifestyle that older generations find unpleasant enough in small suburban traces, but totally repugnant and incomprehensible in its undiluted urban form. A world where teenage males are more endangered, and attract less sympathy, than the spotted owl. A world where, when some politician proposes a "weed and seed" agenda, everybody knows who—and how old—the weeds are.

Never are Americans so pessimistic about their national future as when they contemplate what young 13ers are doing in and to the inner city. Call it America's Beirut. Call it America's Intifada. Veteran SWAT-team leaders call it an L.I.C. ("low intensity conflict") similar to the muck and mire of Vietnam. But it took a 28-year-old movie director to call the place something as nasty, poor, solitary, brutish, and short as the young lives that get lived there: *New Jack City*.

New Jack 13ers perceive an outside world that does not like them, does not want them, does not trust them, and (as they see it) has nothing to offer them. Glancing across at the financial towers and suburban affluence that few of them will ever touch, New Jackers shed even the most basic social conventions that mark a civilized society. Hear them rap a melodyless cant of sexism, racism, and soulless mayhem, celebrating the very nihilism that older generations blame them for. Watch them swagger around in symbolic uniforms—backwards caps, shades, leather jackets, combat fatigues, pump-sneakers, or jackboots—that conjure up the soul-dead violence of robots. Avoid them as their thug-armies rampage for random victims. Hand them the keys—quick—when they carjack you. Fear them as they commit "opportunity crimes" against random passersby, or "hate crimes" against women, gays, or Asian shopkeepers, or "business crimes" against each other. Shoot them down, ship them out, lock them up. If you can catch them. And you'll never catch all of them.

In the 1980s, America became acquainted with a new breed of inner-city youth criminal, a sharp-witted gangster with an all-business attitude toward his mayhem. He uses calculated violence to protect inventory (against smugglers), provide customer service (for "safe house" tenants), build market share (against competing gangs), collect accounts receivable (from addicts), maintain employee relations (with runners), and manage risk (with cops). To run such enterpris-

---

Money and drugs are the obvious immediate rewards for kids in the cocaine trade. But there is another strong motivating force, and that is the desire to show family and friends that they can succeed at something.

Terry Williams,
The Cocaine Kids (book)

One of every four black American men between the ages of 20 and 29 is currently in prison, on probation, or on parole. For urban areas, the figure is even higher. In Washington, DC, 42 percent of all black men age 18 to 35 are either in prison, under court supervision, or sought for arrest; 70 percent are arrested at least once before they reach age 35.

Source: *Washington Post*

We have enough to worry about besides people thinking we are drug dealers. Like the 23 books I have to read in nine months, girls, and dodging bullets.

Damien Oliphant, 15,
Washington, DC

es in the face of like-minded rivals, a reputation for remorseless brutality is an indispensable asset. Fifteen-year-old enforcers brag about their ability to kill for professional reasons only ("no hard feelings," "strictly business," run the movie clichés) and collect murder newsclips as macabre résumés. A young drug-runner, says Washington, D.C., Police Chief Isaac Fulwood, "navigates in a world where most of us couldn't function, a world where you've got to be cunning, slick, and mentally and physically tough." And, of course, a world in which other choices seem even more hopeless.

Where Boomer youths who assaulted Silent victims were often said to have mitigating reasons for their antisocial behavior, 13ers who attack Boomer victims (as in the Bernhard Goetz and the Central Park jogger cases) are condemned in the Boom-led media as "evil" thugs deserving only of execution or, at best, long terms in some boot camp. Back in the late '60s, Boomer criminals were associated with rage and betrayed expectations; today, 13er criminals seem emotionally detached, even insensate. Columnist William Raspberry accuses them of being a "generation of animals," Stanton Samenow of having "the ability to shut off their conscience." At the peak of his boxing career, Mike Tyson bragged that "Sure, I shot at a lot of people . . . . I liked to see them run. I liked to see them beg." A swarm of aspiring street-tough Tysons invented the word "wilding" to describe this kind of behavior.

Like Los Angeles Police Officer Laurence Powell (one of the four cops involved in the Rodney King incident), most of today's front-line cops are 13ers too, scanning the streets from helicopters, with sirens wailing down below as flak-jacketed city troops go head-to-head against a like-aged quarry. The older police leadership is baffled about what to do. "We can arrest them, but jail is no deterrent," reports Washington Long, chief of police in Albany, Georgia. "For them, it's just a matter of fact," says Fulwood. "Oftentimes, they don't say anything. They just sit there and say, 'Officer, do what you gotta do.'" Like the 16-year-old "wilder" Yusef Salaam, who asked his sentencing judge to "Give me the max." (He got it.)

Giving up on rehabilitation or deterrence, growing numbers of older Americans are content to warehouse this generation of criminals permanently, or (as one warden puts it) at least until "about their mid-30s, when their testosterone level drops." Since the mid-1970s, when 13ers first reached adolescence, the U.S. inmate population has

more than tripled, and average sentences for young-adult offenders have nearly doubled. Measured per capita, the 13th already stands as far and away the most incarcerated generation in U.S. history. Even when let out, many 13er parolees are now fitted with electronic necklaces or bracelets so they can be tracked down at a moment's notice—expedients that in the Boomer youth era would have been branded unthinkably Orwellian.

***crasher

>you know, the whole time people have been complaining about the lawlessness and ruthlessness of kids today, I always thought they were talking about someone else! when someone gets stabbed or some baby in los angeles gets its head blown off, I certainly don't think, "well there my kooky generation goes again!" if anything, I'm angrier than you guys ever get, because I understand the horror of senseless violence, but I also know exactly why these people behave like that. so far, I've been lucky not to be as desperate, but if you ignore your dog for three weeks, you can be damn sure he's going to pee on the couch.

   "wilding" is one of those words that some reporter heard somewhere, and in a fit of paranoid journalism, it gave all you baby boomers one more thing to lose your burrito over. around here, nobody under the age of 25 has ever used that word, except to imitate goofy local reporters.

Only five percent of all 13ers (those in inner-city households beneath the poverty line) actually live at the core of the New Jack world. Yet the image of that world exerts a spellbinding power over their entire generation. There's more than a little New Jack everywhere from New Rochelle to New Mexico. In fact, without the huge buying power of white suburban youngsters, the image itself would hardly exist. Gangster rap would remain a cultural oddity, never

It's difficult to tell a young man who is a general in a gang, who has friends who will die for him and power, that he should "Just Say No" and work in McDonald's.

Dr. Jawanza Kunjufu, educator and author of *Countering the Conspiracy to Destroy Black Boys* (book)

producing platinum CDs and "vanilla" imitators and never getting parroted on Disney's Mickey Mouse Club show; paramilitary break-dancing would still be a street oddity, not featured on MTV videos; and the daily chronicle of urban 13er violence would not be dramatized before millions in the *Boyz* movie genre and the Fox-TV real-life manhunt serials.

So why do millions of 13ers, including suburban honors students with Volvo-driving dads, feel drawn to the New Jack rhythm? Could it be because they, too, identify with lone-wolf underdogs struggling to be winners in a world that perceives them as "bad boys, bad boys" (the chanting theme song of Fox's *Cops*)? Is it because, even in privileged surroundings, they perceive a razor-thin line between success and failure, between boys and "boyz"? Is it because the New Jack survivor is a champion for all those who seek out the brutal truth among all the euphemisms, excuses, or flat-out lies of their elders? Is it because they yearn for something that can drain the swamps of endless ambiguity, for a rule-breaking style that *works* amidst the discuss-and-review postures of a legalistic, therapeutic, overcomplicated society? Raised by their parents to resolve schoolyard conflicts with U.N.-style negotiation, every 13er sooner or later reaches a moment—face-to-face with an after-hours bully, a disappearing dad, or a McJobs want-ad—when all those elder-taught rules and procedures suddenly recede to the distance of a million light-years. That's the New Jack moment. Its lessons, once taught, linger for life.

Many 13ers freely admit that, yes, this vision is subversive of what their elders call civilization. But what of it? From their angle, forty thankless years of peddling fries might be less meaningful than one glorious year ruling your own 'hood, creating a surrogate family you can touch and smell, a tight circle you can respect and be respected by. Underneath a committee-built umbrella of technology, bureaucracy, democracy, and civil rights, they perceive much of their own generation sinking into a lawless antiworld whose language only the inner-city rapper understands—where, as Alan Keyes puts it, "the self becomes an anti-self, a moral vacuum that sucks all meaning from the things and people around it."

Against their fascination with the New Jack antiworld, 13ers must always balance their fear of becoming its victim.

Such a fear is rational, since 13ers comprise the majority of today's urban prey as well as predators. Long past are the days when the poor elderly were America's stereotypical crime victims. No, the ones in today's line of fire are those too young to cocoon or commute or retire their way to safety. Who's at risk? The teenage pimps and dealers. The rookie cops who have to bust them. The partying or gambling singles who get mixed up with the wrong crowd. The young-adult tenants who can't afford to live someplace better. The grade-school students and service workers who have no choice but to spend entire days (or nights) in dangerous neighborhoods. Even the college-age elite knows the sniff of fear. Boomers once swept into tranquil Ivy League college towns professing love for downtrodden masses they never saw and hatred for a police establishment they never needed. These days, 13er frosh arrive at Yale or Columbia or Chicago fully aware that their classrooms lie only a few blocks away from New Jack terror, and that the cop you say hi to today might be the one who saves your neck tomorrow.

Viewing crime as an omnipresent threat to the already-fragile security of their lives and income, 13ers take a hard line on what to do about it. Three-quarters believe that courts are too lenient and support capital punishment for murder and rape (a slightly greater share than older generations today, and a vastly greater share than older generations at like age). In the '60s, Boomers grew up with social-conscience movies about ghetto kids unjustly incriminated. In the '80s, 13ers grew up with vigilante movies about violent gang-bangers unjustly let loose. Way back when, the Spencer Tracys asked hard-luck kids to talk about their problems. Today, the Clint Eastwoods no longer expect kids to say anything, but just invite them to try something stupid and "make my day"—as though blowing the head off a male teenager were an event at once trivial and satisfying.

Even if most 13ers lend a hard respect to the inner-city gangster culture, they don't dare sentimentalize it. They don't imagine for a moment that the gangster might have a human soul. That would spoil the image. Who looks forward to words of tenderness or mercy from America's *Public Enemy*? Pepsi's right: Nobody would buy its product if M.C. Hammer stopped his machine-gun rap and started singing "Feelings."

He said he wanted to commit the first murder of the year 1992. He was standing on the street corner looking at his watch and shot the first guy who came around the corner.

Oscar Clarke, policeman in Richmond, VA, describing the motive of an 18-year-old killer

▬▬▬

This is Big Business. This is the American Way.

drug lord defending himself in court, *New Jack City* (film)

▬▬▬

"Look at us, man. Look at you. All we do is walk around these damn projects all day."
"So what you got in mind, Deke?"
"Well, I don't know, brothers. But we gotta get paid. We gotta get paid! Everybody out there's gettin' paid but us."

two youths, *Straight Out of Brooklyn* (film)

Listen up, America, to the philosophy of the New Jack School: When there's one life to lose, it's not mine that I'll choose; winners take over, lose and it's over. That's a rap credo for life at the edge. At the edge of a generation at the edge of American society at the edge of the twentieth century.

> ***crasher
> >this is getting pretty heavy. am I truly the only one out here to respond to this stuff? anyone care to speak?

>16. We Could Care Less, Care Less

"When you get beneath the surface of their cheerfulness," observes Christopher Lasch, author of *The Culture of Narcissism*, "young people in the suburbs are just as hopeless as those in the ghetto . . . living in a state of almost unbearable, though mostly inarticulate, agony. They experience the world only as a source of pleasure and pain." So what's left over, in between the extremes of pleasure or pain? For many, the only alternative is: boredom.

One of the most damning elder indictments of this generation is that they feel no connection to the broader social world beyond their own private interests. It's not so much whether they're smart or dumb, conservative or liberal, miserly or thriftless—but rather that none of the above really matters to them. Thirteeners get scolded for having no civic spirit; for feeling no stake in the nation's past crusades or future ideals; for seldom bothering to read newspapers, learn about public affairs, discuss big issues, or vote for candidates; for just *not caring*.

What about this 13er apathy? Has their civic virtue vanished along with the trucks and cowboys in those desert-mirage beer commercials? To find out, put yourself in the position of a 13er teenager.

You sit in civics and history classes day after day, and then you look around and see what today's adults have been up to lately. You can't help but notice that the last time Americans willingly sacrificed themselves to the public good was way back in the 1930s and '40s. That's decades before you were born, impossibly remote from your own time.

You gaze at the great hero-built edifices that have lasted from that era—NATO, the Pentagon, Social Security, network TV, Aid to Dependent Children, TVA pork barrel, ICBMs, marble post offices—and what you mostly see are dysfunctional irrelevancies sagging with age. Through your eyes, they all seem like some old municipal aqueduct—massive beyond your comprehension, hoisted during some ancient era you can hardly imagine, intended for some grand purpose that no longer matters. Cracks in its concrete reveal a complex network of rusting wires and pipework designed long ago by some whistling young engineer. Maybe he cared about it back then, but he's long since retired on a generous federal pension paid for with the money deducted from your Pizza Hut paycheck.

You know that nobody is about to ask you to build anything to match that old edifice, or even to keep it in good repair. Instead, your task is simply to keep it barely functional, to run to and fro through the cracks—doing errands, delivering messages, fulfilling instant needs of every kind—while your elders are allowed to believe the old edifice still works fine and to reap whatever meager rewards it still has left to offer. Propping it up pays you little today and promises you nothing tomorrow. So you stop caring about the crumbling old thing—and then hear your very indifference used against you. *You're* the ignoramus who can't decipher its ancient inscriptions. *You're* the incompetent who wouldn't know how to rebuild it even if somebody gave you the money. *You're* the barbarian cavorting among its ruins. *YOU* must be the reason it's falling apart.

Then you listen to middle-aged people brag about their grand crusades—civil rights, the Peace Corps, Vietnam, women's lib, Earth Day, the toppling of Nixon—those shining moments when they, as youths, righteously challenged and conquered the great injustices of the world. Here, too, you find yourself at a disadvantage. You're well

Percent Voting in Presidential Elections of 1972 and 1988

	1972	1988	change
Age 18–20	48%	33%	– 15%
Age 20–24	51%	38%	– 12%
Age 25 and over	66%	61%	– 5%

Source: U.S. Bureau of the Census

From 1976 to 1988, the share of high school seniors believing that "most people can be trusted" declined from 32 to 23 percent. In a nationwide 1985 survey, the share agreeing that "most people try to be fair" ranged from a low of 47 percent for 18-to-24-year-olds to a high of 71 percent for people over age 65.

Sources: "Monitoring the Future: Questionnaire Responses from the Nation's High School Seniors" (University of Michigan, 1975–1988); Kantor and Mirvis, *The Cynical Americans* (book)

The attitude seems to be, "They don't care about us, we don't care about them."

Gray Beeker, student, Montgomery College, describing young non-voters' attitude toward politicians

aware that you had no hand in any of that. You suspect that they're exaggerating, but you can't prove it. Watching those crusaders gray in place just ahead of you—ensconced in such culture bastions as college faculties, public radio stations, policy foundations, and trendy rural retreats—you notice how they've redefined every test of idealism in ways guaranteed to make you fail. You're expected to muster passions against political authority you've never felt, to search for truth in places you've never found useful, to solve world problems through gestures you find absurd.

As you assess the bewildering rhetorical legacy of those older crusaders (*make love not war*, *feed the poor*, *off the pigs*, *up against the wall*), here again you're left gazing at the seamy underside of social accomplishments gone awry. Here again you stop caring. And here again any disinterest on your part is interpreted as proof of your moral blight. No matter that it was the crusaders' own self-indulgence that let the system fall apart. The Decade of Greed is your fault. "Compassion Fatigue" is *your* fault. The hunger for sound bites (this from the crowd who once telegenically chanted "Ho, Ho, Ho Chi Minh!") is your fault. "The age of apathy"? Well, that motto, of course, has *YOUR* mindless graffiti splattered all over it.

If you take little interest in the institutional edifices and grand crusades that have always absorbed the energy of your elders, it's because you feel no stake or connection. You sense that much of the debate over the so-called "big issues" is irrelevant to your future—

and that you're powerless to affect the outcome anyway. As such, you feel more alienated from the social legacy being handed to you than your elders were at like age. If you score higher on most measures of cynicism, it's because in your short life cycle you've already witnessed too many grand causes go bust. And because elders seem to think that everything you offer is negative.

Yes, maybe you don't much care about voting—not because you're uncivic in principle, but just because right now, as you see politics, it doesn't make one iota of difference who wins. Policy platforms mean nothing, politicians say anything to win, legislative bodies are gridlocked, and what few measures politicians do enact seldom amount to much (and certainly haven't done squat to fix your own problems). Having grown up in the age of Watergate and Abscam, you look at it this way: When you vote, maybe you'll waste your time, or worse, later feel doublecrossed. If you pin too much hope on a candidate, you could end up feeling like a total sucker. On the other hand, when you give tangible help to your friends and neighbors, you're doing something that matters, if only on a small scale. So you like volunteering for little "c" causes—like bringing food to the homeless, recycling trash, cleaning up beaches, or tutoring the disadvantaged. You express your civic virtue one on one, meal by meal, regardless whether anybody is paying attention. The president of MIT has likened your civic attitude to that of the Lone Ranger: Do a good deed, leave a silver bullet, and move on.

Yes, maybe you don't much care about "current events"—those *boring* newsprinted artifacts that threaten to turn your brain into some overstuffed piece of Victorian luggage. This is an instinct you acquired young, a reaction against what teacher and author Patrick Welsh calls "a world of information overload." Hearing elders declare everything too complex for yes-or-no answers, you've struggled to filter out the noise, cut through the rhetoric, and isolate the handful of practical truths that really matter. Maybe your "aliteracy" prevents you from competing for credentialed sinecures, or from discussing such MacNeil/Lehrer topics as new NTBs at the global phase-two GATT meetings. But it does enable you to forge boldly into the future—by traveling light, thinking fresh, and striking quickly. It's a style you figure elders could learn from. Despite years of testimony and effort, a sixtyish Congress full of voluble readers and talkers can neither eliminate an outmoded spending program nor

We've inherited the disillusionment without ever sharing the feelings that good things could happen.

Patrick Kennedy, 24, Rhode Island state representative

———

"Why do you cry?" "I don't know. We just cry. You know, when it hurts."

11-year-old hustler explaining humanity to a robot, in *Terminator 2* (film)

———

Old at heart, but I'm only 28.

Axl Rose, lead singer, Guns N' Roses

I don't want to be safe, and my vision of safe, the American safe, is corporate America, a lawyer, whatever. That's not safe at all. It's just stupid, myopic. It's nothing, nothing. It really is nothing.

Jason, 18, bike mechanic, Virginia

———

Withdrawing in disgust is not the same as apathy.

tarot card, *Slacker* (film)

———

The images I had were of people being driven mad by living in the city. Images of parents who were so hungry and unfulfilled that they ate their own children. Images of people, teenagers my own age, looking up from the asphalt and being blinded by the sun.

Bret Easton Ellis, *Less Than Zero* (book)

control a deficit everybody knows is wrong and ruinous. But hey, isn't it "aliterate" people like you who are marketing Big Macs in Ukraine and peddling green car designs down in Rio?

***crasher
>good lord, fellow brethren! isn't there a soul out there on the network who is willing to respond to this barrage? where the hell is everybody?

***budster
>you know our wacky generation, crasher. I didn't want to put down my hostess snack cake and surfer magazine. greetings from the budster. yo, net surfers!

***crasher
>where are you, budster?

***budster
>small northeastern state with a funny name. enjoying your witty repartee with the omniscient 2boomers. one question. why hasn't anyone mentioned schoolhouse rock yet?

***crasher
>I don't rightly know.

***budster
>discussion of our generation begins and ends with schoolhouse rock. conjunction junction. I'm just a bill. we the people. I was at the national archives last month and all the kids in line were singing the constitution. and then they wonder why we don't take the heavy stuff seriously.

***pepper
>greetings from maine! I agree totally! I think a generation that relates to each other through a collective consciousness of schoolhouse rock segments, a generation that has a greater affection for snuffalupagus than their fathers, and a generation that can only count to twelve and recites the alphabet only in song--of course we're not going to be too keyed into reality. most of the responses I heard about the gulf war had something to do with the numb sense that someone was hurting and those cool video graphics of smart bombs.

***crasher
>so we can blame tv for all of our apathy?

***taxedout
>hello from st. louis. personally, I was given whirlie-birds and g.i. joes before I knew about vietnam. we were taught about the dangers of the inner cities before "superfly" could teach us about "the man." they sold us pet rocks, pop rocks, cliff's notes, bell bottoms, skoal and mood rings and then categorically dismissed us as the "wasted" generation. I've spent my life trying to filter out the signal from the noise, but for every john-boy on "the waltons" there's a flo on "alice" telling mel to "kiss my grits!" we witnessed the computer revolution, the test tube baby, and the release of nelson mandela, yet we still have to confront the clapper and those insidiously stackable pringles potato chips!

***pepper
>my mom took me to a hearing specialist when I was eight, saying that "she doesn't hear me when she's watching tv." the doctor talked to me and reported to her that my hearing was fine. I just chose to ignore her because I preferred grover or joyce dewitt or j.j. or a commercial for feminine hygiene products--i liked them all better than my mom.

***lizardho
>hello everybody, from seattle. I can't stand tv anymore, so I can't use it as an excuse for being apathetic. my parents rationed it anyway. the overall attitude I see up in the northwest is one of informed concern about social, political, and especially environmental issues. I grew up in a happy two-parent household. I did well in high school and college, I enjoyed learning. steroids are not, and never will be my drug of choice, I didn't vote for reagan or bush, I protested against the gulf war, as did a large part of the youth in seattle...apathetic I am not.
this apathy you talk about isn't apathy at all, it's just that there are so many issues to contend with, our energy gets totally diffused. do I throw my weight behind pro-choice? do I fight for an old growth forest? do I help illiterate adults learn how to read? no wonder most of us say "screw it!"

***budster
>I say that all the time.

***pepper
>pork chops and applesauce!

***crasher
>exactly!

I got no plans, I ain't goin' nowhere
So take your fast car and keep on driving.

Tracy Chapman, "Fast Car" (song)

"What are you looking for?" I ask him. An old habit. "I'm not looking for anything," he says. "Everyone's looking." "Not me," he says, "I'm all looked out."

Emily Listfield, "Porcupines and Other Travesties" (short story)

That's how many 13ers see, and justify, their attitude about public life. In 1989, as East German students poured over the Berlin Wall, newspaper accounts described high school kids as "left flat" and "utterly unmoved" by events that brought their teachers tears of joy. Yet again, older Americans took the opportunity to shake their heads at blasé youth. But what many called "apathy" might also have been described as the weary realism of a generation whose own first-hand experiences have taught them what can happen when barriers are blithely broken down: chaos, confusion, a new mess for somebody to clean up. Today, 13ers are less surprised than other Americans to hear that most of the news from Eastern Europe consists not of constitutions being written or factories being built, but of ethnic warfare, civilian bombardments, mass migrations, and economic panic.

Paradoxically, opinion surveys find that cynical 13ers have more "confidence" in most institutions than their elders. Why? Because they never expected much from any institution to begin with. As long as a corporation makes money, a family stays together, and a government protects the borders, 13ers are satisfied. They wonder why older people keep thinking up loftier goals at which institutions are sure to fail. They also wonder why older people never seem to care whether anything really works.

To find bitter, self-styled cynics—that is to say, disappointed idealists who aren't really cynics at all—check out those older crusaders. But to locate the genuine article, check out 13ers playing in garage bands or delivering pizzas or wandering through malls or ripping down mountains on trail bikes. Older people could swear that nothing's on their mind, that they just "don't care" (*elder translation: selfish, apathetic, uninformed*). It's all a matter of perspective. As the 13ers see it, what elders care about is "history" (*13er translation: dead, past tense, NOT!*). If you're an old crusader yourself, you might want to argue the point. But think it over and save your breath: After all, they'll just turn up their Walkmen and tune you out.

>17. That Funny Vibe

In San Jose, California, a group of young "European Americans" is organizing to "express their ethnicity in an appropriate way" and to protect themselves from "hate crimes and insults." A few miles away at Stanford, "African-American" students are self-segregating where they live, eat, and play, and are quick to accuse the more integration-minded of being "racists." Elsewhere throughout the Bay Area, a region that prides itself in racial tolerance, young skinheads and gangbangers are showing a meaner racial disposition than anybody ever would have expected from a young generation raised on *Sesame Street*, *Roots*, and *The Cosby Show*.

Among white 13ers, college orientation—which once meant barbecues, mixers, and a few laughs for the freshmen—now means seminars instructing them to unlearn their supposedly racist ways. Students hear polysyllabic pronouncements (to quote one professor) about "enriching, expanding, complicating, and contextualizing the curriculum to bring it more in line with international and multicultural realities." They are expected to scribble it all down to pass an exam, parrot the magic words to a dorm proctor, and apologize to a disciplinary committee if they ever get caught in the gears of the multicultural enforcement machine. Told to respect diversity, their own opinions cannot divert. Told not to think racially, they hear other races—and elder-run institutions—stress race again and again. Nothing makes sense.

Among black 13ers, old truisms don't come as easily as they once did for their parents. Their range of individual circumstances is vastly broader than it was for young blacks among the Silent and Boom generations. These elders never saw vast numbers of their friends move directly from suburbs to elite colleges, yet also never knew the utter hopelessness of the New Jack teen. Among young college-edu-

---

Survey question (asked of 15- to 24-year-olds): "Who do you think tends to feel more comfortable dealing with people of other racial and ethnic groups: you or your parents?"

"ME": 43%   "MY PARENTS": 9%

Source: 1991 survey by People for the American Way

No, I'm not gonna rob you . . .
So why you want to give me that funny vibe?

Living Colour, "Funny Vibe" (song)

Today, popular culture defines "diversity" as the differentiation of people by certain biological or sociological traits: race, sex, ethnicity, class. Forgotten is the diversity of opinion and ideas. What a person thinks is unimportant, as long as he represents his "group."

Vincent Cannato, "A 'Curmudgeon' Speaks," in *Diversity and Division* magazine

---

I think blacks could be less defensive about their race. Blacks have put up a wall between themselves and white America, and they have to get past it themselves.

black college student, Houston

cated couples, 13er blacks can now expect to earn nearly as much as 13er whites. Still, on average, the economic position for all black 13ers is sliding backward. Among all *under*-30 households, blacks earn only 51 percent of what whites earn—significantly less than the 58 percent figure for all *over*-30 households. Many success-bound black 13ers are confused: Are they oppressed, or are they stand-ins for others who are (or were) oppressed?

Regardless of individual circumstance, nearly every black 13er sees racism as a problem. Those who live in troubled neighborhoods have difficulty overcoming the common white presumption that they personally embody all that is desperate or dangerous about their environment. When they jog outside in a new pair of pump sneakers, they watch older people cringe and clutch their purses. They avoid asking strangers for the time or directions, to avoid glimpsing fear on white faces. Those who live in the fanciest suburbs are rarely told, but are often made to feel, that they are considered bad risks. Many pursue lives of 9 a. m. to 5 p. m. integration and then 5 p. m. to 9 a. m. segregation. And when they look at the inner city, they shudder at the bleakness that awaits them if they fail. They generally agree with the Malcolm X position that the black urban trauma should be cured— "by any means necessary." But, wherever they turn for specific answers, they see the government starved for money, the white community backing off, and the black community splintering into a hundred rivulets, its middle not holding, a new kind of bitterness brewing.

The issue of race wasn't always this confusing. Thirty years ago, when racial discrimination in America was generally viewed as blatant and pervasive, the 13ers' own parents mobilized to oppose the obvious injustice of it all. The old didn't talk much about race, but the young knew what to do about it. Today, thanks largely to the lifelong civil rights efforts of the Silent Generation, many of the old roadblocks have been removed.

Yet having grown up in the wake of that success, 13ers have been forced by the turbulent social afterwash to question many of their parents' assumptions: that the problem of racial oppression boils down to a single and obvious color line; that overt prejudice underlies America's most important social (or even racial) problems; that racial rewards will be painless to those who give and welcomed by those who receive; and that racial differences can be celebrated even

---

Which would help a lot to deal with racial problems in our society?
(asked of Americans aged 15 to 24)

Get people to take more responsibility for themselves
rather than blaming others for their problems   77%

Punish students who use racial slurs in schools   32%

Require companies to hire and promote more minorities   24%

Source: 1991 survey by People for the American Way

---

while racial animosity is suppressed. To today's coming-of-age youths, the black-and-white assumptions of their elders lie in ruins or at least betray glaring contradictions—even if 13ers aren't yet sure what to put in their place.

In the early '60s, young adults disapproved of the racial barriers with which they had been raised and looked forward to the future of race relations with optimism. They sensed that the various racial prejudices within their generation were softening—and rejoiced when their new pluralism ultimately expressed itself in the heralded "Dream" of Martin Luther King, Jr., and in landmark civil rights and affirmative action laws. Today, polls show that most younger Americans are thankful for what their elders accomplished, yet look forward to the future of race relations with pessimism. Unlike the Silent at like age, they sense that racial attitudes within their own ranks may be hardening—as though each passing year creates new resentments that must eventually explode. It's not that 13ers feel the old civil rights religion is wrong, just that it no longer works. And they suspect that any effort to push forward with the old assumptions may be doomed to failure by a new diversity their parents don't understand and by a new discontent their parents never felt.

The new diversity comes, largely, from immigration. Thirteeners are on their way to becoming the most immigrant American generation born this century. Through the decade of the 1980s, when 13ers entered the labor force, the stream of young immigrants (over one million per year, including illegals) was the largest in U.S. history. These days, Hispanic and Asian 13ers have introduced a complex new overlay of ethnic interrelations. Whose grievance is against whom? Following the Rodney King verdict, the torching of Korean

They think black people are to blame for everything. They don't even want me to be around black people. It's pathetic.

Cindy Yi, 18, speaking of her Korean-American relatives who own small grocery stores

So pay respect to the black fist Or we'll burn your store right down to a crisp.

Ice Cube, "Black Korea" (song)

Why can black people go up to each other and say "nigger," but when a white guy does it all of a sudden it's a big put-down?

Axl Rose, Guns N' Roses

groceries and the mass jailing of Hispanic curfew violators made all the old us-versus-them answers seem largely out of context.

The new diversity also comes from a quickening surge of internal migration—as minority communities fragment into affluent households (that typically move out of depressed areas) and poor households (that typically stay put). Social mobility for all Americans reflects a civil rights triumph, yet also raises new questions about policies that distribute favors solely by skin color. Few Americans complained about the equal housing law that helped today's 60-year-old minority parents, after a life of battling the tide, move into a wealthy suburb. But what about the college-entry quota that helps their 13er children—the ones who *grew up* in a wealthy suburb? Few of today's midlife leaders and parents can recall any of this new diversity from their own youth. Back then, immigrants were rare oddities, and most minority professionals had little choice but to stay in minority communities.

The new discontent arises from the struggle of young adults to get ahead in today's liberated, free-for-all marketplace while trying to abide by elder-run institutions still obsessed with ethnicity and color. White or black, 13ers realize that powerful economic forces are relegating a large and disproportionately nonwhite chunk of their generation to destitution. Whether or not they believe racism is to blame, most 13ers fear that this stretching of the bell curve will have painful racial repercussions down the line. Yet instead of demonstrating any effective control over social change, the nation's leaders (as 13ers see them) obsess over window dressing—banning "fighting words" here, enforcing job quotas there—thereby creating random punishments and windfalls that change nothing and demoralize everyone. Meanwhile, the economic depression surrounding 13ers of both races is pushing many to adopt the survivalist attitude that if playing a racial card can give them an edge in a game they are terrified of losing—then, hey, why not? Put this all together in one big mix, and the pot of racial frustration is near the boiling point.

"My generation isn't racist," says young essayist Robert Lukefahr, "but we certainly have a terrible time with race relations." True on both counts. Although racial tension appears to be mounting, surveys show 13ers to be the least racist of living generations. Questions traditionally designed to test prejudice (Would you mind having a neighbor or son-in-law of another race?) show 13ers to be more comfortable than their elders in dealing personally with other races. They know a lot more about the languages, customs, and (yes, we're talking about 13ers) history of racial and ethnic groups other than their own. Their youth culture is extraordinarily more accepting of individual diversity than anything older generations knew at the same age. From dating and marriage to language, film, music, and literature, never has America seen a generation with so much racial and ethnic crossover.

This shouldn't be a surprise. Theirs, after all, is the first American generation to have been raised in an era when closer contact between different races was deliberately encouraged—with the lowering of immigration barriers, the desegregation of schools and neighborhoods, the shunning of racial epithets in public, the introduction of multicultural school curricula, and the appearance of multiracial programming in the media. White and brown and black and yellow kids can hardly avoid learning a lot about each other. Moreover, 13ers are learning young to be adept at dealing with new or disorienting social environments. Today, few of them are startled when confronting the unfamiliar customs of another culture—given all the weirdness they have already encountered in their own families. When nothing shocks, prejudice has a harder time taking root.

Indeed, if we define civil rights as requiring a strict standard of color-blindness, then 13ers are far and away America's most pro-civil-rights generation. Surveys show that, compared with elders, 13ers are more likely to advocate policies (such as busing) favoring equality of opportunity and less likely to advocate policies (such as quotas) favoring equality of result. They are most attracted to places (like New York or L.A.) where different races live and work side by side and are most critical of places (like South Africa) where different races are segregated. Of all generations, 13ers show the most generous attitude toward immigrants. They are more willing than their elders to grant permanent U.S. residence to political refugees and citizenship to American-born babies of illegal aliens.

I just took the Scholastic Aptitude Test. I emerged from the three-and-one-half-hour ordeal struck by the too large number of questions that emphasized the achievements of minorities, women and third world countries; bemoaned the shortcomings of American society; and advanced fashionable causes . . . . It seemed as if almost half the questions that named real people named blacks.

David Reich, student, Georgetown Day School, in the *New York Times*

How funny the whole thing can be . . . . When a drunken visitor to Mt. Holyoke gets accused of a racially motivated crime for urinating on a door that turned out to be a black woman's, that's rife with hilarity. Sure the guy's a pig for doing it, and sure the accusation is an overreaction, but pigs and overreactions are funny.

David Greenberg, "The Last Word on PC," in *The Next Progressive* magazine

***ankhman
>I'm an african-american in san francisco, and I'm pretty psyched to see 2boomers writing about these racial issues at all. every time I see these generational articles, they tend to focus more on the pop culture. I find it hard to say these things without coming across as a militant hatemonger. the authors of this, I take it, are white?

***crasher
>very.

***ankhman
>what does the rest of the network have to say about this stuff?

***crasher
>I admit I'm trying to stay out of this one.

***ankhman
>why? this is the most important idea that our generation is facing! what kind of future do we have if were going to be so fractious? you have to have an opinion.

***crasher
>I have an opinion, but it changes every day. somehow, every time I get a good theory going on race relations and brotherhood of man, I start talking to someone who either says I'm hopelessly idealistic or inadvertently racist. my own personal theory is to just do unto others as they would do unto you, not sweat the small stuff, and I'll leave the grand debates about racial issues to sociology majors who obviously know more than I do. I'm not hedging the issue, I'm just hedging the issue.

***ankhman
>if everyone thought like that, nothing would get done.

***budster
>look, the only way to get racism out of america is to kill off everyone over the age of 35. they're the ones who can't seem to get a clue. I think if you ever saw a bus with a white line on the floor, even as a kid, you're always going to have that white line in the back of your mind.

***crasher
>that's easy to say, and a tempting daydream at that--but there are lots of young racists here in north carolina. it seems to be a parental gift that's pretty easy to hand down.

***pepper

>yeah, and what's with all the skinheads and klan revivals going on in the midwest? can't somebody get these guys jobs, and perhaps lives?

***taxedout

>they're just bored, I'm convinced! if you give young people all over this country absolutely nothing to do, a few of them are going to dabble in some pretty serious stuff. some of them, like me, got into computers. others sacrifice barnyard animals and burn crosses.

***ankhman

>I'm not even talking about the extreme issues, like the klan and such. I'm referring to the myopic double standard that occurs in college, the stuff 2boomers were mentioning.

***lynnmun

>chicago here. at northwestern, we were all shepherded into this thing called the cultural diversity project that charged us to "leave behind the ugliness, the meanness, narrowness and tribalism" that characterized our "customs and habits of thought." the lecture was followed up by small-group confessionals run by facilitators, and most of us found the discussion awkward and forced. the girl next to me said that she thought that the facilitator was trying to pull out ideas that the people there never had.

***ankhman

>what? being multicultural may seem like an overcorrective step to you, but compared to what's been out there the last 500 years, it's going in the right direction.

***lynnmun

>forced diversity creates an awkward situation that promotes divergence, not growth.

***crasher

>can we go back to talking about tv sitcoms again?

***pepper

>the war of the races is going to be nothing compared to the war of the sexes, once we get older. wait and see.

You grow up in
the ghetto,
living second rate
And your eyes will sing
a song of deep hate

Grandmaster Flash,
"The Message" (song)

If the white liberals
gave a damn about
African-Americans they
would give their own
money instead of
pillaging other people
for it. That's the
difference between
Mother Teresa and
Ted Kennedy . . . .
If we ask for this gift
and that gift just
because we're black, we
are promoting the idea
that blacks are inferior,
and there is no way
around it . . . . We have
to refuse all the
monetary goodies
offered to us by the
white liberal, which
however great the high,
are addictive
and destructive.
Just say no.

Arthur Hippler, graduate
student, Boston College,
"The Liberal Plantation,"
in *Diversity and Division*
magazine

So why do 13ers find race relations difficult? The problem starts at the level of day-to-day life, where today's young people find that speedy and pragmatic choices are necessary for their own survival. Bustling amongst strangers in a world they often perceive as dangerous, 13ers constantly have to size up challenges and risks—on campus, on the job, or on the street. Experience teaches them to ponder the odds that a professor of X race will flunk them. Or that an employer of Y race won't promote them. Or that a passerby of Z race will rob them. If a hard-nosed assessment of such risks requires taking race into account, then many 13ers weigh that race factor and behave accordingly. Those who behave this way do not regard this behavior as racist; they feel they're just exercising personal choice, not imposing their own choice on others. Catch them in a candid mood and they'll probably say they do what everyone else does; it's just that they have to do it more often and that maybe they're less hypocritical about covering it up.

Yet here 13ers feel perversely whipsawed by elders whom they see preaching one thing and practicing another. However they conduct their own personal lives, many 13ers would gladly have every American institution drop the whole race issue and let teachers, employers, and Congressmen treat every individual on equal terms. Their elders, however, often seem to push in the opposite direction. They often insist that 13ers be color blind in their every private deed and thought even while they themselves transact the nation's public business in terms as blatantly color-coded as electrical wires. As the streetwise young see it, race should only be a private issue; as the empowered old see it, race should only be a public issue. Ethnic and racial group-think has thus become a festering paradox that 13ers are never allowed to ignore, or resolve, or work their way past. It has become a poisonous brew of group grievances that older generations keep forever on simmer.

From the 13er perspective, public group-think raises enormous new problems. In their competition for good colleges and entry-level jobs, theirs is the first American generation to come of age second-guessing practically any prize the system hands out. And when the prizes are as scarce as they are now, such second-guessing can easily mutate into cynicism or resentment. If you lose, you wonder whether your group was unfairly handicapped (or whether you let

NEW AND IMPROVED!

STATUE OF MULTICULTURAL LIBERTY

NOW CARRYING A TORCH FOR EVERYONE!

your group down). If you win, you worry others will whisper that your group got an unfair edge (or that you've sold your group out).

Looking down the road, many 13ers wonder how they can ever find peace in a society riven by permanent group tug-of-wars. On campus, most 13ers would just as soon promote individual independence of thought. Instead, faculties enforce canonized thinking by punishing students for gestures deemed insensitive (or, as some would say, "politically incorrect"). On the job, 13ers notice that inequality *inside* each racial group far exceeds the inequality *between* racial groups. Nevertheless, big institutions insist on giving a better break to the child of the Huxtables than to the child of a white migrant laborer (or of a Laotian refugee). In the courts, 13ers would like to see some realistic discussion of how to stop gang violence. Still, they hear older district attorneys and defense lawyers demagogue about the odd case of interracial assault, while ignoring the much vaster slaughter of same-race youths killing one another. Everywhere, they notice that their generation's economic problems—and division—are more fundamental than their racial ones, but they constantly hear older people telling them the reverse.

Older generations sometimes lose patience over what they perceive as the young's mulelike insensitivity about race. But elder accusations incite the young to display just the sort of defensive pragmatism and splinter-group backlash that elders love to lament. Black, white, or whatever, many 13ers feel caught in a circle of blame from which there is no escape. Where, they wonder, is it all supposed to end? With the achievement of social justice, or with endless scams in which each group keeps finding excuses to pick the others' pockets? Opinions vary.

Compare the 13er life cycle perspective on race with that of their Silent Generation critics. Today's midlife Silent stand as the *least* immigrant generation in American history. The years of their own youth—from the 1930s through the '50s—marked an all-time low in U.S. immigration (as a proportion of population). Back then, races didn't mix and nonwhite minorities were systematically denied equal opportunity. Understandably, the Silent came of age aching for diversity. To today's 60-year-olds, the term "civil rights" will always conjure up the schoolchildren of Wichita and Little Rock, the teens sitting in at the Greensboro lunch counter, collegians wistfully singing "We Shall Overcome," LBJ vowing to rebuild the cities, the passage of '60s-era civil rights acts, and sharecroppers lining up for their first vote. From the Silent perspective, explicit ethnic privileges and penalties were a logical answer for breaking down barriers that shocked their conscience when they came of age.

By contrast, 13ers are coming of age in an era in which diversity is so heavily stressed and paraded that they sometimes wonder (as their parents never did) whether centrifugal group loyalties might tear their nation apart. As for the slogans of civil rights, 13ers hear them invoked on behalf of so many trivial or self-serving causes that they no longer automatically assume they signal the moral high ground. Picture the most vivid racial imagery of their coming of age years: Al Sharpton, David Duke, Sister Souljah, urban gangs, an aging cadre of ethnic elites, baton-wielding L.A. cops, rappers chanting about racial violence, George Bush's Willie Horton ads. The people they hear complaining of racist treatment are Marion Barry and Mike Tyson, not Rosa Parks and James Meredith. The "King" in their headlines is Rodney, not Martin. Unlike the Silent in their youth, 13ers have never felt oppressed by cultural conformism and have never yearned for diversity as a liberating agent of social progress. Rather, 13ers view ethnic group-think as an enduring, and sometimes grim, fact of life. They can despise it, game it, price it out in dollars and cents, or react against it—but they can't escape it.

True, white 13ers never had to ask their parents what the word "colored" meant over bathrooms and drinking fountains. Then again, they've gone through other formative racial experiences their Silent parents haven't. White 13ers know what it is to come of age feeling like guinea pigs in some vast and unguided social experiment —to hear elders demand that they relive the fears and wrongs of an era they never experienced—and to suffer the *noblesse oblige* of affluent older professionals who want to expiate adult guilt by requesting sacrifices from the young (in employment and education) that those elders never bore when young. Yes, white 13ers understand that great injustices have been committed against ethnic minorities in the past. But many of them wonder why, since they are the *least* to blame of all Americans alive today, they are the generation that must be *most* burdened with the social remedy.

Quite unlike Silent blacks in their youth, many 13er blacks aren't so sure exactly what anybody can do to "overcome" the injustices they see around them. In mainly white grade schools and colleges, they notice how incredibly popular black slang, songs, and mannerisms have become, with older generations offering courses in black culture and with white peers (so-called "yo-boys" or "wiggers") mimicking the style of hiphopping "gangstas." Yet they rightly suspect that much of this adulation of black "badness" is a double-edged sword that cuts

They will make extreme exceptions for you if you're black. I think they grade you easier on your papers. I did really poorly on this one physics midterm. I went to see the professor about it. He was really easy with me and said, "No problem. Don't worry about it." He said he would drop it off my quarter grade and that it wouldn't even count, which was against his own rules. Right after I went in, this white student went in to ask him if he would drop his midterm grade because he did really bad too. The professor said, "No way."

black daughter of a banker, Stanford University, in John Bruncel, *Race Relations on Campus* (book)

You'll be at the mall. And there'll be a group of white people and a group of black people. The security guards will come up to the black people and say, "How about if we break it up?" But they don't say anything to the white people.

Brandon Davis, a white 18-year-old, Maryland

the other way as soon as both races enter the post-graduation world of work and family. Behind it all, many insist, white racism is on the rise. It's less residual than resurgent, reflecting unease over black ethnocentrism and a fear of urban violence. Black 13ers know that fear themselves, given that nearly all the street-gang victims are black kids, not white kids (nor, for that matter, older blacks). They're far more divided than their elders ever were over the best answers. New legislation? To do *what*? More money? Spent *how*? They don't know what they can do about this generational trauma—except to seek out ways of surviving or prospering on their own. They feel torn between the racial group-think orthodoxy and their own needs as individuals.

Whatever their race, most 13ers are tired of being lectured on the subject—and believe they handle racial problems a whole lot better than their elders. Older generations take pride in having introduced an effusive rhetoric of group justice into such decorous forums as legislatures and universities, while fretting about 13er-style institutions—like small business, pro sports, and the military—where conversations are more to-the-point. Asked to speak their own mind, a lot of 13ers wouldn't mind pointing out the obvious: Where are you most likely to find different races actually eating together and working together, the typical army mess hall or the typical college cafeteria? But 13ers are rarely asked to speak their mind and are usually smart enough not to bother. They already know that the over-30 crowd cares more about what gets said than about what gets done.

Their best strategy, for now, is to keep their thoughts to themselves. On campus, 13ers chat pleasantly in PC lingo with their "multiculti" prof or dean and then think nothing of spoofing the faculty behind their backs (they can't be totally serious, right?) or playfully relaxing with headphones to the racist lyrics of Ice Cube or Guns N' Roses. But to each other, they talk frankly about how to maneuver in a world full of mutually exclusive group loyalties. Individual choices vary. Interracial dating and friendship is commonplace—but so is a crass expediency (that would shock many elders) about what young elites in the film *Metropolitan* refer to as "PLUs"; "It means People Like Us as opposed to People Like Them—who we find threatening," explains 13er producer Walt Stillman. "It's a term of distinction, exclusion, and lately, it stresses defensiveness and escapism."

Racial reactions sometimes go further, especially among non-college 13ers hard-pressed by rampant street violence and economic bad news. Some are tempted to pick up the language of tribalism and suggest a few literal applications—like the rappers who rant about wasting white "pigs" and Korean "parasites," or the white teenagers who burn crosses on black-owned lawns, or the gangs of whatever race who roam against their high-achieving ethnic competitors. (Hey, professor, you want to see group justice in action? These kids will demonstrate.) But for most of this generation, the accumulated failures of elder-built racial policies have led to a very different outcome: a profound skepticism about any social unit larger than the individual or family. Regardless of race, most 13ers rank their own success and mobility above the need to display racial solidarity.

As if to punctuate their skepticism, 13ers are transforming racial images in ways that strip pluralism of much of its earlier poetry and promise. To the youth of the mid-1960s, blacks and whites were symbolically complementary. Blacks (to whites) were rural and spiritual, authors of an expressive blues and folk culture; whites (to blacks) were powerful and disciplined, builders of big things. Trusted leaders spoke of deliverance, giving whites back their virtue and blacks their Promised Land. To 13er youths, all that symbolism has collapsed. Blacks (to whites) have become urban and kinetic, notable for gang violence and a culture of poverty; whites (to blacks) are incompetent and self-absorbed, unable to fix even the simplest public problem. Nowadays, no one trusts group leaders, and no one expects group deliverance. Individual whites affirm their virtue by tuning in to talk-ra-

Counting nonresident aliens, Asian-American males now outnumber black males on American campuses.

Source: U.S. Department of Education

There's no affirmative action, no breaks, no slurs.

Cadet Michael K. Barsella, describing why he chose to enroll at the U.S. Military Academy at West Point

They say two wrongs don't make it right, But it damn sure makes it even.

Sister Souljah, "The Hate That Hate Produced" (song)

We grew up on "Sesame Street." You know, Habla Español, racial harmony on the playground. But you look and you see there are people who are hungry who don't have any place to live.

Julia Ehrhardt, senior, Duke University

dio, and individual blacks reach their Promised Land by moving to the suburbs. White or black, 13ers are coming of age in a world where, as many see it, real racial progress coexists with a new racial cynicism.

Hearing elders preach civil rights while accusing the young of racism, 13ers often feel like they're watching some corny '50s-era Bible epic, full of tribal myth and assembled pageantry and crowds of identical-looking extras—none of which has anything to do with the atomized one-on-one reality they now see around them. Where Silent elders grew up knowing little about real diversity but now are hell-bent on foisting it on the young, 13ers are growing up as America's first-hand experts on the subject. What they want, and what they fear others will not let them have, is a society as diverse and color-blind as common sense will allow.

Where others once talked the civil rights talk, 13ers are now walking the walk—and getting precious little credit for it.

>18. Sometimes We Get Sick of Sex

Follow two 25-year-olds on a dinner date. Maybe he doesn't have a job, but he looks like he just got off work, with short hair and a serious tie. Maybe she does have a job, but she looks like she's leisured, with plenty of time for fussing with makeup and shopping for jewelry. In conversation, both of them list the reasons they enjoy being single, but then confess mutual dread of the Big D (divorce) that might damn them forever to the solo life they profess to celebrate. They chat about romance with all the delicacy you might expect in a steam-drill factory, but then get awkwardly sentimental on the subject of family reunions and baby carriages. They get up to leave. Maybe she pays the bill, and maybe he holds the door. Then they head home—maybe for a PG-rated goodnight, maybe not. It's almost impossible to tell just from looking at them, far harder than two decades ago.

To anyone born before the pill was invented—or who graduated from college still thinking of condoms strictly as a method of birth control—this 13er man-woman scene is full of contradictions. Are the sexual and feminist revolutions entering new phases, turning

HIGH SCHOOL SWEETHEARTS IN "THE BIG STEP"

LET'S GET MARRIED FIRST

LET'S GET STONED FIRST

LET'S GET TESTED FIRST

A.I.D.S. CLINIC

1950   1970   1990

retro, doing both at the same time, or what? Older progressives often complain that 13ers are a generation of sexual reactionaries. So too do older conservatives accuse them of being promiscuous as bunnies, addicted to a sexually charged culture, and brain-dead on the subject of family values. Hearing all this, most 13ers want to point a zapper toward their critics and press hard on the mute button. As they see it, they're sorting their way through a mine field of sexual problems not of their making—and doing a pretty good job at it.

Having grown up during the sexual revolution of the late '60s and '70s, 13ers arrived just after all the traditional rules had just been erased. So they've had to invent their own rules. Sometimes this means experimenting with conventions that most of their elders have never heard of—for instance, dating in groups for mutual protection. Sometimes it means dusting off the most ordinary artifacts (like the lipstick and crewcut so spurned by Boomers) the way earlier generations of kids might have grabbed lace and top hats out of the attic.

> AIDS is definitely a consideration . . . . It's better to meet over coffee and talk, instead of meeting in a bar, drunk. It helps the screening process.
>
> Kevin Lee, 26, San Francisco

> Guys see sex as a sport . . . . Everything to them is winning and losing. They don't like losing and in their minds if they're not having sex with their girlfriends, they're losing.
>
> Charlotte Collins, 17, McComb, MS

Almost always it means making tough, day-to-day choices about all the new dangers, lifestyles, and freedoms passed on to them by older generations—and severing such choices from moth-eaten value judgments that no longer work. Along the way, 13ers are invoking a playful spirit of irony and even self-parody to help ward off the darkness that has fallen over the relationship between sexes and reinfuse it with something that really matters.

The first 13ers entered puberty to the sound of Marvin Gaye humming "Let's Get It On," a time when adults of all ages were emitting erotic signals everywhere and proclaiming their panting obsession with S-E-X. At breakfast, 13er kids could never be sure what overnight companion a parent would bring to the table. At school, their sex education was both antiseptically clinical and unabashedly value-neutral. After school, empty houses provided them with handy trysting spots to test what they had learned. After dinner, pop music and TV programs kept saying "Do it! Do it! Do it! ('til you're satisfied)." Then, on weekends, movies showed them how to close the deal. Through it all, their parents were (says Silent columnist Ellen Goodman) "equally uncomfortable with notions that sex is evil and sex is groovy."

Yet later on, as soon as they reached adulthood in the early 1980s, Atari-wave 13ers found themselves overwhelmed by a plague of sex-related catastrophes—from the burden of past divorce (their parents') to the fear of future divorce (their own), from the unhappy disarray of innocent rituals (like dating) to the rise of a fearsome and deadly sexual disease (AIDS). Meanwhile, elder attitudes toward youthful sexuality turned from celebration to disinterest. America's Woodstock-era fascination with youth and sex transformed into an AIDS-era repugnance. So 13ers had to deal with the dangers largely on their own, by re-erecting age-old defense mechanisms such as platonic relationships, delayed marriages, a personality shell of jaded toughness, and a youth culture in which kids look out for the safety of their own circle of friends. "The sexual revolution is over and everybody lost," concludes Kim Blum of Redlands College, summing up how it feels to be caught in this painful warp of history.

Did you come of age around 1950? If so, you probably remember the sexual revolution as a liberating midlife thaw after having felt boxed in for years by enormous sex-role divisions, a very early marriage, and a hush-hush silence about anything too naughty. Come of age around 1965? Then maybe you recall it as a euphoric challenge to the false consciousness of your parents. But if you came of age around 1980 (or later), the images you associate with both the revolution and its aftermath are probably negative. Yesterday, your Silent parents left you at home to go have fun with *Bob & Carol & Ted & Alice*. Today, grown up, you find that *Fatal Attraction* marriage-destroyers are the demons everyone loves to hate. Yesterday, a Boomer in *Goodbye Columbus* could enjoy shocking her mom by leaving a contraceptive device where mom could find it. Today—big thrill!—your mom would probably be relieved. (Is life unfair, or what?)

In retrospect, 13ers generally regard the era that roughly spanned their years of birth (beginning in 1962 with the mass-marketing of the birth-control pill and ending with the 1981 discovery of AIDS) as a unique window of carefree euphoria that hurt them first as kids and betrayed them again as adults. If many 13ers feel drawn to images of the *Barbarella* '60s, it is a bittersweet attraction to that lost paradise of innocent freedom, a territory that vanished just before they could inherit it. Older generations had fun raising the window and gaping at the ecstasy beyond. Thirteeners not only looked but climbed halfway through the opening—only to have the window slam shut on their bodies.

The number one body-slam has been AIDS. Discovered when the first Atari-wavers were sophomores in college, AIDS is now a fact of 13er sexual life. To the extent 13ers blame it on anybody, they point more to the excesses of Boomers than to the habits of gay men or drug addicts. Here again, Boomers got to pursue the rapture, and 13ers got stuck with the debris. And here again, the 13er view is pragmatic: Disease happens. The task now, pending a vaccine or cure, is for 13ers to protect themselves as individuals. Some do; some don't. They know what they should do, but they're also aware that sexual behavior doesn't get reinvented, nor the human libido controlled, through sex ed classes and safe sex posters. AIDS may be changing 13er sexual *behavior* less than it is changing 13er sexual *attitudes*—turning orgasmic thrill into something akin to Russian roulette. Forty years ago, young adults associated sex with procreation; twenty years ago, with free love; today, with self-destruction.

To most 13ers, AIDS is not just a tangible threat, but an unhappy symbol of all the other trends that have darkened the options in today's post-playboy, post-feminist landscape. Imagine what dating is

"Our girlfriends are most chaste."
"Could be worse, though."
"Yah? How's that?"
"They could be dating our dads."
"Good point, dude. Good point."

Bill and Ted, *Bill and Ted's Bogus Journey* (film)

———

There are more virgins in high school than people think. It's just that virginity isn't the gossipy subject that sex is. Nobody's going to come to school on Monday morning and say, "Hey, guess what I didn't do Saturday night!"

Katherine Reilly, 17, Alexandria, VA

———

Sex outside of a relationship is not so much a question of right or wrong as: Is it really worth the hassle?

Nancy Smith, "25 and Pending," in the *Washington Post*

like for two people who've been hearing as long as they remember that sex is synonymous with getting what you want—that is, with power. He fears both failure to "score" and pressure to try. She fears both date rape and rejection. (And both might wonder why any of it's worth the bother.) Or try contemplating marriage in an era when the ring has been stripped of most of its usefulness—when single women have no problem leaving home, when a house and kids seem unaffordable even on two incomes, and when everyone expects the vows will be broken in a few years anyway. Back in the '60s, Boomers started the trend toward later marriages largely as a lifestyle choice: They wanted time to "find themselves" before getting serious about life. Today, 13ers are pushing the average marriage age even later for reasons that are much less inspiring: poverty and pessimism.

Seen from a positive angle, 13er sexuality is what visionaries have always been waiting for. To the delight of therapists, here is a generation uninhibited and un-hung-up about sex, free of both chauvinism and guilt. To the delight of moralists, here is a generation that confronts sexual hazards with steely-eyed realism. But seen differently, these same traits can and do attract plenty of elder criticism. Some worry that their lack of inhibitions has led to more promiscuity—and point to surveys showing they're "doing it" more often and at younger ages. Others regret that their let-me-sex-you-up bluntness has drained romance of the mystery and sentimentality that (in elder eyes) once gave it beauty.

Thirteeners worry about these things too. They regret that, as children, maybe they overheard too much when adults decoupled sex from emotions—or that, as adolescents, maybe their parents and sex-ed teachers seldom demanded (or expected) that kids could possibly take responsibility for their own behavior. Most 13ers don't congratulate themselves for their ability to deal with sex as casually (to use the old Boomer metaphor) "as shaking hands." Many would be delighted to trade a truckload of condoms for a tiny shred of modesty.

But there are other, more sweeping charges that 13ers widely resent. It's that somehow they've "let down" the progress toward sexual equality gained by earlier generations. That the predatory young hunks featured in bam-bam action movies are a pale reflection of yesteryear's sensitive male. That the mercenary young bimbos cruising in and out of TV sitcoms are an even paler reflection of yesteryear's crusading woman. That, in short, theirs is a generation of sexual re-actionaries.

Once again, it's time to set the record straight. Just as surveys show 13ers to be less racist, so too do they show them to be considerably less sexist than any elder age group. Take a look at today's young men. Ask them if they mind working for a female employer; if women should get equal opportunity in employment; if it's OK when both husband and wife have full-time jobs; if women do as well at most jobs as men; if differences between men and women are the result more of environment than of biology. On all such survey questions, 13er men are more likely to respond affirmatively (with less sexism) than their elder male counterparts. Without complaint, they routinely encounter women in situations that would make older men squirm with wounded dignity—running errands for female professionals, doing sit-ups for female sergeants, depositing girlfriends' paychecks, working to put wives through grad school. Ask employers who's *least* to blame for sexism in the workplace, and they'll admit, yes, it's that same age-bracket of male twentysomethings they love to dump on for their muscle-bound dumbness.

Even more emphatically, take a look at today's young women. They probably represent the largest one-generation advance in de facto sexual equality in American history. The 13th is the first generation of women to exceed men in average educational attainment. They're first to pursue competitive athletics in significant numbers. They're the first to attend military academies, the first to enter the legal, medical, and business professions in double-digit percentages, and the first to approach male salaries in a wide variety of occupations. Knowingly or not, they're the front-line shock troops in America's feminist campaign to achieve on-the-job economic equality. For all full-time U.S. workers, the median earnings of women may linger at only 70 percent of the median for men, but that ratio varies from a low of roughly 60 percent among the fiftyish Silent to a high of over 80 percent among twentyish 13ers.

Somehow older Americans hardly seem to notice—or at least to give 13er women (and men) much credit for this progress. Not even when they watch armed women in their twenties fly behind enemy lines over Iraq or outclass the U.S. men at recent world Olympic events. Not even when they notice women in their teens catch up with like-aged males in such negative indicators as smoking and suicide.

In a 1988 survey, a quarter of junior high school boys and a sixth of the girls said they believed a man has the right to have intercourse with a woman without her consent if he has spent money on her. Also, 65 percent of the boys and 47 percent of the girls said it is all right for a man to force sex on a woman if the couple has been dating for at least six months.

Source: *San Francisco Chronicle*

Personally, I'm scared to death. I've got a friend who keeps a mini-tape recorder beside his bed, and when he reaches over for the condom he turns it on. If she says yes, then he turns it off.

Dave Patton, freshman, on the fear college men have of being accused of date rape

Silent Generation feminists (many of whom discovered their cause as midlife empty-nesters) may congratulate each other for coming "a long way, baby." But any way you look at it, 13ers are the women who are actually going the distance.

Thirteeners can disappoint elders when, as happens so often, they express a "so what—it's no big deal" attitude toward the strides they've taken toward sexual equality. In part, this attitude reflects an instinctive distaste for grand words and principles. Despite their occupational attainments, for instance, 13er women are less likely than Boomer women to identify themselves as "feminists" (and, like 13er men, are less likely to insist that their work is a "career" as opposed to "just a job"). Most of the time, they have more fun playing with sex roles than fitting into anyone's preconceived expectation. They can still shock elders when that young macho-man shows up at a party with earrings and a ponytail—or when that boyish woman in the jumpsuit shows up with permed hair and heels. Sex, like anything else, strikes 13ers as most interesting when it can be turned into a game, an opportunity to have fun by alternately accepting or defying conventions at will.

This 13er nonchalance also reflects a singularly pragmatic outlook about sex. Male and female, today's young people don't feel the same sense of triumph about sexual equality as elders who spent years crusading for it. Instead, they accept equality because they were born into it, grew up with it, and have come to regard it with little more passion than they regard other necessities of life, like food and water. So long as good jobs are scarce, marriages are fragile, and the traditional quid-pro-quos between the sexes can no longer be trusted, the typical 13er woman will speak up plenty when her rights are violated. (How else is she supposed to survive in today's do-it-yourself world?) Otherwise, she may not think about it. She may even wonder, all things considered, whether her grandmother had a better deal. Yes, 13ers are more firmly wedded than any older generation to strictly equal treatment of women as workers, consumers, and spouses. On all these issues, they regard any suggestion to turn back the clock as both unthinkable and impractical. But, at the same time, they're more fatalistic about what's left over after the bras are burned—for instance, by believing more than their elders that the sexual revolution has made life "easier" for men and "harder" for women.

As they strive to reinvent some sense of sexual order, 13ers are confounding the traditionalist and modernist elders on both sides of the great '90s-era culture war. On the one hand, many 13ers openly revere traditional mom-and-dad families that stay intact, show a renewed interest in chastity before marriage, and have a negative opinion of the "no fault" divorce laws their parents introduced back in the early 1970s. On the other hand, these are no Ozzies and Harriets. They are decisively pro-choice on abortion. They are unflinching in their insistence on workplace equality. And they strongly support requirements that employers do much more to accommodate dual-income families.

To blunderbuss crusaders on either side, 13er attitudes about sex appear to be a puzzle of contradictions. Are 13ers turning into family moralists? Hardly. They think people should be free to do anything they want—and that includes the freedom to scope out traditional institutions that might actually work and to steer clear of stuff they'd rather not be around. Are 13ers anti-family? Not at all. They just believe that family-making should be voluntary and that every family, even a single-parent family, should be allowed to make a good living.

Thirteeners find it hard to identify with either side of the raging symbolic battles over sex that so preoccupy their Silent and Boomer elders. As they invade the "flyboy" culture of traditionally male occupations, 13er women are suffering the brunt of Tailhook-style sexual harassment. Even so, this generation would like to scale down the level of the debate. Thirteeners believe that sexual harassment is bad because it's simply unjust, not because it's a symbol of some metaphysical war between the sexes. They recognize date rape as a genuine problem, a reflection of how 13er-era sex has been stripped to its core elements of power, not as proof that women and men are natural enemies. As they see it, such evils can't be ignored—nor can they be stopped by setting up a battery of federal regulators or by sifting every word and gesture through a PC filter. Yet wherever 13ers look—from the Clarence Thomas hearings to the Willie Smith and Mike Tyson trials—they see older people elevating simple questions into grand controversies, with the day-to-day reality lost amid all the inflated rhetoric. Unlike their elders, and because of their own experience growing up, 13ers find man-woman hysteria over sexual issues to be profoundly disturbing. They genuinely want the sexes to get along.

The years between the pill and AIDS were a time of freedom and casual relationships. . . . Those days are over. . . . The idea of casual sex is as inaccessible to me as it was to my mother when she was my age—but with a difference. It probably never occurred to her, while for me it is a lost possibility.

Karla Vermeulen, "Growing Up in the Shadow of AIDS," in the *New York Times*

In 1967, 57 percent of all college freshmen believed that "the activities of married women are best confined to the home and family." Today, only 26 percent of all college freshmen believe that.

Source: "The American Freshman: Twenty-Five Year Trends" (UCLA, 1991–1992)

***crasher
>you know, I have to consider myself a complete romantic, which is weird, since my parents certainly were no model, we didn't go on dates in high school, and I'm surrounded by cynical, sniping bastards who talk of love the same way they would talk of chemical warfare. it's like a strange paradox--there's so little romance in everything I see or do, that I'm completely convinced that it exists in spades. I'm also the farthest thing in the world from being a father, seeing as I can't find a girl I want to spend more than three months with, but then again I get all mushy-eyed at pampers commercials.

***pepper
>I'm amazed I still feel romantic after all the crud I've been through.

***crasher
>I can't remember a single time in high school that I went on a real, honest-to-goodness one-on-one '50s-style pick-her-up-in-the-car, go-to-a-movie-and-talk-on-the-porch date. it was always about five guys and six girls, randomly going to the mall, and then to some goofy pool party, and then maybe pairing off at the end. my prom experience was like some gigantic square dance; ten guys in tuxes went with the same number of girls in dresses. when the photographer asked us to pair off in couples, we couldn't figure out who to stand with. everyone had smooched everyone else at some point in the year, so picking one person seemed a trifle silly.

***pepper
>it's fine as long as you keep it simple. as a girl, I'm better friends with guys anyway. but the minute you go beyond a certain point, all these problems come up and ruin it. guys you thought you could totally trust do the most stupid things, and then all your friendships get ruined. all of the guys I'm friends with now had to go through that stupid period after they kiss me, when none of us knows what's going on.

***crasher
>which is pretty funny, since 2boomers and their ilk are so quick to label us as uncaring and unknowable--I'll bet the farm that if you show me a red-blooded college student on any university campus right now, I'll show you a poor sot who spends 85% of his/her waking hours getting psychotic about the opposite gender.

***budster
>what pisses me off is that we missed the boat, man. no more fun of any kind! you see these movies of these butt-cuts in the '70s going around new york having sex with every thing that moves. nowadays you can get about 30 zillion diseases from a toilet seat. I can name ten folks who picked up something. I feel cheated.

***crasher
>I can't even imagine what it was like, not to worry about all these viruses and infections every time you do anything with anybody. having sex these days is about as spontaneous as the nixon museum.

***pepper
>that guy who tapes his female conquests, to make sure they say "yes" on tape--that's totally gross. I can't believe we've been reduced to that.

***djsalem
>what's up from charlotte. you better believe it, pepper. I'm on the honor court at school here, and you wouldn't believe the number of cases I have to hear involving date rape. there's obviously a lot of sick undergrad boys out there, but there's also a bunch of girls who seem to change their mind the next day. I don't blame the guy at all for covering his ass.

***schpooz
>timonium, maryland here. first, it's "women," not "girls," and secondly, you make it sound like just as many women change their mind as there are boys who force them to have unwanted sex. I'd say there are plenty more would-be rapists than vindictive women. let the guy tape all he wants; I doubt he'd keep a soundtrack of a struggle for your honor court.

***djsalem
>you see, it's people with your attitude keep everyone from getting along. I merely said that the guy should do whatever he wants to without feeling like he's going to have his name trashed by some psycho. I agree with you that date rape is chronic. I see it all the time.

***schpooz
>it's not even guys our age I worry about. when I worked at this specialty popcorn place, the owners were always touching me and making stupid advances. it became clear that I wasn't going to move up on the specialty popcorn ladder unless I went out with one of these turds. they weren't in their twenties, they were older guys, you know, "silents" or "g.i.'s" or something--old farts with their genitalia stuck back in the '50s. they didn't seem to have the slightest clue that I found them and their advances completely grotesque.

***crasher
>my old boss at dr. freeze's ice cream emporium, some fat bald old putz who had the name "scooter" embroidered on his uniform, used to say that his job was a pain in the

A few weeks ago, I got a message on my answering machine from someone I dated in college. I hadn't heard from him since he graduated. He just said, Hi, give me a call. In the time before AIDS, I just would have been flattered and curious. Instead, I wondered why he would call me out of the blue—if that could be why he needed to speak to me . . . . Finally, I returned the call, with great dread. As it turned out, he was just coming to town.

Jill Savitt,
New York City

———

Casual sex doesn't even exist anymore. It's lethal, it's over.

young professional,
Singles (film)

———

Compared to 1975, high school seniors are now more likely to question whether happy marriages are possible— but the share of seniors who "prefer having a mate for most of your life" has risen sharply.

Source: "Monitoring the Future: Questionnaire Responses from the Nation's High School Seniors" (University of Michigan, 1975–1991)

I have a picture in my mind of a tiny ranch on the edge of a stand of pine trees with some horses in the yard. There's a woman standing in the doorway in cutoffs and a blue chambray work shirt and she's just kissed her tall, bearded, and soft-spoken husband goodbye. There's laundry hanging outside and the morning sun is filtering through the tree branches like spider webs. It's the morning after a full moon, and behind the house the deer have eaten everything that was left in the garden. If I were a painter, I'd paint that picture just to see if the girl in the doorway would turn out to be me.

Pam Houston, title story from *Cowboys Are My Weakness* (book)

Median Age at First Marriage

	Men	Women
1960	23	20
1970	23	21
1980	25	22
1991	26	24

Source: U.S. Bureau of the Census

---

ass, but at least he "didn't have to work for some chick." he was referring to the women owners of the fudgery place right across the mall, where all the employees were singing and having sixty times more fun. we had to stand around scooping butter pecan while scooter sat in the back with a copy of hustler. I would rather work for a female boss--i always got along with them better.

***schpooz
>yes, but could you stay at home while your wife earned all the money? could you deal with her being the main breadwinner?

***crasher
>no, that would be sort of humiliating.

***budster
>I'd be happy to stay at home if my wife wanted to work. what, are you kidding?

***crasher
>of all my problems that will arise between now and the time I get married, I'd imagine that one is going to be down there with "should I separate the colors in the dryer?" and "when do I put in the fabric softener?"

***pepper
>I'm scared to death of getting married! what is it, 53% of us come from divorced families? I'm not even going to think about it until I'm 30. my attention span is still about a half hour when it comes to guys. my parents are still together, but I don't see how they made it.

***schpooz
>I plan on spending my twenties becoming at ease with the world around me, before I go screwing it up in marriage. my parents left a pretty elaborate game plan of how not to do it, so I can avoid most of the land mines.

***dungus-b
>after my friend's parents got divorced, I remember thinking it would be pretty cool, because both parents would be extra nice to him and give him lots of things. later on, it was evident that they were "buying off" their responsibility, and he turned into a troubled teen with nothing more than survival instincts.

***cogan
>cogan here from asheville. I was glad when my parents split, man. I could do anything I wanted. liquor cabinet was mine, the stereo played all day. all you guys complaining because you're from broken families. I wish mine had broken sooner! I would have had more fun!

***lizardho
>really, I feel left out. it seems whenever my friends begin a litany of marital disasters, I have to sit back and think of the time I broke my arm on the diving board or something. my parents are so happy together it's really quite disgusting.

***crasher
>don't think for a second that all this shattered family angst gets in the way of me having a good time! I certainly don't sit around, crying in the shower, getting misty-eyed over yellowy scrapbook pictures and writing bad poetry because my folks couldn't get along. all it means is that I'm going to put anyone I meet through a series of mental and emotional trial runs that would put the olympic 800-meter relay team to shame.

This pragmatic view extends to homosexuality. As many 13ers see it, if a person is gay or lesbian, he or she has the right to acknowledge it publicly, and to have the same access to jobs or housing or public office as a straight peer. If not, that person has the right to keep the gay lifestyle out of his or her private space. Unlike many of their elders—who deem sexual orientation to be part of America's defining national credo—13ers generally believe that this live-and-let-live solution is fair and workable. Some 13ers find this new openness threatening. From the Fox-TV *Men On* jokes and macho rap lyrics to hate crimes, something of a homophobic reaction is setting in among the young. Yet, to this point, the bulk of this generation is able to draw

	Freshmen Women in 1966	Freshmen Women in 1990	Change
Primary Career Plan			
business	3%	17%	+ 14%
law	1%	6%	+ 5%
medicine	2%	4%	+ 2%
the arts	9%	7%	− 2%
teaching	34%	14%	− 20%

Source: "The American Freshman: Twenty-Five Year Trends" (UCLA, 1991–1992)

It's like Madonna—she dresses like a whore, but she always knows what she wants. These girls are dressed to kill but ready to fight.

Camille Paglia on "Riot Grrrls," a network of women's rights advocates in their late teens and early twenties

Do you want to know what comes between me and my Calvins? Nothing.

Brooke Shields as a teenager, in 1980s-era TV ad for jeans

I suppose I have a slightly jaundiced eye. I mean, when I look around I try to find one married couple, to find one that's been married for any length of time and is really happy together. It's difficult.

Michael Chabon, author

The 13th is the first generation in American history in which more women than men are entering college or are receiving college degrees.

Source: U.S. Department of Education

the line between having a little fun with a newly acceptable lifestyle choice and engaging in social meanness. The proof is that 13er gays and lesbians are more prominently represented in mainstream professions (the media, especially) than was true for any earlier American generation—certainly more so than was true for the young Silent, who started coming "out of the closet" much later in life.

Likewise with abortion. The way elders talk about it, abortion is the key battle front of the great '90s culture war. But for 13ers, abortion is something more important—a searingly personal and physical event. Of the roughly 25 million legal abortions that have occurred in the two decades since *Roe v. Wade*, more than half were obtained by 13er women. Of all Atari-wave 13er women reaching their early 30s, the data suggests that at least one in four has had at least one abortion. Any national judgment on abortion is thus, by implication, a national judgment on a large share of a generation of women who feel guilty of nothing more than following rules set by others. If they get blamed, it's for the same reason 13ers get blamed for everything else: for doing what they feel they have to do.

The sizable pro-choice majority among 13ers is easy to misinterpret—until you see the issue from their point of view. Imagine growing up, as they have, in a world that condones or at least allows sexual activity in your mid-teens and makes marriage impractical until your late twenties. Then imagine trekking across those ten-odd years with little parental supervision, with few intact courtship rituals, and (if you get pregnant) with no effective means of compelling your child's father to act responsibly. Imagine seeing news stories that equate single motherhood with hopeless poverty. Finally, imagine how creating a single-parent child would be a chilling replay of what you and your peers least liked about your own collective childhood.

You might still think having an abortion is wrong, and you might not have one yourself. But you'd be hard-pressed to persuade many of your friends that their choice reflects a selfish bias against family life. In fact, the declining number of babies (of all races) being handed over for adoption nowadays is evidence of just the opposite. Unmarried 13ers who do give birth are much more determined than earlier generations to raise their kids on their own.

"Even though people today may try to categorize women as feminists or traditionalists," says New Yorker Lisa Pent, age 27, "many of us are both in our thinking and how we live. In our mothers' day, you had to choose." That's the 13er credo: to pick and choose whatever solves the problem at hand. They would like nothing better than to separate what makes sense from what doesn't and to make sex simple and safe again. Their task, as they see it, is to draw lines between danger and fun, between public and private, between work and play, between what's hurtful and what's safe. Above all, they want to safeguard whatever innocence they have left and do something positive with it for their own kids.

THE FRESHMAN

Whatever disagreements arise among 13ers over sex-related issues (and there are plenty), what unites them as a generation is their sense of direction: ruthlessly pragmatic about handling the mess just in front of them, yet entirely selfless, even corny about their ultimate objective. They know their parents grew up absorbing all kinds of sexual absolutes, to which they later added a liberating veneer of individual choice. But looking at themselves, 13ers sense they're on a reverse course. Having grown up ODing on so much lust that *Wayne's World* can mockingly interject a take labeled GRATUITOUS SEX SCENE, 13ers are embarking on a thankless quest to reconnect sex with some absolute larger than the individual—maybe with a workable definition of family, or a personal appreciation of history, or a hopeful vision of posterity.

As Atari first-wavers now pass age 30—many already with growing families—nothing better reflects this quest than their gritty determination to spare their own children much of the child-abusive culture and reality they remember from their own growing-up years. Older

Recently, a 36-year-old colleague giddily announced her first pregnancy. It struck me—27 years old and three years married—that I am of a decidedly different generation than this late-30's crowd haunted by amniocentesis and the tick-tock of biological certainty.
I want children and I want them now. I think I can fuse my family and work life more successfully than the women before me. . . .

Kim Flodin, "Motherhood's Better Before 30," in the *New York Times*

generations are already fawning over a new and no-longer-lost Millennial Generation of youngsters. Yet where Boomer educators and media producers fancy themselves leading a crusade for children—unfurling new banners of innocence, values-training, and civic virtue—13ers see themselves working at a more personal level. Increasingly, they're the parents who actually warm the milk bottles, buy the toys, mount the safety seats, and read the nursery rhymes. As long as they can coax a smile, they won't worry that they never learned much about careful nurture when they were on the receiving end of the parent-child relationship. They'll make up for it by sheer force of will. Unlike their Silent parents, they're in no mood to tolerate family failure.

Having grown up in a culture that celebrated sex more than children, 13er moms and dads are helping America rediscover that sex is also about having children. Like Jodie Foster, playing the tough, I've-seen-everything single mother in *Little Man Tate*, they justify their animal protectiveness with a short and defiant message to these new youngsters: "The day you were born, the first minute I saw you, you know what I said? I said this kid's gonna be special, this kid's gonna be different. And I'm not gonna blow it."

>19. The Choices Are Ugly and Few

Press the generational rewind button. Back in the mid-1960s, *Mad* magazine ran a cartoon spoof about a "new generation gap" twenty years in the future. Seen through the prism of that era, it couldn't have been more bizarre. The middle-aged parents were portrayed as aging hipsters, funky grand-daddios, and graying, free-love radicals; the teenagers as clean-cut reactionaries who despised everything their parents stood for. Readers laughed and shook their heads. Now press fast-forward to the mid-1980s, and press pause at a new sitcom called *Family Ties*. The middle-aged parents? Talkative, sensitive, broad-minded Democrats. The teenager? A cut-the-bull young Republican who argues with dad about Reagan and packs a *Wall Street Journal* under his arm. Viewers laughed, and this time they nodded.

The conservative child of liberal parents. From fantasy to stereotype, this has become the most striking popular image of the 13th Generation's political identity.

Does the image hold? It certainly does if we compare today's 13ers with their older siblings or parents at like age. Twenty years ago,

Percent agreeing that Ronald Reagan's presidency will go down in history as above-average:	
age 18-29	70%
age 30-49	62%
age 50+	48%
Source: Gallup Poll (1989)	

back when mop-haired Meathead was ripping into Archie Bunker, the young were far more liberal than their parents; polls showed self-identified young "liberals" outnumbering self-identified young "conservatives" by nearly three to one. Now that millions of middle-aged Meatheads have their own college-age children, polls show young people no more liberal than their parents—and quite a bit more conservative on such bellwether issues as crime, defense spending, drugs, and welfare. This is true for the poor as much as the rich, for blacks as much as whites.

Yet, this generation has proven that no one party or president has a lock on them. During the 1980s, the partisan tone of young voters shifted from roughly a ten-point Democratic advantage to a Republican edge that, in 1985, reaching 18 points (52 to 34 percent). This made 13ers the first pro-Republican young Americans since the 1920s. In fifteen out of sixteen polls taken between 1981 and 1988, 13ers gave Ronald Reagan a higher approval rating than did any older age bracket. Then, in 1992, 13ers as a whole gave Ross Perot his greatest generational support at the voting booth (22 percent) while married 13ers with children stayed loyally Republican, voting more than 2-to-1 for George Bush. On the other hand, single 13ers switched loyalties and voted three-to-one for Clinton, a self-professed "New Democrat" who promised change (not just from Bush, but from "old" Democrats) and who made at least some effort to speak their language and find out what was on their minds.

So much for the numbers. They confirm that something important happened to America's youth between the "Up Against the Wall!" chants of the mid-'60s and the "USA!" chants of the mid-'80s. But exactly what happened can't be deciphered from polls and surveys alone.

To understand what makes 13ers tick politically, go back and look

Self-centered Republican "values" have crippled the concept of civic duty, while relativist Democratic dogma has led to the fragmentation of American life. In other words, the wasteland before us is the product not only of shortsighted, self-deluded Reaganites, but also of shortsighted, self-deluded and politically incompetent liberals.

Eric Liu, editor,
The Next Progressive

I just feel like my vote doesn't count. They don't reach out to any of us. They could get a major vote if they got students interested.

Shannon Pankuch,
Montgomery College

When asked to rank the actions of living former Presidents since leaving the White House, Americans aged 18 to 29 give the highest score to Reagan—but Americans over age 30 give an overwhelming edge to Carter.

Source: Gallup Poll (1990)

In elementary school, 55 percent of the students believe that elected officials care about young people. In high school, only 17 percent of the students feel that way.

Source: Scholastic Poll of American Youth (1992)

It was pathetically small, pathetically small.

Leo Ribuffo, history professor, George Washington University, describing a student protest against Operation Desert Storm

carefully at the 1970s—that decade of cultural upheaval and institutional decline when grade-school Atari-wavers got their first glimpse of national life. To older generations, this seemed a fine time to turn inward, cast off the burdens of social discipline, and put personal agendas ahead of the larger national interest. But to the opening wedge of the 13th Generation, there was nothing therapeutic in the spectacle of an entire nation letting go. To them, the 1970s unfolded like a grim and horrifying newsreel. Watergate. Oil embargo. The

	College Freshmen in 1970	College Freshmen in 1991	Change
"Liberal" or "Far Left"	37%	26%	− 11%
"Middle of the Road"	45%	54%	+ 9%
"Conservative" or "Far Right"	18%	20%	+ 2%

How would you describe your political views?

Source: "The American Freshman: Twenty-Five Year Trends" (UCLA, 1991–1992)

"Christmas without lights." Impeachment. Collapse of Vietnam. Stagflation. CIA and Lockheed scandals. Three Mile Island. A second oil embargo. More stag- and more -flation. Tehran hostages. Afghanistan. Yellow ribbons. Looking up from the turmoil in their families and schools, 13ers saw a mirror-image welter of political failure and sensed that adults were simply not in control of themselves or the country.

At every turn, it seemed to 13ers that '70s-era America was convulsing over technicalities and symbols that bore no workable connection to real life. While economists bickered about subsidies for residential windmills and methane-producing compost heaps, 13ers wondered if they'd have enough gas to get to the prom. While columnists debated whether Aleuts should be officially recognized as a disadvantaged minority, 13ers feared for their lives in urban subways. While politicians toasted new conferences to redefine the traditional family, 13ers watched divorced moms wonder whether dad's check would ever show up in the mail. Gradually—even before casting its first votes—this generation began to sense its own political agenda: *to make simple things work again.*

By itself, this pragmatic agenda did not compel Atari-wave 13ers to arrive on stage as political conservatives. But they felt themselves drawn in this direction when, in his 1980 campaign, Ronald Reagan asked Americans to stage what amounted to a referendum on the '70s; a vote for him was to be a vote against all that decade had stood for. Hearing the Gipper, and wanting to believe in him, most 13er voters followed his advice and pulled down hard on the "no-more-'70s" Republican lever. They pulled the same lever again in 1984, and again (though with waning conviction) in 1988. During the 1980s, thanks in part to the 13er vote, politicians with the age and temperament of

Maybe our generation as a whole is less politically active. The individuals committed are truly committed to it. They're not just after the fun and drugs—like in the '60s.

Scott Lewandowski, 25, stereo salesman, Washington, DC

By more than two-to-one, students rank the Japanese economy as stronger than that of the United States.

Source: Stuart Himmelfarb, President, College-Track

Most college students would vote. They have strong opinions. But there's such a bureaucracy in getting absentee ballots that when it comes time to register their opinion, they just don't.

Scott Gant, 22, Arlington, VA

their parents (Carter, Kennedy, Mondale, Hart, Dukakis) fell by the wayside, and politicians who reminded them more of their *grand*parents (Reagan and Bush) spearheaded a national conservative revival.

Along the way, with millions of new members reaching voting age each year, the 13th Generation has forged an attitude of political reaction. The 1992 election showed that this reaction can even be against the president and party they once helped elect—if they feel the incumbents just aren't delivering what was promised. Most of today's twentysomethings listen to the partisans of social justice, global compassion, and big government with sharp-eyed skepticism. ("Word, word, word," as a rapper would say.) They prefer the flesh-and-blood loyalties they can count on—family, platoon, gang—over abstract theories, bloated institutions, and political parties that, in their experience, sooner or later let you down. Come election day, most choose not to choose and simply don't vote. Although the 1992 election produced the heaviest 13er turnout to date—they still voted in percentages far smaller than older age brackets. When they *do* vote, they generally prefer the party or the candidate that mainly trusts the simple passions (generosity, honor, even greed) and doesn't try to hector the young into being better people.

Thirteeners who call themselves liberal have absorbed enough of this new mood to trim the horizons of their social agenda. In the late 1960s, young activists could become folk heroes by urging vast new programs for the poor, massive marches on Washington, or spectacular class-action suits against Fortune 500 polluters. By the 1980s, activists stuck to tightly focused projects—like organizing a volunteer soup-kitchen, or getting the dean to approve multi-use recycling, or sponsoring a fund-raiser for something that transcends ideology (like opposing apartheid, or helping Amnesty International).

The 13er drift toward political reaction defies any conventional definition of conservatism. Unlike older traditionalists, they distrust the concept of a collective national will, are suspicious of consensus, and hate to see dissenters coerced. Unlike older supply-siders, they detest deficits and debt. Unlike older libertarians, they don't idealize individualism. To deal with a big national problem like spotty health insurance or failing schools, 13ers prefer flexible, local solutions with op-

How do you think most people feel when they see the homeless?		
	They Feel Upset	They Don't Feel Upset
Age 18–29	35%	55%
Age 30–64	45%	45%
Age 65+	45%	30%

Source: *New York Times* poll (1992)

***rnazezyk
>hello from georgetown. personally, I'm astonished to realize the utter validity of what I've been reading here. it's as though 2boomers are peering into my own deepest feelings.

***crasher
>for christ's sake, don't egg them on like that! that's the last thing we need!

***tmaster
>the whole love affair with reagan was so hilarious--let's face facts, folks. our generation loved reagan when we didn't have to pay for anything. it was easy to love the guy when our parents were writing the checks. you notice that the minute we all started moving out of the house, people started having second thoughts. that's because most of the twentysomethings are right around the poverty line, no matter what their lifestyle. it's all about money, and it always will be.

***schpooz
>what about all of the social questions, like abortion and the environment and foreign policy?

***tmaster
>human interest stories. I don't vote like that. I have two credos I hold above everything else: money is everything. more is better. anyone who thinks differently is completely deluding themselves. art is only art if someone will pay to see it. nothing in life can be accomplished without adequate capital. the only thing money can't buy is good kneecaps.

***crasher
>I think we may have just found the most cynical person in the world.

***tmaster
>on the contrary--i just haven't spent my life trying to fool myself into all these higher ideals you guys have been tossing around. marriage, love, social liberties, they're all fine, but in the end I always ask, "well, who's got the money?" it can all be traced to there. I lost a parent in 10th grade, and since then I've been in control of our family's finances. I'm going to work here in new york until I can retire comfortably, and make sure that I have the freedom to do whatever I want. in the meantime, I consume. I am not going to be denied the amenities that everyone else has had throughout the years. I'm not cynical--I'm going to have some fun.

***schpooz
>don't you care about that kind of senseless consumerism? it seems to me the mess we're all in was caused by that sort of mindset. don't you want a nice, clean country to drive through when you're middle-aged?

***tmaster
>hell, I'm 25. I am middle-aged.

We can't cry over each bum we step over, or every drop of acid rain.

Nancy Smith,
"25 and Pending," in the
Washington Post

Twentysomething doesn't know much about the tax debate, but takes it for granted that politicians lie. Or to put it another way, politicians change their act. Madonna gets a new image every year, so why not George?

Ellen Goodman, in the
Boston Globe

Pacify me, politician
Pacify me with your lies

Living Colour,
"Someone Like You" (song)

There was no one I wanted to vote for. You feel like a little person who can't have an effect on all this crap that is going on.

Julia Guinn, 23,
George Mason University

tions to buy in or opt out. But they do so only because they hate seeing bureaucrats fed and individuals cheated, not because they wouldn't enjoy watching the whole fat status quo turned rudely upside down. Persuade them that a national plan is fair, simple, and will work as intended, and they'll approve it in a flash.

As the 1990 and 1992 elections proved, this generation is no pushover for Republican candidates: By sizable majorities, 13er opinion has run counter to the GOP mainstream on any number of issues involving perceived threats to their personal liberty (abortion, censorship) or to their collective future (environment, public debts). Although polls show that liberals have lost a huge amount of ground among youth over the past twenty years, over half of this shift has gone not to conservatives, but to self-defined moderates.

To understand the 13er political credo, we need a better angle than ideology and more suitable words than liberal or conservative. Try the following five rules:

Rule One: Wear your politics lightly. Sure, 13ers will tell a pollster they're pro or con on taxes or abortion or any other issue. But most do so without deep conviction or ideological passion—and, when asked, a disarming number will admit that "I don't really know enough to judge" or "Yes, I might be persuaded to change my mind." As 13ers see it, that's a lot more sensible than acting like some oh-so-committed Boomer. And since this post-Watergate generation cannot remember a time when Americans actually trusted their government, they refuse to believe that public policies (whether conservative or liberal) really matter as much as elders like to think they do. As they view the world, the most significant social changes take place far from where politicians gather. When they look at government, what they mainly see is a huge, complex irrelevance, seldom staffed by people like them and almost never doing things for people like them. Like the young *New Republic* editor Andrew Sullivan, they consider themselves "post-ideological." To follow every political story in the news is fine, if you get paid for it—but a waste of time if you don't.

Rule Two: Survival comes first. Having learned since childhood that earnest promises can't protect them from harm, most 13ers put great trust in their own survival skills and are deeply suspicious of any attempt to thwart them. They resist political edicts telling a family not to defend itself, or a business not to make a profit, or a nation not to pursue its own interests. This same instinct energizes global warming movements and nuclear freeze campaigns whose purpose is not to be (Boomerishly) one with nature, but rather to save the planet from turning into a very dead asteroid by the time 13ers are due to reach old age. Where older generations give moralistic lectures on "values" issues like abortion, 13ers translate the arguments into immediate human terms. Young pro-choicers point to the impoverishing costs of having a child against a woman's will, while young pro-lifers defend every being's quest for existence. The political debates that matter most to 13ers are about how to help real people thrive (or at least avoid perishing) in a dangerous world.

Rule Three: Try to fix only what's fixable. Ever since 13ers can remember, older Americans have talked endlessly about global maladies no one has any real hope of curing—racism, hunger, poverty, war—while ignoring most of the specific and soluble ills that are gradually undermining the nation and world. In reaction, 13ers show a ruthless focus on problems that are concrete and can get fixed. The global environment? Get real. But limiting greenhouse gases? Yes, maybe that could be done—and off go a bevy of Cal Tech engineers to design hydrogen-fuel cells. Eliminating poverty? As if. But putting an end to urban homelessness? Yes, that's worth a try—and off go a bevy of Miami University architects to design inexpensive wooden shelters and do battle with city regulators and housing codes. While many older Americans tolerate policies that don't work as long as they issue from the proper process and invoke the proper symbols, 13ers work from the other end: They look at each problem as a "job" and look for policies that will "do the job" fastest and cheapest. They don't much care what process is followed or whose ideology is getting stroked, and polls show them less interested than their elders in attaching themselves to "isms" (environmentalism, pacifism, feminism, liberalism—even conservatism). In their lexicon, big words are distractions from the bottom line—and if you talk the big talk, you'd better deliver.

Rule Four: Clean up after your own mess. One of the 13ers' least-favorite '70s-era period pieces is the hippie classic, *Alice's Restaurant.* What especially bothers them is the scene where young Boomers vent their rage on the establishment by dumping a truckload of garbage down a pristine hillside. To 13ers, that scene is a social and political metaphor for their entire life experience. Whatever

You can only do so much. I'm not going to protest either way about the war. I'm not writing to Washington. I'm not sitting on the lawn in front of the White House. Even though I try to keep up with the war and the world in general, these are problems I can't solve, so I might as well try to solve my own problems.

Julie Rim, 21,
government major,
Harvard College,
commenting on the
Gulf War

Politicians. Everyone knows they're the real gang members. Everyone knows that in this country money talks, and that politics is a money thing. It's the politicians who allow the drugs to come here. I mean if I can find the drugs, why can't they?

Robert Penn, 17,
gang member, Omaha, NE

***djsalem

>you know, I find all these "liberal" and "conservative" labels offensive from the get-go. I think it's kind of stupid to be a dyed-in-the-wool anything, especially when life is so complex. I have an oldsmobile I got from my folks, that is still in pretty good condition, and it looks like a nice big gas-guzzling republicanmobile. anyway, my girlfriend thought it would be cute to put a deadhead sticker next to my old reagan/bush bumper sticker. so I walk out of work the other day, and some bonehead has left a note on my windshield that says, "reagan and the grateful dead. how amazing. how typical. how absurd." this person was obviously holding themselves up as pinnacles of cultural grooviness, of open-minded deadhead philosophy, and yet they took two cultural symbols and instantly made all kinds of assumptions about my character. I hate being pigeonholed like that! it makes me furious.

***crasher

>you see stuff like that all the time at school--sometimes I think we are an entire platoon of non-conforming conformers. even the guys who wear all black, dead kennedy t-shirts with nose rings and purple hair--even those dudes seem to have a dress code. and then they snicker when I walk past with my backpack and chuck taylors on, like I'm some sort of freak. you get pigeonholed no matter what you do.

***ankhman

>you guys should try being a black college student for a day.

***cogan

>cogan here again. if you guys are so concerned about being pigeonholed, why do you read this 2boomers stuff at all? talk about being defined, man. I think this generation stuff is all bullshit. 7/8ths of this stuff has nothing to do with me. they ought to call it the 13th generalization. that's all I'm going to say.

***schpooz

>I think we're going to have to act like a generation if we're going to get anything done in the long run. if we had a little bit of a group identity, then maybe everyone would be convinced to help clean up all these messes around here.

***starfire

>personally, I think no one in my generation cares about having a group identity.

***crasher
>but just by saying that, you give us all away. if anything, the absence of caring is enough to bond a group of people together.

***budster
>crasher, you sounded very 2boomers-like just then. are you losing it? are you going over to the dark side of the force?

***crasher
>look, like it or not, we are chronologically following the biggest pile of demographic dung in american history, and if that means categorically rejecting everything that they stand for, then I don't mind being pigeonholed for a bit. my hatred for everything they represent is as real as it is irrational.

***skari
>hello from new york. I wanted to say that everything I have to deal with is the result of bloopers from the generation ahead of us. it is like we are going through the backwash of life from a grimy, scuffed-up coca-cola can that has been slurped of all its fizz.

***djsalem
>I can be a little more specific. at the honor court, I work on both the regular court and the court of appeals. the regular court is just us students, but the appeals court judges are comprised of two students and three faculty members, all three of them in their forties. every time we rule on a case that goes to the appeals court, those professors reverse it, as if to say that we can't do our job. I fight to get this conviction through on some student who has flagrantly cheated on some exam, and the professors will smile and let the guy go. they live by the same waffling, vague rules that they inflicted on society all during the '60s and '70s, and I just feel like getting some giant hook and yanking them off the gong show. let someone who can do the job in there. enough of this namby-pamby crap.

***schpooz
>I like the idea of being in a generation. I don't think there's anything wrong with that.

***sfynktur
>hello there from iowa. they're defining us as having a lack of definition. It's like writing a poem that doesn't rhyme about how hard it is to rhyme a poem.

***crasher
>I'm going to have to think about that one for a while...

I think it's so much easier to accept the fact that nothing is going to change rather than to think, try to think optimistically that by voting something is going to change.

22-year-old graduate of Morehouse College

We see no connection between our concerns and the ballot box. National politics, for my generation, has become irrelevant.

Jonathan Cohn, assistant editor of *The American Prospect*

"Croatia's Gotta Be Free"

title of a popular song that helped rally the 1992 Croatian drive for independence, written by three American college students the issue—pollution, schools, families, deficits, jobs, sex, race, housing, trade, public works—today's young people have repeatedly seen elders act out noble emotions and then allow the consequences to crash down on somebody else. Already resigned to the task of cleaning up after the mistakes of others, most 13ers are determined not to repeat those same mistakes in their own turn. What this means, as they see it, is learning to say "no" to programs that finance adult consumption on the backs of children, "yes" to equitable sacrifice on behalf of the future. Candidates who try to appeal to 13ers' generational self-interest are wasting their breath. This most destitute of generations reports the most negative opinions toward welfare spending. Two-thirds believe that, if they ever end up unemployed, it's their own fault. Thirteeners are determined to shoulder their own hardships, to be generous toward others when the facts warrant, and to prod government to treat a new batch of kids far better than it ever treated them.

Rule Five: Personal style matters. To 13ers, the personal style of a candidate reveals more than credentials, platforms, or ideology about how that candidate will actually perform in office. They are comfortable with charisma, because they appreciate the animal element that energizes the small household and workplace groups that help them through their daily lives. While the over-30 crowd pores over the endless policy papers, this generation zooms in on the pluses and minuses of human detail: what Boris Yeltsin said while staring down the barrels of enemy tanks; what joke Reagan cracked while being wheeled into the hospital with a bullet in his chest; how Mike Dukakis answered the question about what he would do if his wife got raped; or the way Bill Clinton jived his sax on Arsenio. On the job or on campus, 13ers themselves often cannot explain why they are drawn so magnetically to the Ronald Reagans, Jesse Jacksons, and Ross Perots of national politics. They feel at ease with leaders who charm without effort, who don't mind hamming it up, who exude confidence in crowds, who sleep easy after making big choices, who understand—whether you're dealing with Congress or walking the mean streets—that who you *seem* can be just as important as who you are.

Right now, this generation remains politically up for grabs. Thirteeners have recently pulled away from Republican and big-C "Conservative" banners. This latest turn in what Coupland calls the "microallegiances" of today's young people reflects a toxic reaction to what Boomers have done to the G.O.P. (even right-wing 13ers shuddered when they heard the Quayle and Quayle "values" preaching) as well as a backlash against the entire two-party status quo.

Among older Atari-wavers, there's also a feeling of disillusionment about the Republicans' twelve-year record in the White House. Yes, the final triumph of individuals over institutions has pretty much completed the "Reagan Revolution" that most of them cheered when they first came of age. It has happened not only at home, but in Russia, Eastern Europe, Sweden, and China—not only in the marketplace, but also in politics and families. But now, what's left to be done? Besides, who is the young, unskilled, I'm-getting-exactly-my-market-wage sucker who's going to have to pay back all the '80s-era debts? A decade that started with 13ers cheering Reagan's "Morning in America" ended with 13er author Andrew Shapiro arguing that *We're Number One!* only in items that are either undesirable or don't matter. And the new decade began with first-time voters turning against an aging caretaker president presiding over a nightmare youth economy.

The younger Nintendo wavers are just entering college at a time of long youth unemployment lines—and are showing renascent support for social activism on issues like national health care, environmental protection, and abortion rights. On campus, the once-ascendant "New Rights" clubs and Dartmouth Review-type publications now have to compete for student attention with the once-scorned tie-dyed activists and a new-leftish underground. But the recent 13er surge toward the Democratic Party is powered by a perilously unstable mood of economic alienation, and by a thirst for generational change that (given the 13er hostility toward Boomers) could turn sour at any time. An all-Democratic and Boomer-led government had better do its job well. Otherwise—especially as more 13ers get married and have children—their generation could return to its Republican roots, this time with enough electoral clout to spearhead a sweeping political realignment.

In a 1987 survey, only 1 of 365 Yale seniors expressed an interest in a civil service career.

Source: National Commission on Public Service

When . . . young people were asked if they would consider public service or government work, the words most often used in reply were "big," "intransigent," and "stifling"—the same words applied generations ago to business.

Washington Post

If you could make $100,000 a year at any of
the following jobs, which one would you pick?

Teacher	49%
Lawyer	17%
Investment banker	11%
Politician	6%

Source: 1992 survey of college students, *Esquire*

Today's 13ers don't hear any national party or candidate express more than token interest in who they are or where they're going. No one has caught fire on campus. To young zap-TV viewers who are redefining the role of images in our national media, George Bush declares he won't appear on "a teeny-bopper show" like MTV. To young workers who equate a politician's mendacity with the length of his sentences, Bill Clinton offers a 47-point economic recovery program. To busy young people with no time to waste, the fickleness of Ross Perot's grass-roots movement is proof positive of how those who "get involved" can end up feeling tricked. To young non-voters waiting for messages to turn them on, older civic groups try dumbing down the threshold of voter participation through "Rock the Vote" or "motor-voter" registration schemes. It's almost as though America is content to ask 13ers to vote even if they *don't care* who wins.

True, a few young public-interest entrepreneurs are making the news through daring efforts to bypass the official party system altogether. Check out Gregory Watson's effort to get 38 states to ratify a forgotten Constitutional amendment blocking Congress's lame-duck pay raises. It worked, catching the House and Senate leadership completely by surprise. Or check out Wendy Kopp's "Teach for America" movement, which is scandalizing teachers' unions by placing thousands of uncredentialed college grads into grade school classrooms all across the country. Or Vanessa Kirsch's Public Allies, mobilizing inner-city kids to apprentice with D.C. civic groups. Or Owen Byrd's GreenVote, a wedge group for young eco-activists. Or, especially, Jon Cowan's and Rob Nelson's "Lead . . . or Leave" campaign to get congressional candidates to sign a pledge guaranteeing that they will either halve the deficit or resign after their first term. Now *that's* in-your-face lobbying.

Yet ask most bright 13ers about politics, and many will tell you they're either dabbling privately with some alienated fringe (socialists, libertarians) or have simply given up. When they zap into a televised debate, maybe they'll make a quick joke about a candidate's hairline before zapping on to the next channel. Back in the 1960s and '70s, young Americans made raucous appearances at national party conventions, hooting speakers from the floor or battling police outside the doors. Today, party conventions don't even show up on their radar screens. Small wonder that columnist John Leo, during the 1992 campaign season, dubbed them the "Unplugged Generation."

Seldom does anybody take the trouble to present political choices in a way that makes sense to young voters in their teens and twenties. Why should anyone bother? Older folks always have the last word, right?

Wrong. The ticking of the demographic clock will have the last word. Not so long ago, Americans used to assume that time was the ally of young crusaders and the enemy of old fogeys. But today the tables are turned—in favor of the *young* fogeys and against the old crusaders. In 1992, the first 13ers won elections to the House of Representatives (Richard Pombo in California and Cleo Fields in Louisiana), while George Stephanopoulos and Paul Begala emerged as key members of Bill Clinton's inner circle. And that's just the beginning. With the passing of each two-year interval between national elections, 8 million new 13ers will join the nation's electorate, and 6 million G.I. and Silent Generation voters will disappear. By 1998, 13ers will comprise the largest American generation of voting-age adults—larger than Boomers, twice as large as the Silent and G.I.s combined.

Inexorably, national politics will drift toward the personal, no-nonsense, survivalist approach of the 13th Generation, leaving mainly the new Boomer hegemony to fill in for everything that's vanishing: the expertise, sentimentality, and optimistic memories of today's 50-and-over crowd. The constellation of generations is turning. Unnoticed amidst all the media celebration over the Boomer rise to national leadership, the voting muscle of this rising "just do it" crowd is starting to transform American politics—and, with it, our identity as a nation.

***End of file. Upload completed.

***Select: (D)ownload, (U)pload, (M)enu,(Q)uit? q

***Exit USA-TALK.

***Log off at 1:23:39am 11/30/92.

More Americans, and more young Americans, are volunteering today than at any other time in our history.

Brian O'Connell, president of Independent Sector

I like politics because at the end, they count it up and stamp you on the head, and you're a "winner" or a "loser."

Paul Begala, 31, campaign adviser to Bill Clinton

Students don't vote. Do you expect me to come in here and kiss your ass?

Senator Wyche Fowler, Jr., responding to a request to take the "Lead . . . or Leave" anti-deficit pledge during his 1992 reelection campaign. (In a very close race, Fowler lost to an opponent who did take the pledge.)

C:> ph.bill

ATOT 1(703)555-0991. . .Phone number being dialed. . .Connection made. . .

<TRAN>told you that would rile'em up. now we're cooking.

<RECV>bet that would show the publishers 13ers have more than just microwaves in their skulls. it was surprisingly upbeat.

<TRAN>well, crasher, in case you're tapping in, we're moving onto your turf now. pop culture. the 13ing of america. you must something to say about that. same time tomorrow night.
———————————— computer log OFF at 1:29:16am 11/30/92 ————————————

PART 3

THE 13ING OF AMERICA

C:\usa-talk

ATOT 1(202)555-3850. . .Phone number being dialed. . .Connection made. . .

***Welcome to USA-TALK On-Line Bulletin Board.

***Your handle is: 2boomers

***Log on at 10:33:14pm 11/30/92.

***Messages to/from other current USA-TALK users will appear in upper-right cb box. At any time press alt-e to enter cb box.

***SELECT: (D)ownload, (U)pload, (M)enu, (Q)uit?u

***Upload channel currently open. Specify file at prompt:

>C:\13th-gen\part-3.doc

***USA-TALK uploading 13TH-GEN\PART-3 by 2BOOMERS at 10:33:45pm: stand by. . .

>20. We're This and That's That

In 1970, Coke ran a memorable ad showing barefoot and bellbottomed Boomer collegians holding hands atop a grassy Italian hillside, singing "I'd like to teach the world to sing in perfect harmony." In 1990, Coke resurrected that same scene and song—except this time the flower-bedecked singers were fortyish and accompanied by sweet little children. No college-age kids were anywhere to be seen. To find them, you had to watch Pepsi's competing ad showing a black-clad adolescent careening through a haunted fun house before getting dumped on a pile of junk.

Anyone who has lately turned a TV dial or browsed through a magazine rack has seen recurring 13er symbols that could not be further from the "natural man" youth image of two decades ago. Take the media-crafted personalities of 13er pitchmen: Coke's Max Headroom, R.J. Reynolds's "Smooth Character" (alias "Old Joe" Camel), the Marine gladiators on a chessboard, Nissan's faceless Bob, Reebok's Dan versus Dave. Splice on the cult movies, from time travel to alternate futures, from the "Dark Ages" of *Terminator* to the "Lite Ages" of *Buffy the Vampire Slayer*. Add a few well-known pitch-phrases: Bud Dry's "Why Ask Why," Diet Pepsi's "Uh Huh," Reebok's "Pump Up, Air Out." Toss in dozens of other imagistic 13er icons in TV graphics, magazine layouts, product and team logos, sales bites, videos, movie posters, book jackets, T-shirts—even graffiti on urban walls.

Now transform all this into some 13er *Mondo 2000* virtual reality world of shared generational experience where the only reality is sensory input. Play brain games programmed by market researchers who know (after countless teen and twentysomething focus groups) exactly how to sell products and messages to today's young people. Don

---

Let's cut the chitchat... It's it and that's that

TV ad for Miller Lite beer

C'mon, you like me. I'm an acquired taste.

young corporate wannabee, *The Secret of My Success* (film)

From 1975 to 1988, the share of all high school seniors who agreed that "there is nothing wrong with advertising that gets people to buy what they don't need" rose from 16 to 34 percent.

Source: "Monitoring the Future: Questionnaire Responses from the Nation's High School Seniors" (University of Michigan, 1975–1988)

I believe in beer commercials. There's a lot of fame and glory in it.

soldier, 23

the electronic helmet and gloves, and imagine yourself wandering around a digitalized refraction of 13er life and self.

It's quite a scene.

The setting is a big wasteland, a bleak and baked desert-beach with bright sun and no shade. Scattered about are piles of postmodern ruins, abandoned huge hulking things that once served a function but now don't. Everything is either urban density or nothingness—no fringes, no towns, nothing pastoral. Here stands a bridge going off into space, there a careening blimp, yonder a top-heavy building, on the horizon some space-age elevator or cantilever leading someplace nobody is going. Roads streak to nowhere, populated only by RVs whose sole purpose is touring, racing, or fun—nothing civic or industrial. City streets are dank and dangerous. Whatever little there is of nature (bushes, trees) is discolored, contorted, Scissorhandian, in flux. Colors are black and metallic, accented by hues not normally found in nature (the *Dick Tracy* palette), splashed around randomly or glowing in garishly tubescent neon. Occasionally a sign pops up, with few—or changing—words.

Enter the young people. They're the total Anti-Boom, a mongrelized cross between beasts of pleasure and genetically manufactured androids. Names are unimportant, at most one syllable long. Stares are vacant, eyes shielded or averted, faces turned or in shadows. Hair is antiBeatle—asymmetrical, ornamented, pushed up rather than hanging down, carved into topiary hedges. Bodies are rippled, bulbous, armor-plated. Makeup is accented, jewelry big and shiny. Clothes are walking billboards complete with logos and dollar signs. The human shell is not to be measured by what it contains, thinks, or says, just by what it looks capable of doing or selling. Were we to ask anybody a question, we couldn't easily tell whether a *Homo sapiens* or a computer answers back. Man is no creator here, just a terminator. Maybe he's engaged in some gladiatorial competition resembling a lethal game of lacrosse. If not presently competing, he's pumping up for his next event.

Everything is Yes-No. Life is full of code words and secret places, iron doors separating the welcome from the strange. The rich reside in luxurious transmillennial penthouses, enjoy unimaginable opulence, and immerse themselves in high-tech games and illusions. Down below, the poor scurry about in social chaos, scrounging through debris left over from some earlier grand age. Bars are jammed with barbarians. On the streets or in the outer wasteland, people have frenetic fun and take physically impossible risks: maybe jousting on a skywire, or bicycling out of a plane, or skiing straight down a skyscraper. From time to time, an instrument of earthly pleasure arrives—some punked-out Aphrodite on a dog biscuit—and the barbarians celebrate. This lets them forget, for a few precious seconds, the vast expanse of time and geography separating them from what they really want. The pleasurable things disappear as if by magic—into the sand, into the air, into some technologic contraption. No one seems to care, and the barbaric hubbub continues.

Nature is perverse. Clouds come, and go, then move upside down. Objects zoom by, slow down, spin around, turn upside down. Textures twill, reverse, decompose, disappear. Life is just trompe l'oeil, a world of Claymation or "computer morphing" in which anything can turn into anything, for any reason or for no reason. Cars become animals become people become things become nothing. Human emotions get tricked so often that even the thought of having feelings seems pointless. The scene itself is presented as no unaided eyes and ears would ever see or hear it. Cameras bounce. Editing is quick, jarring, clumsy. Words are artificially stuttered. Music is nonacoustic, synthesized, lip-synched.

It is as though we, as viewers, are also to be transformed into computerlike robots absorbing inputs in binary bits and bytes, to be remembered only if we take the trouble to push the "record" button. But, of course, we seldom do take the trouble.

Baby Busters' Vernacular:

BLIP-MITMENT: Stunted relationship characterized by shallow talk, malt liquor and infrequent (but safe) sex.

PAISLEYITES: 1960s–1990s cross-pollinators . . . affiliation with '60s consciousness ends with clothing.

DISPLACED NOSTALGIA: Wistful feeling stirred by another generation's music . . . .

Anne Gowen, 25, and Sean Piccoli, 28,
"A Generation Lost in Time," in the *Washington Times*

Hamburger ads pop up
in my head
On the edge of Aquarius

B-52's, "Channel 2" (song)

———

Part of the appeal of MTV is that anything can happen next. This is a world without perspective: Paula Abdul dances with a cartoon cat; a clay hammer spurts from Peter Gabriel's clay head; David Byrne of Talking Heads is a child one minute, a face projected on a house the next. For 16 minutes—the network's estimate of the average viewer visit—logic takes a break.

John Leland with Marc Peyser, in *Newsweek*

———

Slacker . . . portrays a network of cultural bottom-feeders, living off scraps of the mainstream culture which drift down to them. People try to sell T-shirts or a Madonna pap smear; they wander around with tape recorders and videocams . . . . *Slacker* makes me wonder: Can art redeem wasted time? And that's not a rhetorical question. I really want to know.

Scott McLemee, "Notes of a Slacker," in the *Next Progressive*

For visitors over age 30, this surreal world is like some postapocalyptic sci-fi 13erland of public wreckage and private survival. It could not be further from the old Disney Tomorrowland on which Boomers were weaned—a happy place where progress was public, institutions were all-powerful, markets were weak, and individuals were compliant cogs in a well-ordered civilization. In this 13erland, progress is personal, institutions are enemies, markets are everything, life is decaying, and individuals are either lonely nomads or mutant musketeers belonging to small warring tribes. To elder eyes, this 13er theme park is the juvenile embodiment of national decline, the total decay of the American Dream, a dreadful vision of a declinist *Road Warrior* future in which thuglike teens wage war over three drops of gas.

Thirteeners see all this too—*as a game*, a way to fool older people. Yes, surrealism speaks to them, but they don't take it all so literally. (If they did, they'd be out hoarding gold, not putting on ties and going to job interviews.) To them, this is also a pastiche of pleasure and play in a fantasy trick-universe. In such a world, all human response is just some mimic of real life. What *is* real is how young people cope with whatever weirdness their environment dishes out; what matters is *private* reality, not public reality. What matters is not *why* you pick up the weapon, or even whether it's a seventeenth-century saber or a twenty-seventh-century laser sword. All that matters is whether you're brave and quick enough to slay your enemy. The game's context is nothing; the game's outcome is everything.

Hardly born when Marshall McLuhan declared that "the medium is the message," 13ers are growing up as America's first truly McLuhanesque generation, young men and women who have learned far better than their elders how to separate media form from message content. They can appreciate a movie (like *JFK*) or an ad icon (like "Old Joe" Camel) for its extrinsic entertainment value while disregarding—or, at least, *claiming* to disregard—its intrinsic ideology or sales pitch. They can appreciate a "star" (like Madonna or Michael Jackson) whose principal talent lies in being, well, a *star*.

Whether born in the '60s or '70s, 13ers passed through childhood gaining an easy familiarity with all of today's modern media and their various blended applications. Atari-wavers were just learning to read when *Sesame Street* first used ad constructs as learning tools (with "commercials" for letters and numbers) and were just reaching ele-

DAN & DAVE'S MOST EXCELLENT DUDE-ATHLON

DOWNHILL SKATEBOARD SPEED RUN

UPHILL MOUNTAIN-BIKE SPRINT

HANG-TIME GLIDE

BUNGEE JUMP

HUMAN FLY

VELCRO VAULT

GALE FORCE WINDSURF

PEC FLEX BREW SLAM

mentary school when *The Electric Company* used kinetic videos to build self-esteem and social skills. These babies of the '60s entered adolescence when TV advertisements attained a new level of sophistication and entertainment value. They joined the job market during the explosion in cable programming, sound bites, commercialized logos, parallel-think messages, and "production values" in advertising. The Nintendo-wave babies of the '70s differ only in that they didn't grow up with this transition: They've been exposed to "edutainment" and "infomercials" all their lives, from computer games to Whittle's Channel One.

"Post-literate" 13ers don't draw the division between fiction and reality the way older people do. In this age of participatory technoculture—of hand-held video cameras and digital editing—13ers know that anyone can reveal the news and, conversely, that anyone can lie. Unlike Boomers at the same age, 13ers don't have the option

There's our "attitude," a coolness, a detachment. There's the way we dress—"mock" turtlenecks, way-too-big suits. And the way we speak: ironic, flip, uncommitted, a question mark at the end of every other sentence.

Nancy Smith,
"25 and Pending," in the
Washington Post

Word	Meaning
Not!	Used at the end of a statement of fact, expressing denial, negation or refusal. (Similar to how a negative symbol at the beginning of a mathematical subset renders that subset negative regardless of any possible positive integer within said subset.)

Mike Myers and Robin Ruzan, *Wayne's World Extreme Close-Up* (book)

of watching Cronkite, then *Gunsmoke*, then a politician on the late-night news, and lastly an entertainer on a late-night talk show. Now, everything is interwoven in one big national *Soapdish*: Sister Souljah holding a press conference, Bill Clinton on MTV, a police drama reenacting a "true" story. These days, any high-class techie with the right equipment can make a video purportedly showing politician "X" having sex with bimbo "Y" or robbing bank "Z." As 13ers see it, everything in the media is (or can be) one big tangle of fact and fancy.

Today, when Boomer viewers stumble across some 13er romproom, they feel a little like Moses returning from the mountain. Hands full of abstract principles, they look down with a mixture of pity and horror on these reveling young celebrants of the Golden Calf—pity that the young were born too late to defy the Pharaoh, horror that they've lost all faith in the Promised Land. So these latter-day Moseses do what prophets must and command the young against worshiping Graven Images. But the young stare back without comprehension. They refuse to trust anything they can't see and feel with their own eyes and hands. And what they do see and feel is where their Virtual Reality machine tells them they really are: in the middle of a wilderness, a million miles from nowhere.

According to Wimbledon athlete Andre Agassi, IMAGE IS EVERYTHING. But for most of this McLuhanesque young generation, the truth is better stated the other way around: everything is image. In such a world, the purpose of Virtual Reality is not to persuade you to trust appearances, but rather to teach you to distrust any interpretation of reality that is not vitally, immediately *necessary*.

>21. It's Our Culture, So Naturally We Use It

Peruse today's mainline media. Notice how '90s-era America is becoming a somber land obsessed with values, back-to-basics movements, public and private rectitude, harsh punishments, and a yearning for the simple life. Moods, messages, even popular pigments have turned somber. A neopuritanical black adorns everything from sequined gowns to the sleek Lexus crunching leaves like some brooding, unforgiving demigod. Life's smallest acts exalt (or diminish) one's personal virtue. That's what you get when Boomers start tightening their midlife grip on the nation's *haute couture*.

But look again. This time, notice a counter-mood popping up in college towns, big cities, Fox and cable TV, and the various ethnic side currents of the national culture. It's a tone of physical frenzy and spiritual passivity—a pursuit of cutting-edge, high-tech, guiltless fun. Watch *In Living Color* or Arsenio Hall, read *American Psycho* or *Sassy* magazine, buy a ticket to *Wayne's World, Slacker*, or *Singles*. Find bits of Americana by, of, and for people in their twenties. This is the real 13er stuff. *Basse couture?* Maybe. Nothing but noise? Only to the uninitiated.

Any voyage through the 13er cultural landscape has to begin with a car. Not some finely-tuned Lexus, but a rugged RV, a banged-up beater with a sound system costing half the car's total worth. Thirteeners don't select wheels the way their elders did, as some chrome-plated V-8 cruiser to vent conformist frustrations, or as some Beetle-ish ethical rebuff against Detroit. No, they mainly want cars that can go absolutely anywhere, fast and enjoyably. With an RV, a 13er has got *potential*, he's got the confidence that he can handle anything at any time—and handle it on his own. If life ever gets to be a hassle, he can get away to literally anywhere he wants: onto some remote beach, across some river, up some mountain track, far away from those canyons of Wall Street where the sun has to reflect down off all those big yuppie office buildings.

Cars help a 13er zip a state or two away not to save distant souls or launch grand political movements, but just to have some raw, uncerebral, unpunished *good times*. Maybe she'll track down some all-night word-of-mouth ingenue-organized maxi-party "rave" with nonstop bands and a $15 cover. Maybe she'll find a little fresh terrain and dig through dunes in a buggy, pop down paths on a trail

> **D**on't ask me why I play this music It's my culture, so naturally I use it
>
> Living Colour, "Pride" (song)

> **I**n the new recombinant rock, the pacing has sped up to match the zap-around-the-dial mentality of a generation brought up with electronic toys. For them, stylistic purism can seem quaint and limiting. With a world at your fingertips, why not try everything in reach? Maybe the music should be called zap-rock.
>
> Jon Pareles, in the *New York Times*

> **I**t's an incredibly active scene. People hang out, dance, drink, yell, and the work is very urban, very rhythmic, full of sex, drugs, violence, politics, anger, humor. And it's not a depressed scene, it's not introverted or tortured; that's a '50s image.
>
> Eve Packer, a New York City "performance poet" describing Greenwich Village "Poetry Slams"

bike, do a Spiderman climb up some urban brick wall, or plunge off cliffs on a rubber band. Maybe she'll get hard exercise, take crazy risks, dare a competitor not to quit, or do some triathlonish mix of the three. Polls show 13ers not especially interested in going to national parks, full of slow-moving G.I. Winnebagoes and Boomers in search of their own personal *Grand Canyon*. Today's young people are more attracted to places where life moves a little faster, where they can do pointless things without attracting the gazes of elder disapproval.

Like every generation, 13ers are finding youth Meccas. Senior citizen G.I.s took their big band swing culture to CCC camps and military bases. The Silent carved a *Lonely Crowd* ethos and Design Research culture out of new suburban tracts. Boomers discovered their souls in university towns, pasturelands, and wilderness communes. For 13ers, the hot youth spots are teeming immigrant cities—places with style and frenzy, offering the most jobs and the best fun. These days, youth trends don't spring from Berkeley, Boston, or other tony places where Boomers are busy cruising around with that PC air. No, for 13ers, the gotta-be-there urban zones are the cityscapes stretched across America, the deal-making bazaars of Manhattan, Miami, L.A., Minneapolis, and Seattle ("the new Liverpool"), with their platinum bands and hot club scenes; the mirrored, air-conditioned towers of Atlanta, Dallas, and Charlotte, where low-wage kids help hot new businesses rocket past the competition; and the agewave oases of Tampa, Tucson, and Palm Springs, where there's plenty to do helping out the old and moneyed. Industrial towns? Forget it, unless you like bagging fries for blue collars. Small towns? Boring, Boomer-infested. Rural isolation? Only if friends are along, the weather's good, and there's plenty of vertical rock or white water nearby.

Like members of other twentieth-

century American generations, young 13ers are drawn overseas—but not to the same places others went when young, and certainly not for the same reasons. The G.I.s liberated, and fell in love with, England, France, and Italy. The Silent went to Ethiopia, Peru, or the Philippines to swear a (temporary) oath of poverty and do a little Peace Corps good. Boomers went anyplace they could export their draft-dodging, drugged-out blue jeans scene: Canada, Mexico, Sweden, Holland, India, Polynesia. But 13ers? Their preferences are shaped by the economics and politics of the New Word Order. Western Europe? Why—to pay $5 per cappuccino waiting for some Eurocrat to process a work permit? The Third World? What for—to get sick, shot at, or taken hostage? No, a 13er would rather journey off to Taipei to make money teaching English, to Japan to help the locals buy U.S. assets, to Santiago to start a shoe franchise, or to Prague to build a venture capital company.

On the overseas youth circuit, a common experience is to make a little money for a while, travel around until it's gone, and come home broke. By then, chances are a 13er's sublessee-friend has found another sublessee who found another sublessee, each of whom split after a few months, so every rent check has had to cross two or three oceans before reaching a furious landlord. So the nomad moves on. When picking a new place to live, a 13er doesn't much care about the view, the garden, what the neighborhood's like, or even the size of the apartment. What he *does* care about is nearness to friends, a parking space, and having space, time, and money for all the techno-gizmos he craves. Forget fancy furniture, save for one cozy spot to sit with headphones and a Radio Shack programmable wand, the sorcerer's stick for a dozen digital devices.

For entertainment, a typical 13er mainly watches movies—*six decades* of movies, all at her fingertips, any one she wants any time she wants, an average of 89 movies a year. She likes everything from '30s classics to '60s nostalgia stuff to modern-era downmarket junk. Thanks to VCRs, she watches 'em forwards and backwards, slo- and fast-mo, as many times as she can bear. Sex and violence doesn't bother her much; by now, she considers herself something of a student of all that. She chortles over gratuitous scenes and has an eye and ear for the scenes and words that earned a film its R rating. She can recite all the best car chases, bun scenes, sequel rip-offs, and latest technologies for faking blood, severing limbs, and making aliens drool.

Fans of politically conscious "message rock" by artists like U2 and Suzanne Vega prefer tie-dye fabrics, Indian prints, leather sandals, and little or no makeup. But fans of heavy metal groups like Bon Jovi and Van Halen choose designer clothes, watches, lingerie worn as primary clothing, heavy eye makeup, and stiffening hair gels.

American Demographics

———

I liked Arnold's wit and his charisma and his ability to throw in good punchlines before he blows someone's brains out.

Jason Quinn, 16, Arlington, VA, commenting on the movie *Terminator 2*

———

In 1987, the typical teenager watched an average of 89 films—10 of them in a movie theater, 27 on cable TV, 25 on broadcast TV, and 27 on a home VCR.

Source: The Gallup Organization, *America's Youth, 1977–1988*

***crasher

>hello again, boys. thank the good lord above you're finally talking about the culture-- that's the only thing I find interesting in the long run anyway. it's probably the only thing I'm particularly good at.

***2boomers

>your culture isn't easy to define, much less be "good at."

***crasher

>well, my housemates and I got together and came up with a few lists for your reading pleasure. this first one I call "the top 10 movies that have come the closest to depicting life as people our age know it." shall I paste it on to the network?

***2boomers

>be our guest!

***crasher

>1. "fast times at ridgemont high" - this was the first classic of my movie career. in fact, I think it was the first time I paid for my own ticket. it looks a little dated now, full of zipperheads wearing members only jackets who say stuff like "put on 'led zep iv,' man--works every time"...but the feeling is still there. phoebe cates weighed heavily on my sexual psyche after this one.
2. "sixteen candles" - the first of the john hughes teen movies, depicting me and my high school chums as cuddly yet wacky cherubs falling in like with the world around us. anything can happen in a world with the thompson twins on the soundtrack, you know.
3. "the breakfast club" - ya got your basic nerd, jock, outlaw, priss and pariah--and by the end everyone's smooching. this was "our movie" at the time, and while the boomers tried to pooh-pooh it by calling it "the little chill," we knew it was cooler. and I thought ally sheedy was prettier before molly ringwald gussied her up.
4. "ferris bueller's day off" - perfectly describes going to high school in the '80s, with kids asleep at their desks bathed in drool. probably the finest moment I remember from that whole period was when ferris's friend cameron looks deep into the eyes of a seurat painting at the chicago art museum, while the smiths wail softly in the background. tortured youth, man, I loved it.
5. "repo man" - car fresheners, plates of shrimp and other non sequiturs that are as much fun to watch as it is to make your parents squirm. having the circle jerks as guest stars has got to count for something.
6. "say anything" - totally the right combination of bleakness and humor. the scene at the end, where the father accuses john cusack of hopeless mediocrity, was worth the price of a large buttered popcorn ($4.75).

7. "river's edge" - kids doing drugs, failing school, operating heavy machinery while intoxicated, and killing each other. not a great movie to take your first date to, but powerfully depressing for those who want to wallow.

8. "risky business" - most people don't see it, but this flick has exactly the same story line as dr. seuss's "the cat in the hat," only with whores. i guess the message here is that your parents are far stupider than even you thought they were.

9. "boyz 'n the hood" - pretty eerie, all of those nice, well-kept houses in south central, the very same cleaver-esque homes my folks grew up in down there. it's amazing that one person my age can make it out, let alone make such a cool movie.

10. "slacker" - to me, this is the best and most sublime treatment of directionless young folks there is, and it doesn't have any themes or morals to staple-gun to your forehead. no story line and no swelling soundtrack to give you those warm fuzzy feelings, just a beautifully orchestrated day in the life. i'd like to go to a bar and do shots with richard linklater.

***2boomers
>maybe if more older people saw these films they wouldn't treat your generation so badly.

***crasher
>if they saw them they might treat us worse.

In between movies, he watches TV programming, but not exactly as yuppie producer-writers might intend. Apart from one or two favorite shows, TV is, to him, mostly a wondrous font of games. Maybe he'll invite friends over to watch vapid *Love Boat* reruns, assigning each guest one celebrity character and making that guest take a chug every time that character utters a line. Or he'll watch *Beverly Hills 90210* to compare notes on what to wear and what lines are cool. With friends or solo, he'll spend an hour or two playing zap-TV, switching from channel to channel like a control-room editor,

Number of times key words appeared in three N.W.A. albums:

I	426
you	351
motherfucker	194
bitch/ho	161
police	61

Source: *Spin* magazine

On my ideal vacation, I would like very much to . . .

	age 18–29	age 30–49	difference
go to a national park	42%	58%	– 16%
see mountains and lakes	66%	74%	– 8%
stay in one place	30%	36%	– 6%
go to a U.S. city	32%	29%	+ 3%
be active and sightsee	58%	49%	+ 9%
go on a Caribbean cruise	80%	59%	+ 21%

Source: Gallup Poll (1991)

punishing the slightest on-air stupidity with a flick of a thumb. He'll tune in to Fox (median viewer age: mid-twenties) ahead of the networks (median viewer age: early forties), less from any sense of taste than from a sense of absurdist humor.

As she sees it, life is like a big cartoon. Little surprise that, on Saturdays, this twentysomething will get up early to watch the same cartoon shows she watched as a kid. She tunes in faithfully to Fox's *The Simpsons* and Nickelodeon's *Ren & Stimpy*—anti-Disney characters whose eyes are bigger than their brains, and whose most interesting noises don't come from their mouths. Traditional satire and corny humor doesn't ring her funnybell. To make her laugh, comedy has to

Would you say that it is very important to . . .

	age 18-29	age 30+	difference
work for the betterment of society?	58%	70%	– 12%
follow a strict moral code?	53%	62%	– 9%
have a nice home and car?	44%	40%	+ 4%
have an exciting, stimulating life?	63%	46%	+ 17%

Source: 1989 Gallup Poll

blam through a tough outer shell: It has to be beyond exaggeration, totally un-PC, and full of stupid characters, pointless plot pivots, and ridiculous cultural connections. "Firehouse Bob" scenes of self-destruction. Def Jam jabs at total incompetence—in government, on the job, in family life. *Men On* swipes at gays, women, and ethnics that she'd be crucified for if she dared to utter herself. Comedy Channel coverage of political conventions. MTV technoparodies. *Saturday Night Live* jokes without punch lines. Something pop but overdone—like *Batman* logos on McDonalds Fries, or *Malcolm X* potato chips—can be very funny. So can going to a concert to see a rapper holding a baby pacifier in one hand and an Uzi machine gun in another.

He likes writers and musicians his age who revel somewhere around the furthest boundaries of modern American culture. His reading taste runs to social ephemera—fantasy fiction, acid lampoons, zany fun books, cataloguey pop culturamas. His musical taste is a combination of the centrifugal and the gravitational. On the one

Usually, it's got to be something just wacked-out and interesting and different and fresh. This generation, if you want to get their attention, you're going to have to blast it wide open.

Bob Rice, ad copywriter

All of a sudden, from Tarzana, California, to Tarrytown, New York, everyone with a teenage daughter was wondering: "Is she one?" A Valley Girl, that is. If she was from a fairly well-to-do family and between the ages of 13 and 17, chances are she was. If her passions were shopping, popularity, pigging out on junk food, and piling on cosmetics, the answer probably was, "Fer shurr." If her speech was almost unintelligible, the verdict could only be, "Totally." Particularly if she pronounced the word "toe-dully."

New York Times (1982)

hand, some of his favorite musical groups stay away from the high-tone mainstream, leave The Big Issues alone, and produce studio-made technopop sounds that bubble with imaginative synthesis. Their songs aren't singalongable and often aren't even performable live. He likes rap, his generation's only original genre, although (and partly because) he knows it might set the standard as the meanest music ever written. He likes "alternative" and "progressive" rock, and heavy metal, now fusing with rap in a transracial genre of alienation. The farthest-out edge of a 13er's musical taste hits occasional dead-ends, and other times pushes further out into frontiers leading from bad to who-knows-what. But our Walkman-wearing, CD-playing 13er has a more traditional side to his taste. His collection includes everything from New Wave jazz to reggae, from acoustic revival to a capella voicestras, many of which are creations of young performers trying to get somewhere interesting by retracing the steps and undoing the excesses of those who came before.

For a 13er teen, MTV videos provide surrogates for the *Hit Parade* countdowns familiar to earlier generations: They create a shared musical experience for people her age. At an average of three seconds between edits, MTV has enough self-contained zapping to satisfy her thumb at its twitchiest. Whether watching Nirvana throw their bodies at speakers or rappers dance across *Baby's Got Back* landscapes modeled after human posteriors, a 13er can always count on MTV to indulge her visual impatience, absurdist humor, and alienation from an elder-built society. She watches MTV for only an average of 12 minutes at a time, but those are high-intensity minutes that leave indelible memories.

Ask a 13er to show you his favorite music, and he might not turn on MTV, but instead take you to the best garage band in his own neighborhood. To him, that music is *real*, authentic, unfiltered. Once fame strikes and a hot band gets pop-anointed, the question arises in a young fan's mind whether that band is now selling out, more interested in pushing twenty-dollar T-shirts than in making authentic sounds. (Hey, it's great they're making money, but it doesn't have to be my money!) By the time that band hits platinum, they're already history—among the youth cognoscenti, at least. So this generation never develops its own equivalent of Elvis, the Beatles, or Simon and Garfunkel. U2 is the closest anybody has gotten, and that's not very close. (Most people over 40 still associate the alphanumeric "U2" with Francis Gary Powers, not Bono Vox.) Lollapalooza is the closest they've gotten to Woodstock, and few elders even know what it is.

Thirteener music has real trouble cracking the consciousness of older generations the way G.I., Silent, and Boom music once did. As hot groups rise and fall in reputation, as "bootleg" tapes proliferate, and as video asserts itself as the dominant driving force of rock, "Top 40" stations (and lists) evaporate. Since 13er-oriented songs seldom make "classic rock" or "adult contemporary" radio play lists, it has become extremely difficult for Boomers-on-up to stay current with 13er musical trends. Not many bother trying.

Thirteeners *like* their culture and resent elder criticism of it. Yes, some will say, it doesn't approach what Boomers had two decades ago. That's often just a self-effacing answer to elders, as if to say "Sure it's garbage, whatever you say." But others defend their 13erama as extraordinarily diverse, technologically advanced, and capable in its odd way of giving comfort to kids who grew up too fast in a world grown too complex. It's their carnival culture—and, in the '90s, it's helping 13ers to find their elusive generational core.

>22. Trying to Strip Things Down and Simplify

Imagine yourself as an older visitor wandering through a college dorm, glancing at memorabilia on walls, floors, shelves, and tables. Sometimes you see a bare ensemble of nearly nothing. Mostly, you find what students might describe as stream-of-consciousness stuff that represents their life. There won't be many works of art, just collages of a zillion cut-up things. Retro tapestries. Deadhead knick-knacks. A U2 Amnesty International concert bulletin. Posters of R.E.M. and various alternative bands. Cards from overseas friends on various trips. Cute family photos. Plus countless guitars, amps, and high-tech gizmos lying around.

Looking closer, you find a number of crazy little icons that bring to mind the 1970s. Nothing related to any of the countless "isms"

I was in this mode of trying to strip things down and simplify . . . . I had a desire to clean out.

Steven Soderbergh, film director, describing his mood before making *sex, lies and videotape*

I cannot stand stories that lament the emptiness of pop culture, TV, fast-food. No one needs to read a story to learn this.

Debra Spark, *20 Under 30* (book)

"Man! Forget the '70s! We're the youth of the '90s! This is our decade, man! We shape the future. You've gotta stop living in the past! Say—mind if I borrow this 'Dead' tape?" "Yeah—when you return my Hendrix album!"

Jeff Shesol, *Thatch* (book)

you remember from that era—but junky things, ugly things, ranging from the tacky to the moronic. Not a grand memento of the feminist movement—just some bald Barbie doll hanging from a doorknob, a Kiss LP cover, or an old *People* magazine with John Travolta or Olivia Newton-John on the cover. Not a photo of Planet Earth from space—just some dog-eared poster of R2D2 or C3PO, Farrah Fawcett or Cheryl Tiegs, David or Shaun Cassidy, Leif Garrett or Scott Baio. Not a *Whole Earth Catalog*—just a lava lamp, a flowered pillow, a Pacer ad, a *Flintstones* toothbrush, or an *Incredible Hulk* lunch pail. While older generations link their '70s-era memories to the vast causes, great events, and theme-setting books of that decade, 13ers remain bonded to its detritus, to the throwaway tokens left over from a decade of throwaway children.

Of all that '70s junk, of all that 13er childhood salvage, the most treasured icon might well be something Brady.

The Brady Bunch is one bit of the great American culturama that 13ers have elevated to the status of generational hymnal. The show originally ran from 1969 to 1974. From the mid-'70s through the mid-'80s, old Brady episodes appeared twice a day all over the country. Since then, it's been a staple on cable. Thirteener fans are quick to describe the show as inane, but admit they're driven to watch it out of some herd instinct, like penguins flapping their way home. *The Brady Bunch* depicts a widow and widower, each with three children, who get together and form a happy family unit. Their problems, always little ones, get neatly solved in 22 minutes (plus commercials). On circa-'90s campuses, with Boomer professors lecturing them about political correctness—or off in today's urban world, where hard-laboring youths face hopeless complexities and low wages, America's 20- to 30-year-olds can ease their minds by escaping to that simple little show.

The Bradys were of a piece with other large and happy TV families of the 1970s: *The Waltons*, *The Partridge Family*, and the families on *Eight Is Enough* and *Little House on the Prairie*. All of them had a powerful appeal to little kids. In an era when families were ungluing, adults looked incompetent, and kids felt alone and unimportant, these shows offered an imaginary world where families were regluing, adults got things done, and kids felt part of something. Amidst all the social and family chaos of the '70s, they provided an unremittingly wholesome—and simple—cultural artifact for kids.

SOME DAYS IT TOOK *HOURS* TO GET DRESSED . . .

/ 193

Whatever was then happening in their own private sphere, 13ers could subliminally fantasize about being just like the Bradys.

To the 13ers' Silent parents, the '70s were a decade of catharsis, a time when they felt personal releases (what Gail Sheehy called *Passages*) and discovered postmodernism, multiculturalism, decentralization, multilateralism, and countless other polysyllabic adult bliss machines. In *Future Shock*, the book that keynoted the decade, Alvin Toffler sounded the Silent trumpet for an "ad hocracy" stressing complexity over simplicity, participation over authority, process over result. A decade later, Tom Peters's peers were clearly *Thriving on Chaos*—and, in *Megatrends*, John Naisbitt lovingly chronicled his generation's success in transforming America into a more decentralized, complicated, high-speed, therapeutic society.

Yet where the Silent grew up feeling an overweening center to American life, 13ers grew up feeling no center at all. Were a 13er to read those three Silent theme-setting books today, she might suffer a little *Past Shock* and conclude that, by *Surviving Amid Chaos*, she and her friends set a few *Microtrends* of their own. It's one thing to reach

I collect young artists that I like, just because I think they're good, not because some museum tells me they are.

Perry Farrell, singer, Jane's Addiction

The game ended. Alec wanted to go home, but once again his father was bending low over the table and breaking the rack. Sound pierced the room for an instant. The balls scattered, some careening sharply off the bumpers. Alec watched their movement and thought again of the science film he had seen, of destruction theory, of how the flower had split apart into millions of particles. The table seemed to grow brighter as he stood there looking at it, as if it too might burst apart at any second. And he felt suddenly as though it was happening all around him, the coming apart of things.

John Burnham Schwartz, *Bicycle Days* (book)

***crasher

>jesus, what did you guys do? get a ladder and look inside the 4th floor dorm room of some ucla english major? put a hidden mike in the flower arrangement at the pi phi house at carolina? you scare me sometimes.

***2boomers

>you wouldn't be reading this if everything we said came with a long footnote. but all this is relentlessly researched, we promise you.

***crasher

>want another list to add to your already-bursting knowledge of our culture?

***2boomers

>that depends.

***crasher

>I entitle this list "the top 10 seminally formative rock albums of our era that, thank god, you won't hear on dinosaur rock stations," and believe me, my housemates fought over this one for three hours. I narrowed the list down to the albums that are the most important, nostalgia and ground-breaking-wise.

***2boomers

>careful, crasher, you're slipping into boomer territory. who decides what's "important"?

***crasher

>why, I do, of course! you guys can't have all the pompous, overgeneralizing fun!
1. "the knack"- I put this one on because if it weren't for "my sharona" in 1979, we'd still be listening to "le freak" and "boogie oogie oogie." this song cut through the flaccid am disco top 40 like a buzzsaw through butter, and the lyrics are nice and pornographic, just like we like 'em.
2. soundtracks to "grease" and "xanadu" - two olivia newton-john favorites, one with john travolta and the other with elo... what more could you ask for? "summer lovin'" and "magic" put me right back on the roller rink at skate town, usa, clutching a soggy fresca and a copy of "dy-no-mite!" magazine.
3. duran duran--"rio" - these guys were the absolute coolest when I was in 9th grade, and their hair defied most of newton's gravitational laws. anyone who doesn't get a little misty-eyed hearing "hungry like the wolf" probably wasn't breathing in 1983.
4. ac/dc--"back in black" - angus young for president, man. such charisma!
5. r.e.m.--"murmur" - out of nowhere came these guys from athens, georgia, and suddenly everyone and his cousin has a garage band. they proved to the world that you didn't have to have a ph.d. from juilliard to write great pop songs.
6. the police--"synchronicity" - it seemed like a whole year was filled with police memorabilia, and sting promptly became the literary (and oh so sexy) patriarch of rock and roll. they broke up when I was in high school, but not before legions of new

wave teenage philosophers dog-eared all the books by jung and nabokov at the library.

7. grandmaster flash and the furious five--"the message" - when I first heard this song on my car stereo, I thought I was seeing god in a 1982 chevy citation. this was the first rap song to make it big, and it caught most of us white kids off guard. "did you hear that?" my brother asked. "he used the 'n' word!"

8. the smiths--"the queen is dead" - right at a time when most of my friends were becoming sort of tragic and nihilistic, along came the smiths, to put it all to music for them. when morrissey sang "i wear black on the outside, 'cause black is how I feel on the inside," he doomed pastel fabrics for those under 30 forever.

9. public enemy--"fear of a black planet" - it's not that rapper chuck d. is brilliant, it's not that the stuff he sings about is real and frightening, it's not that you can dance the hell out of it--it's that it scares the crap out of older boneheads who have no idea what they're talking about. put this one on in the car and drive through nice neighborhoods, and you'll see them drop their hoses and run for the tool shed.

10. jane's addiction--"nothing's shocking" - these guys sum up all that is good with alternative music, thinking, and lifestyles. perry farrell and friends gave us three loud, rapturous, transcendent rock albums and then bolted--some goofy schlock magazine called them the "led zeppelin of the twentysomething generation." I would take that as an insult.

***2boomers
>hey, crasher, how come michael jackson and madonna didn't make your list?

***crasher
>because I was the only person at franklin jr. high that didn't have "thriller," and please don't get me into the madonna fight I just had with my housemates.

***2boomers
>excellent taste. but do you really think any 45-year-old would ever buy, much less listen to, any of your ten albums?

***crasher
>you have two choices: either you can get used to it now, or you can wait until you are doddering, incontinent septuagenarians puttering around in your rickety old volvos, and when your trembling hand reaches for the radio to turn to your beloved classic rock station, gone will be simon and garfunkel. gone will be peter, paul and mary, the eagles and janis joplin. you'll be blasted with our classic rock, which will be stuff like this, and our victory will be complete.

***2boomers
>yeah, over some aging boom producer's dead body.

***crasher
>whatever it takes, boys.

Time says we have no "original youth culture" of our own. It insults us when it dismisses our music as retro, pointing to the plethora of remakes of '60s and '70s songs as proof of our lack of originality. If punk, new wave, new age, house, new jack swing and rap sound to *Time* like Herman's Hermits, I have no defense.

Emily Posby, recent graduate, Yale College, in the *New York Times*

Two kids (in unison): "Radical grub!"
Adult: "Groovy chips, eh boys?"
Two kids (to each other): "What'd he say?"

TV ad for potato chips

When one compares them musically and lyrically with the powerful pop music of the late 1980s and '90s, pop music that encapsulates the real emotions of the times, such as that by Public Enemy, the Jesus and Mary Chain, the Replacements, and Nirvana, much of that written by the Beatles and Bob Dylan looks embarrassingly self-indulgent.

Halle Winkler

To superserve the 48 million baby busters age 18 to 29:

- Stage singles parties or advertise singles connections; promote safe sex.
- Institute a job line or bank; hold job fairs.
- Give away exotic trips or more leisure time.
- Focus public affairs programming on the environment . . . .
- Advertise the value, ease, simplicity, and practicality of clients' products.

radio marketing bulletin

midlife in a world where barriers are falling and time is accelerating. It's quite another to begin your life there.

From the 13er perspective, Silent-style postmodernism pushed America from institutional cohesion toward the kind of atomization and fragmentation in which all the pieces keep getting smaller, going faster, losing direction. A society in which everybody is liberated from everything but interlinked with everywhere, in touch with everyone, updated everyday. A society of easily broken barriers in which behavior has to get ever more extreme to have any shock value. A society of instant replay and relitigation in which nothing is final, negotiations repeat every second (what's my market worth now? now? now?), and network ratings are microcalibrated minute by minute. In such a world, young people feel like Max Headroom, stuck in a spinning spiral, stuttering for sound-bite answers and expected to say they love it. If there's a coup in Rwanda or a monsoon in Bangladesh or a bad harvest in Uruguay, it affects *you*—and must immediately be added to the list of 10,000 world problems the Union of International Associations can declare in dire need of solution.

To all of which, 13ers want to say: Enough, please. Chill. Instead of opening more things up, start filtering a few things out. This most ethnically and culturally diverse young generation in living memory is starting to push America back toward a simpler core.

Examples abound. In a 13er culture where overproduced zap-video and high-tech special effects are still king, a growing 13er minority is bucking the trend by filming, singing, and writing works that veer back toward minimalism. Kids still line up to see the $100 million high-tech blockbusters, but 13er-made movies like *Slacker*, *Met-*

ropolitan, or *sex, lies and videotape* use eyelike cameras to follow people in and out of casual conversations. In music, the down-and-dirty lyrics of rap and heavy metal keep selling, but increasingly share shelf space with genres in which words and themes are low-tech afterthoughts—muffled, ordinary, or absent altogether—as though young songwriters and performers have grown exhausted about the very notion of giving their songs any message.

In 13er literature, fantasy writers remain big, but young authors with blunter (Bret Easton Ellis) and simpler (Pam Houston) styles put the most basic elements of the young-adult world in the sharpest possible relief. Their emphasis is on Anglo-Saxon monosyllables; on nouns and verbs; on setting scenes without shadow or nuance, as though stage lights were always glaring; and, especially, on pop culture. In nonfiction their prose style brings to mind *USA Today*. 13ers use prose that is spare and unforgiving, with just a twist of irony. Today's youth magazines are trim and blunt, and adult comic books are enjoying a renaissance.

In fashion, the garish and gaudy still sell, but compete for rack space with a more utilitarian-industrial look that emphasizes plaids, flannels, and cottons. Hundred-dollar Reeboks and Nikes are still hot items, but clumsy old thirty-dollar Chuck Taylor high-tops are the latest fad on college campuses. Designer boutiques get their traffic, but the true 13er clothes-shopping experience is to head for The Gap or, alternatively, to buy wack slacks, fuzz, plats, and kickers and go for the "grunge" look. The latest styles draw crowds, but the foremost selling point for 13er clothes is to be practical, to be durable, not to require constant washing or pressing, and (above all) to be cheap.

In food, the exotic and the ethnic maintain their appeal, but 13ers are moving toward a functional style of eating. They take microwaves and Big Macs for granted. Food has to be cheap, quick, filling, with a basic taste. The best bet is some preprepared food that offers a meal for pennies like macaroni and cheese (a *Wayne's World* favorite). Jolt Cola's double-dose sugar and caffeine. (Why, 13ers wonder, would anyone but a Boomer waste fifty cents on a sugar-free, caffeine-free, color-free cola?) You won't find much Dijon mustard or radiccio on 13er tables. If any food item smacks of symbolic gesture, of consumption for the sake of making a point—*forget it!*

After lunch, 13ers care about trash disposal. That's both ironic and

Look back at those junior high school photos of yourself—no doubt you're wearing either a cowl-neck sweater, aviator glasses, and Farrah wings, or a Jack Daniels T-shirt, a Scott Baio haircut, and painter's pants. Like Patty Hearst, you probably weren't yourself in the '70s.

Pagan Kennedy, "Ring My Bell-Bottoms," in the *Voice Literary Supplement*

In the 1960s, when I was a student, we used to say "cool it" to encourage calmness when all hell breaks loose. The expression has changed slightly; the word is now "chill" (another usage derived from street talk), usually spoken as a command . . . . "Chill" seems a useful and even instructive term. It puts the ice on humiliation, muffles it in the comfort of jargon, helps the sufferer to feign a bit of indifference . . . .

Richard Bernstein, "Youthspeak," in the *New York Times*

fitting, because the packaged fast food they prefer produces far more paper and plastic debris than do more natural, cooked-from-scratch meals. But they hate garbage, because it further messes up a world that, as they see it, is already garbagey enough. They take recycling and other day-to-day envirodeeds for granted, and despise peers who leave little messes for other people to clean up.

In 1990, Alvin Toffler published *PowerShift*, a prophecy of a hyperventilating future in which the trends of the 1970s and '80s will race ahead like a runaway exponent, a future where the speed and complexity of everything will keep accelerating beyond presently imaginable limits. In the Tofflerian universe, only the most inexhaustible can expect to thrive. To the aging Silent generation, that's a thrilling dream. To young 13ers, it brings to mind their worst nightmare: an infinite extrapolation of trends that started in the '70s, the decade in which (say the authors of *Stuck in the Seventies*), 113 things "screwed up" their childhood world.

The very thought of lots more elder-imposed complexities, entanglements, interdependencies, expert committees, due processes, polyculturalisms, therapies, and lawsuits is enough to make a 13er sneak back to her one-room efficiency, put a Pop-tart in the microwave, and bake her brains watching morning-to-night reruns of (what else?) *The Brady Bunch*. Sure, she recently learned that the Brady dad turned out to be gay, and that mom dated one of the sons. (That just makes the family all the more authentic, doesn't it?) But back in the '70s, when the Bradys mattered most, they were everything she ever imagined a family could be.

>23. The Bottom-Line Generation

Madonna. Michael Jackson. Spike Lee. Cartoonists Matt Groening, Bill Watterson, and Berke Breathed. Ice T. The creators of Def Jam rap, of *Max Headroom*, of the *Teenage Mutant Ninja Turtles*, of *Ren & Stimpy*, of *Batman Returns*, and of Fox TV entertainment programming.

What do all these people have in common? First, they are important forces shaping the culture and reputation of the 13th Generation. Second, they produce images of dark comedy, frenzy, physicality, alienation, and low self-esteem—all of which resonate with 13ers. Third, *they are not 13ers*. No, they are all in their early to middle thirties, all part of that final wave of Boomers, born in the mid- to late 1950s, who pushed social pathologies way up (and SAT scores way down) just in time for the first 13ers to step in and take the blame.

These "Madonna-wave" Boomers are the leading cultural mentors for 13ers—much as young Silent Generation songsters like Paul Simon and Bob Dylan once were for Boomers (though to very different effect). Whatever today's Madonnaish thirtysomethings do with their sociocultural palette, 13ers are the ones left sitting there with the paint covering their faces. That paint provides an opaque generational veneer that accurately shows what many 13ers are like today, but tells little about what will someday emerge when that veneer gets chipped away.

To find out what personality lies underneath, waiting to be revealed, we have to discover what's going on in those realms of day-to-day life that are already dominated by 13ers themselves. When we do, we find a generation in relentless pursuit of the bottom lines of life.

With each passing year, the 13th Generation is deepening its stamp on American society. Look around in your daily life and see them as Particle Man, single-purpose tools for getting jobs done. If they look disconnected or lopsided, they're simply focusing mind and body on the job at hand, applying that uniquely 13er ability to safeguard themselves from the chaos around them. They have the hunter's gift of being patient to the point of numbness—then striking quickly and decisively. They do outrageous things without carrying emotional or ideological baggage, without pondering the symbolism of it all.

Picture the urban Speedo corps. The bicycle messengers, decked in Spandex, bristling with mirrors, walkie-talkies, and spray-cans for defense against attack dogs, breaking every traffic rule to deliver packages of memos to skyscraper honchos who never imagine how many near-accidents almost sent those memos flying into traffic. The cops-on-a-bike, shrieking out mock siren-like wails while pedaling to the most routine of calls, mixing a little fun with the danger. The pizza jobbers, rushing quick bites to distracted yuppies, ducking new regulations prohibiting their companies from guaranteeing 30-minute deliveries. It's the standard 13er predicament: do the job slow and get no business; do it fast and get punished.

Picture the Richmeisters in the copy room. Temps with dreary jobs, eight dollar an hour wages, no career ladder, no benefits, zero job security—and a crazy sense of humor. When they don't have to focus on what they're doing, they feel totally free to play, to bring their friends in on a joke. They're experts at disconnecting their real selves from their job. When they hear some wiseguy in the Japanese Parliament harp on them for spending Fridays planning and Mondays discussing their weekends, their attitude is: Hey, Toyota-san, get a life.

Picture the national nerd network. Self-proclaimed hackers, phreaks, and pirates gulping down Cokes, munching HoHos, clicking keys and flicking disks, delving into their dungeons-and-dragons world. To what end? Maybe they're linking up with some big new board, or cracking a hot new game, or sneaking into some county files and shaving some traffic-ticket points off a friend's driver's license. Inside this modem-connected realm of amber and black, complexities constantly give way to shortcuts, and elder concepts of privacy and fair process matter not. Personal messages pop up for everyone to see, opening up the sender to anyone who's out there and to anything that might happen next. If a rule doesn't make sense, nobody follows it. If rules are absent where rules are necessary, some Legion of Doom will invent them, and the rest will enforce them in the unforgiving court of network reputation.

Picture the Air Jordan sports stars. Emperor-gladiators, strutting in bright lights in colosseums full of yuppies putting thumbs up or thumbs down. Crowding the limos on the way in and out, picture the anonymous losers of asphalt hoop- (or pigskin-) lotto, grasping for icons from the celebrated winners. Money—not civic loyalty—rules this bread-and-circus athletica. The next year, half the team might be gone, and half the fans will wear the badge of a rival. Winner or loser, everybody has a logo on his jacket—the only difference being that

The world of computer hacking is a lot like Mexico: There's no middle class. There are a million little kids screwing around with their modems, trying to snitch long-distance phone codes, trying to swipe pirated software . . . . And then there are the heavy dudes. The players. The Legion of Doom.

Bruce Sterling, "The Hackers Who Came in from the Cold," in *Details*

———

There's something about making a tangible product, something you can put your arms around.

Harvey Packer, recent graduate, Wharton School of Business

***2boomers
>where are all your crasher friends tonight?

***crasher
>what? it's monday night. you're lucky you have me to talk to. it ain't the most hoppin' night on this network, y'see.

***2boomers
>so all your friends are watching tv?

***crasher
>no, but if you caught us ten years ago, you would have been right on target.

***2boomers
>so what do you watch these days?

***crasher
>I watch random cable things. but it's not like the old days, when my entire week was defined by network television. we were talking about this today, and we came up with the most battle-scarred list of them all. once again it took me forever to get everyone's opinions from turning into popcultural warfare over this stuff.

***2boomers
>what could it possibly be?

***crasher
>"the top 10 tv shows that irrevocably shaped our shattered thought processes":
1. "the brady bunch" - this one has become a natural phenomenon--old faithful will erupt, the rains will come to india, the big one will hit los angeles, and the "brady bunch" will be on after school. it's as simple and beautiful as that.
2. "sesame street" - before I got out into the harsh, uncaring world, jim henson had me convinced that the whole world was free of racism, sexism, and pollution, and that I could probably count to twelve with relative ease. that was also the last time most of us saw hispanics, blacks, and white folks singing anything together.
3. "the dukes of hazzard" - bo and luke (along with starsky and hutch) made me ask my dad why he didn't weld his car door shut. this may have been one of our first "of course it sucks, that's why I'm watching it" shows.
4. "the shazam/isis hour" - this one was so cool, and it represents all the other great saturday morning shows: "grape ape," "hong kong phooey," "scooby do," and "h.r. puff'n' stuff," to name but a few. also, the only reason I still know my "7 times table" and how congress works is because of "schoolhouse rock." I can't wait until someone who can sing "we the people" actually gets elected.
5. "the a-team" - this was the kind of show that was so guilelessly inane that my mom would get physically ill whenever she saw my friends and me glued to the set. I would

try to explain to her that murdoch and b.a. "bad attitude" brackus (mr. t) were simply metaphors for an american justice system gone awry, but I don't think she bought it.

6. "mork and mindy" - I was in love with pam dawber, and all the girls in algebra were in love with robin williams. later on, I started to understand mork's sexual innuendoes and discovered that they lived in a really trippy college town!

7. "happy days" - speaking of spinoffs, this was the father of them all. you should have heard the buzz in the third grade lunchroom when the fonz tried to jump the cars with his motorcycle. in fact, with "happy days," "laverne and shirley," "grease," and "american graffiti," I can't remember having much of a '70s. it seems like I lived the '50s instead.

8. "the love boat/fantasy island" night - yes, for two hours on saturday night, you and your slumber party guests could be assured of having the best time aaron spelling could offer. first, you could take a pleasure cruise with captain stubing, gopher, and his other lobotomized pals while they immersed themselves in the romantic lives of poor actors in the sunsets of their careers. then ricardo montalban and herve villechaize would submerge your 10-year-old brain further into the netherworld of modern american teleplay. I'd be hard pressed to find anything more fun these days without serious chemical alteration.

9. "roots" - this was "required watching," much like "the day after" and many super bowls thereafter. I was living in iowa, playing on swingsets and well fed on corn, when this series hit me over the head like a plank. I still have nightmares about the slave ship scenes, and for the first time I felt really guilty for being so privileged. such p.c. thoughts for a 9-year-old!

10. "the simpsons" - of course, we didn't grow up on it, but thank god somebody else is.

***2boomers
>wait a minute. what about "melrose place" and "beverly hills 90210" and "class of '96" and all that?

***crasher
>those shows aren't about anyone I know. my friends have lives that don't translate at all into successful sitcom ideas. we are all conversation and very little action. we'd probably make one hell of a funny radio show.

***2boomers
>so what are those tv shows about?

***crasher
>beautiful, preening, pretty, smart-ass twentysomethings with lots of money and beer-company-endorsed angst, i.e., nobody I would want to know. this whole "ain't this a cruel world for us busters on our own" schtick was obviously conceived by some overzealous network exec who read one too many copies of sassy magazine and wanted to sell time to the gap. forget it, boys, we've got less important things to do.

I wonder whether, 27 years ago, Kathy's mom thought about what she'd be doing today— battling "Ice" with a pugil stick.

announcer, "American Gladiators," describing 27-year-old Kathy Mollica, Costa Mesa, CA

I don't know anything about Angola, except that Angola's in trouble.

Basketball forward Charles Barkley, on the eve of the U.S. "Dream Team"'s Olympic match against Angola

PARIS, May 26—John McEnroe didn't lose at the French Open today simply because he is older and slower and tamer than he used to be. He lost because a bam-bam player of the younger generation showed him no mercy.

Washington Post on McEnroe's (age 33) loss to Nicklas Kulti (age 21)

the winners might get paid for it and the losers might get killed over it. A pro sports championship can mean big money flying like beer foam over thousands of youngsters, from the MVPs to the on-line bettors to the kids with card collections. And, for others, an easy excuse to get wild.

Picture the troops of Desert Shield and Storm. Leave it to 60-year-olds to James-Baker their way through the complexities of the "peace process." These young men (and America's first-ever combat women) will step in to do the one-syllable jobs when the process fails. Sweat. Hide. Move. Hunt. Hit. Kill. Leave. Ask them a question, and you'll hear no discourse about whether the war is just. Instead, you'll hear how they're getting the job done, and what it feels like to do it. They're totally focused, with few signs of the disabling personal entanglements that characterized the sensitive Silent in Korea or the spaced-out Boom in Vietnam. For the parents of 13er troops, olive drab was once a symbol of repression—but for 13ers themselves, desertwear has become the symbol of small-group teamwork, of platoons that care more about each member than many of their families or schools ever did.

Where history shows Silent foot soldiers having fought to a stalemate, and Boomers having been the only battlefield losers in U.S. history, Desert Stormers ripped through a once-mighty enemy in 100 lightning hours. Then they shipped out. Maybe a few fiftyish generals got snookered into not finishing Saddam for good, but nobody can say the Stormers didn't get their assigned jobs totally done. Afterwards, they became CNN-style instant heroes—*briefly*. They got scant benefits for it—and got mustered out to a wretched young-adult economy. A year later, most of the elder talk about them was of sexism, bad behavior, and celebrations that went way too far. Big surprise. Even so, the Gulf War stands out as a positive collective moment for a generation that has had precious few.

Finally, when the job (or war) is done, picture 13ers returning to their *Melrose Place*, without the upscale address and without the Hollywood glitz. It could be anywhere: a singles condo, a club, a campus dorm, an inner-city street corner, an Army rec room. It's a place to which they can retreat, shut down every cranial neuron that thinks about problems, and splash around awhile with friends. A place where they can avoid worldly realities, be themselves, and enjoy a little un-hung-up fun. A place where kids once pressured to grow up

"NO SWEAT. I USED TO PLAY THIS AT CHUCK E. CHEESE!"

fast can find a little young-adult respite and slow down. A place where the daughters and sons of divorce can band together and invent their own fully functional surrogate families. A place where a generation raised to distrust everything can build small circles of total trust.

Do 13ers symbolize national decline, as so many elders fear? Think again. Strip away that Madonna-wave Boom veneer, look carefully at those Speedos and Richmeisters and hackers and Air Jordans and Desert Stormers, and what you'll find is a generation that knows—and has got—what it takes to win.

These days, America's greatest need is to find new ways to clear out the social and political underbrush and get some things done. Others don't yet see it, and not many young people yet sense it themselves, but this Particle Man generation brings a bag of savvy tricks its elders lack. In some ways, this is a bad generation—but so too is it a necessary generation for a society in dire need of some serious survival lessons.

There are bikers among us who are less than ideal. The majority of messengers, however, are hard-working, intelligent, exotic, funny and fun-loving people . . . . What people see as reckless riding is really the art of survival in these streets that became a jungle well before the idea of bicycle messengers was conceived.

D. Wayne Thomas, bicycle messenger, Washington, DC

I didn't think about being the first woman. I thought about doing my best, and concentrating on the puck.

Manon Rheaume, 20, goaltender for the NHL Tampa Bay Lightning, who became the first woman to play in a major professional sports league

Sometimes I think that the person who said winning isn't everything never won anything.

TV ad for athletic shoes

>24. Dead, Famous Wild People

On the cover of its July 16, 1990 issue, *Time* magazine labeled 13ers America's newest "lost" generation. In a twentysomething feature later that year, the *New York Times* described them as "a lost generation, an army of aging Bart Simpsons, possibly armed and dangerous." On everything from Day-Glo book jackets and CD rap labels to anticrime editorials and self-esteem manuals, the word "lost" keeps snapping back to zap this generation like a Nintendo blaster, a laser-guided smart bomb—or a hammering rabbit punch from the glove of Jack Dempsey.

The last time the word "lost" was attached to American youth was in the aftermath of World War I. Today's Atari-wave 13ers have only the dimmest personal memory of this "Lost Generation," the ex-flappers and veteran doughboys whom they vaguely recall from childhood as the burned-out old codgers of the 1960s and 1970s. But when they see them in old movies and newsreels, they know the label fits. Kinetic Lost as in Jimmy Cagney and Charlie Chaplin. Evil Lost as in Boris Karloff and Edward G. Robinson. Adventuresome Lost as in Humphrey Bogart and Douglas Fairbanks, Jr. Mischievous Lost as in Mae West and the Marx Brothers. Tough Lost as in "Give 'Em Hell" Harry Truman and "Blood and Guts" George Patton. In *18 Again*, 13ers can even get a few personal tips from nonagenarian George Burns about how the Jazz Age kids of his day got the job done.

On one side, take the young Lost Generation (born between 1883 and 1900) and line up all their barnstormers, jazzmen, admen, newsies, and rumrunners. On the other, take the 13th Generation (born between 1961 and 1981) and line up all their cyberpunks, rappers, Wall Streeters, telemarketers, and inner-city gangsters. Compare the two. What you'll find are enough parallels to persuade you that 13ers aren't alone—and that others have gone down a similar life cycle path before them.

Survey question: Who would rank among America's three greatest Presidents?

	George Washington	Franklin Roosevelt
teenagers	46%	21%
all adults	25%	41%

Source: The Gallup Organization, *America's Youth, 1977–1988*

For starters, take a look at the world in which the Lost Generation grew up as children. "Gay Nineties" America was an era of spiritual and ideological upheaval—of anarchist violence, agrarian populism, muckraking, race riots, and student missionary and settlement house movements—which gave birth, after the turn of the century, to the Bible Belt and the I.W.W., to Greenwich Village and the Women's Suffrage Crusade. It was an era of widespread substance abuse, when alcohol consumption rose rapidly and newly-popular drugs like *cannabis* (praised by doctors) and cocaine (back when Coke had the *real* thing) went entirely unregulated. It was an era of rising immigration, which reached flood tide during precisely the decades (the 1900s and '10s) when the young Lost entered the labor market. It was an era of prosperity mixed with a crisis of confidence—when America suddenly became aware of long-standing institutional failures, when "good government" became synonymous with committees and process, when urban wildness was blamed for destroying the family, and when Deweyesque educational reforms were all the vogue.

All this might sound familiar. But what about the kids themselves?

Were they, perhaps, just a wee bit "bad"? Yes, from the time they first hit their teens. Like 13ers, the young Lost grew up with a nasty reputation for crime and violence. Popular magazines featured stories like "Bad Boy of the Streets" and "Making Good Citizens Out of Bad Boys." From the decade just before to the decade just after 1900, the number of published articles on "juvenile delinquency" rose ten-fold. From 1900 to 1920, while the Lost came of age, America's homicide rate rose by 700 percent. By the time the murder binge peaked in the early 1930s—along with imprisonments and executions—the extralegal entrepreneurs of this generation had put the "roar" in the Roaring Twenties, matured into this century's most notorious crime kingpins, and become the principal objects of Prohibition-era "vice squads."

Were the Lost reputed to be a little dumb? Yes again. Like 13ers, they came right behind a generation that marked huge academic progress—but they showed little or no improvement themselves, from first birth cohort to last. When young Lost men took the first-ever I.Q. tests during World War I, the results shocked the nation by showing that half the draftees had a "mental age" of under 12. During the 1920s, what some called the "threat of the

Do sound bites swallow substance, as the critics say? Read Einstein's lips—"$E=mc^2$"—and a scientific revolution is born; the Ten Commandments—the Ten Sound Bites—and monotheism makes its debut. Jefferson pens "Life, Liberty, and the Pursuit of Happiness" and a sound bite is heard 'round the world.

Andrew Savitz and Mark Katz, "Sound Bites Have Teeth," in the *New York Times*

▬▬

As Pericles said to the Athenians, I really need another beer!

young man, *Opportunity Knocks* (film)

▬▬

That little dead dude?

response given by 15-year-old tennis star Jennifer Capriati, when a Parisian reporter asked her about Napoleon

▬▬

"Socrates!"
"Yeah, we know that name."
"Hey, look him up. It's under 'SOW-KRATES.'"
"Oh yeah, here. 'So-cra-tes: The only true wisdom consists of knowing that you know nothing.'"
"That's us, dude!"

Bill and Ted encountering Socrates, *Bill & Ted's Excellent Adventure* (film)

Are we living in the most exciting time in history?

YES	38.5%
NO	61.5%

Source: 1992 *Spin* magazine campus survey

feeble-minded" turned many older voters against foreign immigrants (then a code word for stammering young workers) and prompted an older psychologist, Henry Goddard, to invent technical terms like "moron," "idiot," and "imbecile" to identify every gradation of stupidity. By the time the Lost filled America's elder age brackets in the late 1960s, the educational gap between all adults over age 25 (who averaged 12.2 years of schooling) and all adults over age 65 (who averaged 8.7 years) was the largest ever measured.

Did they show a bent for self-destruction? Like 13ers, the Lost had unusually high suicide rates during their youth, higher than for any other child generation ever measured—until 13ers themselves came along. From youth forward, moreover, the Lost were more suicide-prone at every phase of life than were any of the next three generations—G.I., Silent, and Boom. In longitudinal surveys taken from the 1960s through the 1980s, Lost elders scored higher in "suspicion" and lower in "self-sentiment" than later-born G.I.'s did at the same age.

A yen for the buck? Like 13ers, the Lost gained an early passion for making (and spending) money. As children, they entered the cash labor market at a higher rate than any American generation before or since. Unsupervised by parents or government, they liked to work for themselves (as newsies, bootblacks, scavengers, messengers, cashboys, or piece-rate homeworkers)—and built America's first big child cash economy around candy stores and nickelodeons. These kids grew up glorifying self-sufficiency. The word "sweatshop" was coined *for* them, and the motto "It's Up to You!" was coined by them. Later on, as young adults during the 1920s, they resisted collective action in favor of independent entrepreneurship—resulting in a steep decline in union memberships. They became, as F. Scott Fitzgerald described them, "a new generation devoted more than the last to the fear of poverty and the worship of success."

Politically retrograde? Yes, so others told them. Coming of age, their women disappointed older suffragettes, and their men turned a deaf ear toward such older campus-touring radicals as Jack London and Upton Sinclair. "College students are more conservative than their professors," reported one disappointed organizer, "because they too often regard college as a back door to big business." As Fitzgerald afterwards observed, "The Jazz Age . . . had no interest at all in politics." Starting in the 1920s—after their newly-enfranchised young women infuriated midlife feminists by voting for Warren Harding—the Lost blossomed early into this century's most Republican-leaning generation.

The list of similarities goes on and on. Like 13ers, Lost kids had to grow up fast. "At 17, we were disillusioned and weary," recalled Malcolm Cowley. Like 13ers, they learned early that they had to be tough to survive, to flaunt the physical, to avoid showing fear. Like 13ers, they came of age with a reputation for shameless cynicism ("the Flapper of 1915," complained the older H.L. Mencken, "has forgotten how to simper; she seldom blushes; and it is impossible to shock her."). Like 13ers, their nomadic young men and garçonish women were drawn to cities, to markets, to risk, to the dizzying glamour of new technologies, to a frenetic, *Metropolis*-like pace. Like 13ers, they expected and received little help from government throughout their lives. And like 13ers, they didn't mind helping to protect the kids born after them (the G.I. Generation) from all the shocking labor, drug, and educational abuses that had shocked no one during their own youth.

The Lost even had their own Boomerlike nemesis to contend with. They knew what it felt like to be upstaged by an indulged "postwar" (in their case, post-Civil War) generation just older than themselves. These next-elders prided themselves on having come of age while the fires of spiritual discovery were still burning, and on being smarter and more culturally correct than those younger than themselves. By the time these next-elders reached midlife, their narcissism, pomposity, and moral zealotry were a blight on youth. Today's 13ers look up the age ladder and see yuppies and born-agains, Greenpeacers and ex-Weathermen, pro-lifers and feminists, William Bennett and Rush Limbaugh, Angela Davis and Tipper Gore. Yesterday's Lost looked up and saw Babbitts and Klansmen, missionaries and wobblies, prohibitionists and suffragettes, Andrew Volstead and H.L. Mencken, Emma Goldman and Jane Addams.

The Lost did not assume a generational identity until it had filled the twentysomething age bracket around the time of World War I. Their young men soon became memorialized by F. Scott Fitzgerald

---

Ancient history.
Artimese Williams, 17, student body president, Berkeley High, describing the Beatles

---

Compare and contrast Christopher Columbus's discovery of America and Doogie Howser's discovery of girls. What were the social and political implications of the two events for contemporary culture? Did their hairdos or clothing have anything to do with their ultimate success? Why or why not? How and how much? Who cares? Please discuss.

Zillions magazine, spoof on school essay questions

"I'm sorry. The notion of two people spending their entire lives together was invented by people lucky to make it to twenty without being eaten by dinosaurs. Marriage is obsolete."
"Dinosaurs are obsolete. Marriage is still around."

two recent college graduates, *St. Elmo's Fire* (film)

Right here, right now Watching the world wake up from history

"Right Here, Right Now," Jesus Jones (song)

The shows were broader, the buildings were higher, the morals were looser, and the liquor was cheaper; but all these did not really minister to much delight. Young people wore out early—they were hard and languid at twenty-one . . . the city was bloated, glutted, stupid with cakes and circuses, and a new expression, "O yeah?" summed up all the enthusiasm evoked by the announcement of the last super-skyscrapers.

F. Scott Fitzgerald (1896–1940)

The young men of this land are not, as they are often called, a "lost" race—they are a race that has never yet been discovered. And the whole secret, power, and knowledge of their own discovery is locked within them—they know it, feel it, have the whole thing in them—and they cannot utter it.

Thomas Wolfe (1900–1938)

My candle burns at both ends
It will not last the night

Edna St. Vincent Millay (1892–1950)

as *All the Sad Young Men* of a war that (elders feared) closed the book on western civilization. The actual "Lost Generation" tag was invented by Gertrude Stein and adopted by Ernest Hemingway in the beginning of *The Sun Also Rises*. But they had already earned their black-sheep reputation. Years before Eddie Rickenbacker buzzed the Kaiser's troops, and years before composer Virgil Thomson chose Paris "to starve where the food is good," those smug next-elders were already finding plenty they didn't like about these daredevil-but-smooth, hard-to-know young people.

In 1911, the fortyish Cornelia Comer—sounding exactly like a circa-1990 Boomer—penned an *Atlantic Monthly* "Letter to the Rising Generation" accusing them of "mental rickets and curvature of the soul," of a "culte du moi," of growing up "painfully commercialized even in their school days." While admitting that "you are innocent victims of a good many haphazard educational experiments," Comer asked "What excuse have you, anyhow, for turning out flimsy, shallow, amusement-seeking creatures?" Responding to Comer in the *Atlantic*'s next issue, 25-year-old Randolph Bourne defended his generation as a logical "reaction" to universal parental neglect. "The modern child from the age of ten is almost his own 'boss,'" he observed, adding that while "it is true that we do not fuss and fume about our souls, . . . we have retained from childhood the propensity to see through things, and to tell the truth with startling frankness."

Like Lost, like 13th. "The 'New Jack' philosophy," says the 29-year-old producer of the 1991 youth gang movie, "is to give it to you straight, no chaser. The tension that underlies much of our daily life is the rage of a generation left behind." In his answer to Comer, Bourne had said essentially the same thing.

The lesson of history is simple. Matching up 13ers with other generations in America's past, we can see that theirs is by no means the first to be regarded as "bad" almost from birth. Nor the first to mark a one-generation backstep in educational or economic progress. Nor the first to see their own lives in sharp relief against a world overburdened with phony

America's "Bad" Generations	Birth years
13th	1961–1981
Lost	1883–1900
Gilded	1822–1842
Liberty	1724–1741
Cavalier	1615–1647

rhetoric and needless complexity. Nor the first to see in themselves a persona defined more by individual deeds than by collective heroism, refined sensitivity, or crusading rhetoric. Nor the first to resent the hypocrisy of those just older than themselves.

In fact, several earlier American generations have faced a similar gauntlet, owing to their similar location in history—as the children of an era of spiritual upheaval and confusion over values, as teens who came of age just after a crowd of self-righteous moralists, and as young adults whose pleasure-seeking drew condemnation from 40-year-olds who had once had plenty of less hazardous youth fun themselves.

Thirteeners can find another kindred bunch in the Gilded Generation (born 1822-1842) of Ulysses Grant, Mark Twain, Louisa May Alcott, and John D. Rockefeller. These were the hardscrabble children of the "Second Great Awakening" who came of age in a freewheeling era of torrential immigration, gold fever, frontier boom towns, and rising national tempers. They bore no resemblance to their next elders, those holier-than-thou Emersonians and narcissistic Whitmans. Instead, they were a young generation of metal and muscle, excoriated for their dumbness and greed, in an era when (wrote the Lost historian Van Wyck Brooks) "the young men who

What is moral is what you feel good after, and what is immoral is what you feel bad after.

Ernest Hemingway
(1899–1961)

Did other generations ever laugh so hard together, drink and dance so hard, or do crazier things just for the hell of it?

Malcolm Cowley
(1898–1989)

The rising generation has a very real feeling of coming straight up against a wall of diminishing opportunity. I do not see how it can be denied that practical opportunity is less for this generation than it has been for those preceding it.

Randolph Bourne
(1886–1918)

Our generation has seen the horrors latent in man's being rise to the surface and erupt.

Paul Tillich (1886–1965)

might have been writers in the days of *The Dial* were seeking their fortunes in railroads, mines, and oil wells."

Or 13ers can compare themselves with America's Liberty Generation (born 1724–1741) of George Washington, Patrick Henry, and Benedict Arnold. Raised in an era of growing economic mobility and spiritual turbulence (the original "Great Awakening"), these were the bounty-chasing kids who came of age as the disillusioned foot soldiers of the French and Indian War. Scattering across the colonies, they became a cynical "Don't Tread on Me" cadre of "Yankee Doodle Dandies" who raised hell as heavy drinkers, daring pioneers, and angry orators attracted to high risk and decisive action.

Or 13ers can look all the way back to America's Cavalier Generation (born 1615–1647). These peers of Nathaniel Bacon and William Kidd were perhaps the wildest and least-lettered of all American generations, cursed and punished by high-minded next-elders as "unconverted" and "lost" to God. Raised in New England theocracies, they were the alienated offspring of God-intoxicated parents obsessed with creating a New Jerusalem. Toiling in the Chesapeake tobacco fields, they were the hungry young servants and royalist refugees fleeing the madness of England's Puritan Revolution. Up and down the eastern seaboard, young Cavaliers entered adulthood as lonely risk takers and irascible judgment evaders—merchants, explorers, pirates, planters, and soldiers.

Where each of these ancestral generations reached roughly age 30—matching the 13ers' present phase-of-life—the comparison has to stop. Or does it? Perhaps some of the mysteries of the 13th Generation's own purpose and destiny can be deciphered if we take a look at what happened to these other "bad kid" generations through the rest of their respective life cycles.

As they aged, all these earlier 13ish generations showed remarkable parallels in their behavior at each phase of life. In midlife, they excelled at practical realism, just the talent they needed to lead America through a stormy era of crisis. In elderhood, they were generous to their juniors and thought little of themselves—hardly protesting the political reprisals and witch frenzies that incriminated mainly their own peers.

Specifically, the Lost entered midlife with a Crash (of 1929), after which they changed character completely. In families, they protected children almost to the point of suffocation. In the culture, they were the Frank Capras and early radio stars who pushed the media back to practicality and community. In politics, they turned isolationist and conservative. They were the biggest Roosevelt-haters and the Martin-Barton-and-Fish types whom FDR blamed for blocking many of his New Deal crusades. During the 1940s and '50s, the Lost tenure in governorships, Congress, and the White House was relatively brief. Their two Presidents (Ike and Truman) were stolid, get-it-done old warriors, known more for personality than candlepower. At the peak of their earning years, the aging Lost tolerated crushing 91 percent marginal income tax rates to support the Marshall Plan for world peace and the G.I. Bill for a younger generation of veterans. As elders, they took pride in having ushered in the prosperous "American High," even while younger people accused them of being cynical rock-ribbed reactionaries. Back in the 1950s and '60s, America's old people were extremely poor, relative to the young, yet they repeatedly voted for candidates who promised to cut their benefits.

The Gilded? Decimated by the Civil War, they matured into midlife "pragmatists" who bet their lives on what William James called "truth's cash value" and who led America through an era of technological innovation, political machines, Victorian prudery, and no-holds-barred economic growth. They were attracted to big, strong, worldly projects—steam turbines and Brooklyn Bridges—anything that could make them forget the ugly introspection and destructive moral zealotry of Americans just older than themselves. Late in life, they ended up on the "industrial scrap heap" in an urbanizing economy that rewarded youthful energy and offered old people nothing.

The Liberty? They supplied most of the signatories of the Declaration of Independence and the Revolution's bravest patriot officers—as well as its most infamous traitors. Stigmatized for wildness by their next-elders (the peers of Sam Adams and Ben Franklin), they sank into exhaustion after their mid-forties. In old age, they became suspicious "Anti-Federalists" in local politics and exercised extreme prudence as national leaders, eager to secure for their own children the close family and peaceful community life they had been less able to find for themselves.

The Cavaliers? In midlife, they faced rebellions, wars, and plagues with quiet courage, bore crushing emergency taxes without com-

What is the chief end of man?—to get rich. In what way?—dishonestly if he can; honestly if he must.

Mark Twain (1835–1910)

We are a crooked and perverse generation....

Josiah Bartlett (1729–1795)

We have not men fit for the times. We are deficient in genius, in education, in travel, in fortune—in everything. I feel unutterable anxiety.

John Adams (1735–1826)

We, poor we, alas what are we! It is a sad name to be styled "Children that are Corrupters."

William Stoughton (1631–1701)

If the body of the present generation be compared with what was here forty years ago, what a sad degeneracy is evident in the view of every man.

Increase Mather (1639–1723)

plaint, and watched over their own children with a close protectiveness they had been denied when young themselves. Their life spans were shorter than those who came before. Those lucky enough to avoid untimely death from disease or violence became self-effacing elders who took great pride in community survival and in preparing the young for a dawning age of imperial prosperity.

Lost, Gilded, Liberty, Cavalier: All these ancestral generations had the ill fortune to be, as historian David Hackett Fischer describes the Liberty, a "generation whose unhappy fate it was to be young in an era when age was respected, and old in a time when youth took the palm." Yet they all brought to America a style and an attitude that 13ers are beginning to notice in themselves. Whatever went right, they always got less than their share of the credit; whatever went wrong, they always got more than their share of the blame. Even now, 13ers know the feeling. They'd better get used to it.

>25. The 21st Century Breathing Down Our Necks

So where *are* 13ers heading?

To figure out where any generation is heading, you have to know two things: its current location and its future direction.

Location is the easy part. You can find out where a generation is today by identifying its collective personality, its cultural center of gravity, and its attitudes, habits, and skills. To answer any number of trivial questions about the future, current location may be all you need to know. Take music, for example. Even in old age, a generation retains a special fondness for the songs it first hears in its mid-teens to early 20s. Thus, we could have predicted many years ago that today's G.I. senior citizens would still be listening to Glenn Miller and Benny Goodman. And we can safely predict that, sometime around 2040, America's 70-year-old 13ers will feel a special nostalgia for (believe it or not) the staccato rhythm of a vintage urban rapper.

Yet even if a generation can't alter many of the specific traits it acquires young, it is equally true that such traits get applied to new purposes and are shaped by new attitudes over the course of its life cycle. Along the way, a generation typically finds that its personality in old

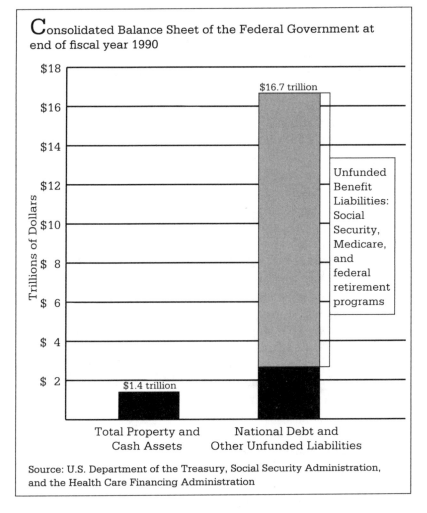

Consolidated Balance Sheet of the Federal Government at end of fiscal year 1990

Trillions of Dollars

$18
$16.7 trillion
$16
$14
$12
Unfunded Benefit Liabilities: Social Security, Medicare, and federal retirement programs
$10
$ 8
$ 6
$ 4
$ 2
$1.4 trillion

Total Property and Cash Assets

National Debt and Other Unfunded Liabilities

Source: U.S. Department of the Treasury, Social Security Administration, and the Health Care Financing Administration

age is very different from its personality in youth. (That old 13er may still feel a nostalgia for rap, but what will it mean to him? And will he want to play it for his grandchildren?)

To make more important predictions, therefore, you need some understanding of a generation's sense of *direction*—what Ortega y Gasset called its "preestablished vital trajectory" and Karl Mannheim its "essential destiny." It's not easy to identify this direction. It's like unwrapping some hidden sociogenetic code. You have to read motives and questions and dreams that are hidden inside a generation like an oak within an acorn and that don't become fully apparent until they are expressed in history.

But one thing is certain: If you don't know the direction, you'll be

Unfortunately, our dream—and it's still a dream deferred—is just to make ends meet.

Andrew Cohen,
New York City

▬

Lou, you don't bet horses, you bet dogs. Horses are a gamble. Dogs are an investment. Smart guys are dog guys.

young hustler,
Opportunity Knocks (film)

clueless about the future, because no generation ever starts and ends its collective journey in the same location. Consider a generation (like the G.I.s) that comes of age saving, working, and building big things. Who would guess that this same group of people, entering retirement, would create the biggest consumption and leisure lobby in world history? Or consider a generation (like the Silent) that spends the first half of its life doing everything by the rules—and ever since midlife yearns to break all the taboos. Or consider a generation (like the Boom) that celebrates the libido at age 18—and then three decades later begins to engage in what marketers call "non-ism," the ascetic art of celebrating whatever it is you're *not* enjoying.

To understand how generations acquire a sense of direction, you have to ask how they interpret their world early in life. Coming of age, what is their agenda? What's their greatest challenge—the biggest problem they want to solve or the obstacle they need to overcome? For G.I.s in the early 1930s, the challenge was national poverty and pessimism—which helps explain the affluent, upbeat image of today's senior citizen. For the Silent in the early '50s, it was "yes sir" determination and conformism—hence the ambivalent, open-minded image of today's midlifer. For the Boomers in the early '70s, soulless abundance and complacency—hence the (still evolving) values-fixated image of today's 40-year-old.

This brings us to the future of the 13th Generation. What is it about America's current social mood that is likely to leave the most lasting impression on Americans now coming of age? We don't know for sure, but we can make some fair guesses: chaotic individualism; social fragmentation; cultural openness; institutions grown over-complex and irrelevant; a consumption-based economy that devours its own future; a political system that debates everything but chooses nothing. Were you to extrapolate the future strictly on the basis of how 13ers are now coping with this world, you could indeed draw a very dismal scenario. Imagine a place in which civilization has crumbled into dust, leaving only a bunch of aging Road Warriors and Blade Runners. But this scenario is likely to be as wildly inaccurate as the totalitarian *1984* projections made for the compliant young Silent Generation in the wake of Hitler and Stalin. It's wrong because it looks at where a generation is without paying attention to what's happening *inside* that generation—where it's going, what it's on the way to becoming.

So what *is* the 13er direction? Here's where history helps. Suppose 13ers follow the trajectory of prior generations—the Lost, Gilded, Liberty, and Cavaliers—that started out life much like the 13ers themselves. If so, we can make a good number of informed predictions about how their collective personality will evolve as they grow older; which attitudes and habits will stay constant, and which will reverse; what lifelong lessons they will carry with them from the circa-'80s and '90s world in which they are coming of age; how they will behave toward other generations, and how other generations will behave toward them; what kind of leadership they will someday provide; and how history will someday remember them.

The most important lesson of history is this: Once these previous 13er-like generations reached midlife, they underwent a profound personality transformation. Their risk-taking gave way to caution, their wildness and alienation turned into exhaustion and conservatism, and their nomadic individualism matured into a preference for strong community life. The same unruly rebels and adventurers who alarmed older colonists during the 1760s later became the crusty old Patrick Henrys and George Washingtons who warned younger statesmen against gambling with the future. The same gold-chasing '49ers and Civil War brigands whom Oliver Wendell Holmes, Jr., called "a generation touched with fire" later became the stodgy "Old Guard" Victorians of the Gilded Era. The same gin-fizz "Flaming Youth" who electrified America during the 1920s later became the Norman Rockwells and Dwight Eisenhowers who calmed America during the 1950s.

With history as a guide, we offer 13 predictions for the 13th Generation:

1. Over the next fifteen years, the festering quarrel between 13ers and Boomers will grow into America's next great "generation gap." As their stamp on American culture increasingly looks, tastes, smells, and sounds anti-Boom, everything 13ers do that Boomers already consider frenetic, shallow, or shocking will grow even more so, confirming public opinion that this truly is a "wasted" generation. Like the Lost during the 1920s, 13ers will have their greatest cultural impact on the marketplace (entertainment, products, styles, advertising), yet over time their what-you-see-is-what-you-get brassiness will spill over into religion and politics. Thirteeners will vent their social alienation by stressing bucks and deals where their next-elders once talked about

We won't have a bad backlash against our lost idealism, which previous generations have had to fight. We never had that to begin with.

Richard Linklater, 29, director of the film *Slacker*, interviewed by Diane Kadzis, in the *Boston Phoenix*

———

By the time I'm sixty-three There won't be nothin' left for me When all the Boomers have retired And bought a house in Santa Fe

Susan Werner, "Born a Little Late" (song)

ideas and values. In response, midlife Boomers will try to insulate their families from a mainstream culture gone rotten and will project heavy-handed value judgments into public life. Interpreting these judgments as pitiless and Scroogelike, 13ers will blast away at Boomer hypocrisy and pomposity—and get blasted back for their own cynicism and wildness. Only during the first decade of the next century, when Atari-wave 13ers reach midlife, will this age war subside.

2. Thirteeners will never outgrow their "bad" image. The children allowed to grow up unskilled, unschooled, and unwanted in the 1970s and '80s will carry those pathologies with them. They will be just as unemployable and socially undesirable at age forty as they are today at age twenty. Remedial adult education will lose funding, young-adult welfare will be cut further, and expanded health-care benefits will help young parents only to the extent that it targets their kids. Many of today's youth gangsters will ripen into their adult facsimile, waging Capone-like wars with police. Already the most incarcerated generation in American history, 13ers will in time be (thanks to Boomer legislators, judges, and juries) the most executed generation as well. Efforts to prevent antisocial behavior and to encourage cooperation and teamwork will be focused exclusively on the young. By the year 2020—roughly thirty years from now—Americans in their fifties will be generally regarded as worse-behaved (and worse-educated) than Americans in their twenties—exactly the opposite of today.

3. The 13th will become one of the most important immigrant generations in U.S. history. Ultimately, its membership will include the highest percentage of naturalized U.S. citizens of any generation born in the twentieth century. The politics of ethnic group rivalry and the cultural impact of racial diversity will play a far more serious role in the lives of 13ers than they ever did in the lives of the Boom and Silent. As immigrants and nonwhites flaunt their unique identities, many white 13ers will see themselves as endangered, sparking social movements that others will regard as know-nothing nativism. Over time, the perception that large numbers of 13er immigrants threaten to fragment society beyond repair will persuade Americans of all ages to clamp down on immigration—ensuring that the foreign-born share of the next (Millennial) generation will be smaller. Meanwhile, foreign-born high-achievers will catapult new ethnic groups, especially Asians and Hispanics, into national prominence—much as the Lost

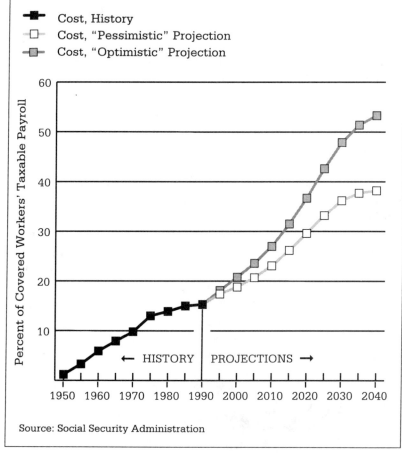

Total Social Security and Medicare benefits as a percent of taxable payroll, history and projection, 1950–2040

- ■ Cost, History
- □ Cost, "Pessimistic" Projection
- ■ Cost, "Optimistic" Projection

← HISTORY | PROJECTIONS →

Source: Social Security Administration

Generation did for the Italians and Eastern Europeans and the Gilded Generation did for the Irish and Germans.

4. Early in life, the most successful 13ers will be risk takers who exploit opportunities overlooked by established businesses. The leading 13er frontier will be overseas, where this generation can most fully apply its entrepreneurial instincts and take advantage of its linguistic, computer, and marketing skills. At home, 13ers will revitalize the unskilled service sector, turn small manufacturers into exporters, mount gray-market challenges to credentialed monopolies (law, medicine, finance), and set up profitable alternatives to rule-encrusted state enterprises (mail, schools, waste disposal, secu-

As we move into the next century, will the minorities of this country—immigrants and otherwise—come to see the Social Security system as a mechanism by which the government robs their children of a better future, in order to support a group of elderly white people in a retirement that is both too luxurious and too long?

Dorcas Hardy, former U.S. Commissioner of Social Security

The day is coming when you are going to see someone like Janet Jackson on cereal boxes.

Dell Furano, president of a music merchandising firm

We're not trying to change things. We're trying to fix things. We are the generation that is going to renovate America. We are going to be its carpenters and janitors.

Anne McCord, 21, Portland, OR

rity). As contract work employees, many will dart from job to job, while others mix steady wages during the day with get-rich-quick deals at night—discouraging companies from offering job training, career ladders, or pension programs. As managers, 13ers will seek market niches where quick deals matter more than long memos. Professional and union loyalties will continue to decline. The bottom line is that 13ers will leave public and private bureaucracies leaner, more personalized, and more oriented toward doing the job than staffing the process.

5. Reaching midlife, the 13ers' economic fears will be confirmed: They will become the only generation born this century (the first since the Gilded) to suffer a one-generation backstep in living standards. Compared to their own parents at the same age, the 13ers' poverty rate will be higher, their rate of home ownership lower, their pension and health care benefits skimpier. They will not match the Boomers' inflation-adjusted levels of disposable income or wealth, at the same age. Thirteeners will also experience a much wider distribution of income and wealth than today's older generations, with startling proportions either falling into destitution or shooting from rags to riches. They will change the focus of class politics—away from raising low-income families to the median toward preventing the root-

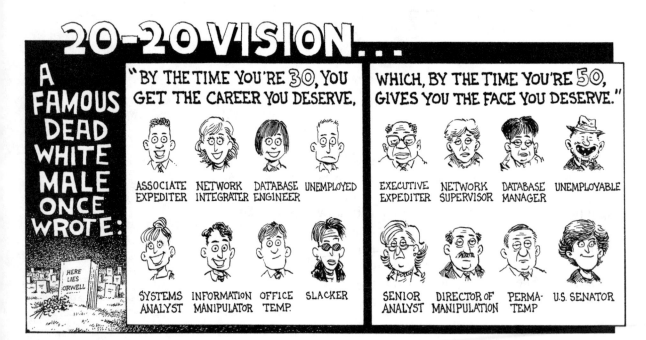

less poor from sinking into a total abyss. Finding their youthful dreams broken on the shoals of marketplace reality, 13ers will internalize their disappointment. Around the year 2020, accumulated "hard knocks" will give midlife 13ers much of the same gritty determination about life that the Great Depression gave the midlife Lost or Reconstruction gave the Gilded.

6. Thirteeners will restrengthen the American family. Dedicated spouses, they will work hard to shield their marriages from the risk and stress of their work lives. Around the year 2000, these efforts will be reflected in a marked downturn in the national divorce rate. First as parents and later as community leaders, 13ers will practice and advocate a heavily protective, even smothering style of nurture. They will revive the innocence of childhood by deliberately shielding their own kids from the harsher realities of life, and by prohibiting those kids from taking the same liberties they themselves once took at the same age. Having no illusions about sex themselves, they will appreciate the advantages of creating illusions (and resurrecting modesty) for their children. In their style of parenting, midlife 13ers will be much the opposite of the midlife Silent who raised them as kids during the 1970s—and much more similar to the midlife Lost who raised the Silent as kids during the 1930s.

7. Reaching their fifties in a mood of collective exhaustion, 13ers will settle into the midlife role of national anchor, calming the social mood and slowing the pace of social change. As senior educators, political leaders, and media executives, 13ers will reverse the frenzied and centrifugal cultural directions of their younger years. In alliance with old Boomers, they will clean up entertainment, de-diversify the culture, reinvent core symbols of national unity, reaffirm rituals of family and neighborhood bonding, and re-erect barriers to cushion communities from unwanted social upheaval. As architects and civic officials, they will oversee the rebuilding of urban America and pioneer the next great era of (high-tech) infrastructure. Cities will define and energize them—but Boomer-run exurbs will surround them and constantly preach to them. As cultural mentors for the younger and more favored Millennial Generation, they will play a crucial formative role—reintroducing wholesome songs and friendly humor. As elder role models, 13ers will make near-perfect 50-year-olds: irascible, full of mischief, with that Twainlike twinkle in the eye, but also worldly wise and experienced in the stark realities of pleasure and pain.

I think when I'm my parents' age, the world will be worse. But I want to fall in love and have two kids and a house. I want my husband to be an athlete, with good muscles, who has a sense of humor and is sensitive too and is good with kids.

Denise Parker, 14, archery champion

My generation will be the family generation. I don't want my kids to go through what my parents put me through.

Mara Brock, 20, Kansas City

When I raise my children, my approach will be my grandparents', much more serious and conservative. I would never give my children the freedoms I had.

Kip Banks, 24, graduate student, University of Michigan

While a new set of youths comes of age turning to pedantic old Boomers for the stern ought-to-dos of life, they will turn to avuncular midlife 13ers for the fun *want*-to-dos of life.

8. Throughout their lives, 13ers will be America's most politically conservative generation since the Lost. Until their mid-40s, the dominant brand of 13er conservatism will have a strong libertarian and free-market leave-me-alone flavor; later in life, it will lean toward cautious, pragmatic stewardship. Their attachment to the "conservative" banner will be sealed if aging Boomers rely on liberal standards to rekindle a spirit of national community and to rally younger generations to their cause—say, through some new CCC-like mandatory youth service. Ever the social contrarians, 13ers will be tempted to take the other side and try to keep their elders (and juniors) from going off the deep end. Regardless of party or ideology, 13ers will be drawn to candidates who avoid hype, spell out the bottom line, do what it takes to get the job done, and shed no tears. In politics as in other spheres of social life, they will be most effective where the issues are local and personal. They will press to simplify the complex, narrow the bloated, and eliminate the unworkable. They will gain their first Senate seats and governorships before the year 2000. Their weak political profile in national affairs, however, will prevent them from winning a generational plurality in Congress until relatively late in life, perhaps not until around 2020, when the (by then) burned-out Atari wave is reaching age 60.

9. As they reach their turn for national leadership, 13ers will produce no-nonsense winners who will excel at cunning, flexibility, and deft timing. If 13ers turn out like every earlier generation of their type—Lost, Gilded, Liberty, and Cavalier—they will ultimately become a stellar generation of get-it-done warriors, able to take charge of whatever raging conflicts are initiated by their elders and bring them to successful conclusions. In the tradition of George Washington, Ulysses Grant, and Dwight Eisenhower, the most memorable 13er Presidents may themselves be ex-generals. Military or not—and regardless of sex—13er leaders will be cagey, jockish, unpretentious, inelegant with words, more inclined to deal than to argue, and more admired for their personality than for their vision or learning. As they come to power around the year 2020, younger voters will view them as a welcome change from the ponderous, principles-first Boomer style. In public, they'll come across a bit shallow. But, as any 13er al-

```
***2boomers
>well, crasher, we're nearing the end of the transmission. are you going to be sad to see us go?

***crasher
>actually, this is the most interesting thing that's been on here in ages. this prediction stuff is bothersome, though.

***2boomers
>why?

***crasher
>how can I possibly worry about the future when my present is so whacked? how can I contemplate being a "midlife national anchor" when I can't get my bike unlocked?

***2boomers
>watch out, crasher--history may be counting on you.

***crasher
>yuck.
```

ready knows, low expectations can be a game you can use to your advantage—in a poker game or in the White House.

10. Before the year 2030, events will call on pockmarked 13ers to make aging Boomers get real—and, perhaps, to stop some righteous old Aquarian from doing something truly catastrophic. Gazing down the road, some 13ers already wonder how they're going to cope with their next elders when those crusading Boomers finally go gaga. It's not an idle worry. Just think about it: Of all of today's living generations, which one is someday most likely to risk blowing up the world just to prove a point? When that nightmare possibility appears, it may compel a grown-up cadre of shouted-at Breakfast Clubbers to insist on having the last word after all—and to demand that principle defer to survival. The day may come when 13ers do to Boomers what the Gilded did to Union Radicals and Confederate Fire-Eaters after those aging enthusiasts had razed half the continent: In the election of 1868, Gilded voters touched off the biggest generational landslide in American history and slammed their next-elders out of office. Or what Harry Truman did with grandiloquent old crusaders like Douglas MacArthur and John L. Lewis: With few words and no ceremony, he just gave them the boot.

11. Throughout their lives, 13ers will neither ask for nor receive much assistance from government. In their thirties, they will vote to cut young-adult welfare benefits. In their fifties, they will vote to raise income taxes. In their seventies, they will vote to cut Social Security.

It's not the baby boom that's going to fight the next war. It's more likely that the baby boom will start it.

Julie Phillips, "Boomed Out," in *Seattle Weekly*

As a generation, we've grown up in a time of accelerated history and experience. We are prepared for anything, surprised by little. When our turn comes to slay the deficits, to hold restive and separatist peoples together, to fight off economic competitors, to articulate national strategies, we will not wring our hands. We'll just do it.

Eric Liu, editor, *The Next Progressive*

A generation of low collective self-esteem, 13ers will never voice much objection to their own "bad" reputation in the eyes of others (today their elders, forty years from now their juniors). Nor will 13ers ever effectively organize or vote in their own self-interest. Instead, they will take pride in the handouts they don't receive, in their life-long talent for getting by on their own, and in their ability to divert government resources to help those younger than themselves. Policy experts who today worry about the cost of Social Security and Medicare past the year 2025 seldom reflect on the political self-image of those who will then be entering their late sixties. Will they become entitled "senior citizens"? Hardly. Like Lost Generation elders in 1964—who voted more for Barry Goldwater than any younger generation even after he promised to slash their retirement benefits— old 13ers will feel less deserving of public attention than richer and smarter young people who lack their fatalism about life.

12. As mature leaders and voters, 13ers will favor investment over consumption, endowments over entitlements, the needs of the very young over the needs of the very old. Whether by raising taxes, by freezing the money supply, by discouraging debt, or by shifting public budgets toward education, public works, and child welfare, elder 13ers will tilt the economy back toward the future. They will use any available policy lever to raise national savings far above what private households would otherwise choose on their own—exactly the opposite of the national choice they will remember from their own youth. Like the post-Civil War Gilded, who led the nation through twenty-eight consecutive federal budget surpluses, 13ers will leave behind a smaller federal debt than they inherited. Like the postwar Lost, who resisted the call for Keynesian pump-priming, 13ers will prefer recession to an out-of-kilter national balance sheet. Either way, elder 13ers will be national survivalists, determined to store up capital for future contingencies and opposed to doing anything too risky, too wasteful, or too ambitious. Exiting power, they will—like the elder Washington, Twain, and Eisenhower—warn against the danger of pushing too fast in world rigged with pitfalls.

13. Thirteeners will make caustic, independent, yet self-effacing elders. When old, 13ers will watch America (once again) lose interest in people their own age and rediscover a fascination with the energy and promise of youth. They will watch younger generations

MT. RUSHMORE (OR LESS) – 2050 A.D.

ignore their "old fogey" warnings and unleash new dreams of national ambition. They will watch younger people zoom past them economically. But 13er oldsters won't mind. They'll have reason to take pride in what they see happening down the age ladder. Pride in having pulled America back together and in having restored ballast to the ship of state. Pride in having rebuilt the social foundations that will by then be supporting a renaissance in public confidence and cultural optimism. Pride in having produced more than they consumed, in having made simple things work again, *in having done more for others than others ever did for them.*

Life is a sneaky fortune wheel for the 13th Generation. It spins, it turns—and just when you think you've lost, it tantalizes. Just when you think you've won, it clicks again, and you lose. But, by losing, 13ers help others gain. That could well be the story of their future.

History is not invariant, with predetermined outcomes. Any generation can bring forward good or bad leaders, or just run into good or bad luck. But each generation gets only one script. And how history turns out often depends on how well each generation plays its script.

***2boomers
>so have you gotten anything from all this, or is it still just a "sack of dung," as you might say?

***crasher
>I'm not sure yet if I can buy this whole "generational" thing, it seems so touchy-feely, sweeping and full of horrible news most of the time. I remember in high school we had this sociology class that went through all the gory definitions of human social activity. one day, the teacher was going through gender roles, and he said that boys always carry their schoolbooks in one hand down by their side, and girls always carry them with both hands clutched against their chest. I remember it had something to do with men instinctively carrying their books like the hunting spears of early man, and women clutching their valuables close to the chest as though they were nursing a baby--but mostly I remember the class disagreeing entirely that we did it like that at all. so the teacher had us stay after class to peer out the window while the other students were being let out, and sure enough, there were the boys and girls, all holding their books exactly like the teacher said. and I remember we all looked at each other with this curious sort of disgust, like we were a bunch of goofy robots, and we'd fallen for some giant galactic trick. he let us go with a victorious smile, but as we left the room, you can be damn sure the girls were clutching spears and we were nursing babies.

If there's a generalization you can make about all of us, it's that we all hate generalizations. especially the ones that are frequently true. whenever someone starts some sappy, solipsistic drone about being a vacuous twentysomething, I get that nappy feeling I had in that sociology class, like I was automatically being included into a club without my permission. people my age are way too cynical and untrusting to feel an allegiance to anything as pompous and nebulous as a "generation," with a capital "g." if we're anything, we're a generation with a small "g," but the thought of us doing anything idealistic in tandem is kinda dumb. what we do have in common are about three trillion bits of similar information: mikey from the life cereal commercials, fruit stripe gum, ms. pac-man, jeff spiccoli, "purple rain," and the episode where jan gets a curly black wig. past that, we diverge like wounded warplanes, most of us scurrying off to our jobs, hobbies and projects with self-obsessed tenacity. we're a generation of winks and nods, not protests, disco and cocooning. I feel a slight twinge of generational happiness whenever I peruse a friend's tape collection, but certainly not by spending three days in the mud with some girl named rainbow in upstate new york.

so our american dream, if you can even call it that, is going to be likewise as cynical and full of low expectations. you guys are going to think that is necessarily a bad thing, but that's where you're wrong. we know the value of being naturally happy more than you guys did. we understand the inherent good feeling of a hostess ding-dong, and we appreciate why the glory of a spontaneous road trip to tennessee eclipses that of a good study weekend. while the rest of the country gets immersed in best-selling diet plans and codependency workshops, my friends and I are going to be down here in the basement cranking the clash, raging on this computer line, trying to get to the adam and eve electronic sex catalog.

I am scared to death of permanence; there is something about the idea of sticking at a job for fifty years that makes my blood clot into tiny icebergs. so the entire concept of becoming the world's lovable yet crusty custodian, mopping ocean floors and stopping global wars until we're 90--it's going to scare most of us to death. the ability to drop everything, hop into a car and drive to mardi gras--that's what makes my life worth the trouble. that's my american dream, the ability to do these silly things without worrying. I desperately need to bleach out the extraneous garbage that pollutes the minds of my elders, and then someday teach my kids to do the same. I'd say all of that is going to take about 20 years and 1.6 million dollars. oh well.

I tell you, boys--last night the student union showed the movie "the wall," and I sat nestled between two guys: one dude on my left had a nose ring that was chained to his earring, and the other guy on my right had taped-up horn-rimmed glasses and ocean pacific corduroy shorts on. when the "comfortably numb" part of the movie came on, I could hear the "s" sound of all the lyrics come from both of my partners as they silently sang along. eventually everyone in the whole place was singing along to themselves, and I felt a wonderful tingle down my back each time I heard that "s" sound swirl around me. and for a tiny second, I was happy to be a part of it all, singing that silent little consonant to myself, with dreams that we might all be a part of something amazingly special after all...

I'm going to go now, before I bust out crying.

***2boomers
>crasher cry? not! anyway, good talking to you, good luck with everything.

***crasher
>adios, my friends. (soundtrack swells)

When they are the leaders, they are going to say, "Where were you when I fell down and hurt myself when I was a kid?"

Fay Crowe,
divorced mother of three latchkey children in Fairfax County, VA

——

We may not get what we want. We may not get what we need. Just so we don't get what we deserve.

two law students,
in unison, *True Colors* (film)

——

"Only the most serene and enlightened souls shall gain audience [in heaven]. Bill, dude, these people seem pretty easygoing, but I have a feeling this serene enlightenment stuff is something they take most seriously. It's like a house rule." "Serene and enlightened souls? Dude, we're in big trouble."

Chris Matheson and Ed Solomon, *Bill and Ted's Bogus Journey* (film)

To date, 13ers are a generation without a self-perceived mission. They know full well that they can't do or be what the G.I.s or Silent or Boomers did or were. Unite in the face of global crisis? Add nuance to a conformist society? Scream out against spirit-dead affluence? It makes no sense for them to attempt even a pale imitation of their elders—nor for those elders to condemn them for not following the paths others blazed in youth. Instead, 13ers have to find their own path, to develop their own sense of mission, to follow their own script.

Over a half-century ago, historian James Truslow Adams first defined the "American Dream" as giving every young person "the chance to grow into something bigger and finer, as bigger and finer appeared to him." This Dream is each generation's unique vision of progress, each generation's unique sense of how to improve on the legacy that has been handed down by its ancestors. The G.I.s defined their Dream through economics. The Silent defined it through social justice. Boomers defined it through inner consciousness.

So where do 13ers fit in? Have all the dreams been defined? Is anything left for them?

Yes, 13ers *do* have a mission. Theirs is the American generation that history has charged with the task of cleaning up after everybody else's mess. (Somebody had better—before it's too late.) So too is theirs the generation charged with showing others how, in this millennial era, Americans can still enjoy "life, liberty, and the pursuit of happiness" without letting the world fly to pieces, without bankrupting the nation, and without squandering scarce global resources. History is calling on the 13th Generation to provide the youthful entrepreneurship, midlife investments, and elder generosity that will enable future generations once again to define the American Dream in economic terms, if that is what they wish to do.

Do the dirty work, have a little fun, help the kids behind them. Not bad. Let others call 13ers "underachievers." They can take it. We, their elders, will never live to see how their story turns out. They will. The rest of us can only imagine how, when their job's done, they'll look history straight in the eye, give a little smile, and move on.

***End of file. Upload completed.
***Select: (D)ownload, (U)pload, (M)enu,(Q)uit? q
***Exit USA-TALK.
***Log off at 1:04:09, 12/1/92.

C:> ph-bill

 ATDT 1(703)822-0991 . . . Phone number being dialed . . . Connection made . . .

<TRAN> hey bill, remember that thomas wolfe line you like so much? what he once said about his own lost generation? "you're a part of it whether you want to be or not." well, that's our friend crasher.

<RECV> he's finally getting around to using the g-word, even if it is with a small g. maybe there's hope for this project after all.

<TRAN> how about those lists of his?

<RECV>they're kind of like a personal inventory of pop 13erama. maybe we should use them. wish i'd saved the whole thing.

<TRAN> no problem. i've been keeping a log of all these uploads on my hard drive.

<RECV> know what? maybe we stumbled across a book after all. why not send this whole thing, crasher and all, off to some publisher?

<TRAN> yesss. crasher'd better get out his ding dongs. maybe we'll make him a small s spokesman for his small g generation. that'd really send him packing.

<RECV> watch out. crasher might be listening. if so, I'll bet he's hacking into our conversation and figuring out some phreaky way to cut us off. don't know how, but 13ers can be very good at doing things we older guys don't expect and don't even think are possible.

<TRAN> not this time. anyway, i'm signing-off. don't wanna be like a typical boomer who never knows when to s

C:> top talking.

———————————————————— end of session ————————————————————
———————————————— computer log OFF at 1:10:31am 12/1/92 ————————————

Neil Howe and **Bill Strauss** are the authors of *Generations.*

Neil Howe, an economist and historian, is the co-author of *On Borrowed Time* (with Peter Peterson). He is currently writing a book on federal entitlement programs. He lives in Great Falls, Virginia.

Bill Strauss is director of the *Capitol Steps* political satire troupe. He is also the author of *Fools on the Hill* (with Elaina Newport), *Chance and Circumstance* (with Lawrence Baskir), and *Reconciliation After Vietnam* (also with Lawrence Baskir). He lives in McLean, Virginia.

Ian Williams is a resident of Chapel Hill, North Carolina. He is currently at work on his first novel.

R. J. Matson is the political cartoonist for the *New York Observer* and staff illustrator for *Roll Call.* His work has also appeared in *The Single Woman's Guide to the Available Men of Washington* and *Fools on the Hill.* He lives in New York with his wife, Samantha.